Presidential
Influence
and
Environmental
Policy

PRESIDENTIAL
INFLUENCE
AND
ENVIRONMENTAL
POLICY

Robert A. Shanley

Contributions in Political Science,
Number 307
Bernard K. Johnpoll, Series Editor

Greenwood Press
Westport, Connecticut • London

Library of Congress Cataloging-in-Publication Data

Shanley, Robert A.
   Presidential influence and environmental policy / Robert A.
Shanley.
       p.   cm.—(Contributions in political science, ISSN 0147–1066 ;
no. 307)
   Includes bibliographical references and index.
   ISBN 0–313–25883–X
   1. Environmental policy—United States. 2. Reagan, Ronald.
3. Bush, George, 1924– . I. Title. II. Series.
   HC110.E5S47   1992
   363.7′056′0973—dc20   92–15584

British Library Cataloguing in Publication Data is available.

Library of Congress Catalog Card Number: 92–15584
ISBN: 0–313–25883–X
ISSN: 0147–1066

First published in 1992

Greenwood Press, 88 Post Road West, Westport, CT 06881
An imprint of Greenwood Publishing Group, Inc.

Printed in the United States of America

The paper used in this book complies with the
Permanent Paper Standard issued by the National
Information Standards Organization (Z39.48–1984).

10 9 8 7 6 5 4 3 2 1

Copyright Acknowledgment

The author and publisher gratefully acknowledge permission to quote from
the following:

"Presidential Executive Orders and Environmental Policy," by Robert A. Shanley,
Presidential Studies Quarterly, 13, pp. 405–16. Copyright © 1983 The Center for the
Study of the Presidency.

"Franklin D. Roosevelt and Water Pollution Control Policy," by Robert A. Shanley,
Presidential Studies Quarterly, 18, pp. 319–30. Copyright © 1988 The Center for the
Study of the Presidency.

Dedicated to the
memory of Lawrence H. Chamberlain,
scholar and friend

Contents

Abbreviations

ATB	America the Beautiful Program, Department of the Interior
ANWR	Arctic National Wildlife Refuge
BLS	Bureau of Labor Statistics
CAFE	Corporate Average Fuel Economy
CDC	Centers for Disease Control
CEQ	Council on Environmental Quality
DOE	Department of Energy
DOI	Department of the Interior
EIS	Environmental Impact Statement
EPA	Environmental Protection Agency
E.O.	Executive Order
EOP	Executive Office of the President
FY	Fiscal Year
GAO	General Accounting Office
HHS	Department of Health and Human Services
IRLG	Interagency Regulatory Liaison Group
NAPA	National Academy of Public Administration
NAS	National Academy of Sciences
NES	National Energy Strategy
NEPA	National Environmental Policy Act of 1970
NRC	Nuclear Regulatory Commission
OSHA	Occupational Safety and Health Administration
OIRA	Office of Information and Regulatory Affairs
OMB	Office of Management and Budget
OSM	Office of Surface Mining Reclamation and Enforcement
PRA	Paperwork Reduction Act of 1980

QRA   Quantitative Risk Assessment
RARG   Regulatory Analysis Review Group
RIA   Regulatory Impact Analysis
RCRA   Resource Conservation and Recovery Act
SMCRA   Surface Mining Control and Reclamation Act of 1977
TIA   Takings Information Assessment
WRC   Water Resources Council

Acknowledgments

My thanks to Michael Kraft, who read the chapter on the politics of risk management and made valuable suggestions and criticisms. I am also grateful to Fred Kramer for his comments and suggestions in initial stages of this study and to Bob Gilmour for his suggestions concerning material to be included in the final chapter.

I would also like to express my appreciation to the governmental officials and former governmental officials, including EPA officials, staff members of congressional committees, and specialists in environmental and public interest organizations, who were interviewed or provided background information for this study. Stuart Eizenstat, former assistant to President Carter in Domestic Affairs and Policy; Erik D. Olson, Conservation Foundation; Morton Rosenberg, Congressional Research Service; Debra A. Jacobson, counsel, Subcommittee on Oversight and Investigation, House Committee on Energy and Commerce; Roger L. Sperry, former senior GAO consultant for the Senate Committee on Governmental Affairs; Gary Bass of OMB Watch; and Stephen Jellinek, former staff director of the Council on Environmental Quality, were especially helpful.

I would also like to thank Bill Thompson and the staff of the Government Documents Division at the University of Massachusetts for their assistance; Doris Holden, for her ability to decipher my scrawl in typing the drafts of this book; Charlotte Belenky, for her encouragement in writing the book; and the Greenwood Press staff for their cooperation and patience in making this book a reality.

Presidential
Influence
and
Environmental
Policy

Introduction

Presidents influence environmental policy through strategies affecting legislation and through administrative tactics and means. In this study the administrative presidency and its resources are examined more as a means of influencing the course of environmentally related policies than as a vehicle for presidential coordination and oversight over a complex federal bureaucracy. The tools of the administrative presidency are analyzed as a means of promoting presidential policy goals in advancing environmentally related objectives as well as in constraining them, for example in the Ronald Reagan administrative presidency strategy. Some of the problems associated with both approaches are also explored.

Some presidential achievements and problems are examined in advancing conservation policy objectives in the first half of this century during the presidencies of Theodore Roosevelt and Franklin Roosevelt. More recent presidents have faced environmental policy problems more complex than the conservation policy goals that the two Roosevelts addressed. The presidencies of Jimmy Carter and George Bush are evaluated in their commitments to promote environmental goals through administrative means. They have been confronted with the challenges of maintaining economic growth and promoting greater energy supplies and balancing such goals with environmental protection.

Since F.D.R.'s presidency, chief executives have sought to achieve greater managerial control over a burgeoning federal executive establishment. Given the pressures and expectations of executive leadership by Congress and the public, presidents of both parties promoted the centralization and politicization of the institutional presidency, particularly through the Office of Management and Budget (OMB), in order to promote their policy objectives. The trend continued throughout the Reagan presidency, primarily through the White House's controversial administrative presidency strategy.

A major purpose of this book is to extend the analysis of the Reagan administrative presidency strategy and its impact on environmentally related policies throughout the Reagan years and to examine its legacy for the Bush Administration. Previous administrations attempted to provide coordination and cost considerations in selected regulatory programs, but the Reagan Administration initiated a more centralized review and an integrated system of controls of agency activities that had substantive impacts on some agency programs. The role of the OMB in the centralized review system of agency information requests, proposed agency regulations, and risk assessments relating to environmental policies is examined as an instrument of the Reagan administrative presidency strategy in promoting regulatory relief and a reduced federal presence.

The first vantage point of the strategy lay in selectively shaping regulatory programs dealing with environmental and social policies through interpretation of the Paperwork Reduction Act (PRA) of 1980 and the role of OMB's Office of Information and Regulatory Affairs (OIRA) created by that act in reviewing agency information requests. OMB's reports, for example, indicated that the Environmental Protection Agency (EPA) had one of the highest percentages of information requests withdrawn by an agency or disapproved by OIRA during the Reagan presidency. A comprehensive study by the General Accounting Office (GAO) analyzed the limitations of OIRA in assessing agency information requests of a complex scientific nature. Another study conducted by the Harvard University School of Public Health and Mount Sinai School of Medicine documented OIRA's selective bias against environmentally related research requests submitted by the Centers for Disease Control (CDC). The Reagan White House's use of the resources of the administrative presidency also had special impacts on the statistical policy of regulatory agencies, including EPA and the Occupational Safety and Health Administration (OSHA).

Presidential executive orders and presidential proclamations have long been significant vehicles in promoting conservation policy and environmental policy. However, the Reagan Administration revoked President Carter's executive orders in environmental and natural resources activities as part of its goal to reduce the influence of the federal government.

All of President Reagan's executive orders dealing with environmental and natural resources areas are described, with special analysis of Reagan's key orders, Executive Order (E.O.) 12291 and Executive Order (E.O.)

12498, dealing with regulatory policy. E.O. 12291 provided OMB with considerable power and discretion in a centralized review system of major rules proposed by regulatory agencies. The order had a demonstrable impact on EPA and some other agencies, with EPA among the agencies highest in withdrawing its proposed rules or revising them and in meeting delay in obtaining OMB approval throughout the Reagan Administration and into the first year of the Bush Administration. E.O. 12498 represented the capstone of the Reagan strategy, requiring proposed agency regulatory agendas to be submitted to OMB to ensure their conformity with presidential priorities unless prevented by statute or court order. E.O. 12291 and E.O. 12498 also served as important bases in the administrative presidency strategy's promotion of a scientifically justifiable but more risk-tolerant approach in risk assessment in regulatory policy. E.O. 12630, the "takings" order, represented one of the Administration's last efforts to constrain the regulatory process and minimize the intrusion of federal regulations on private interests.

In response to Reagan's administrative strategy, Congress required greater public disclosure and reporting requirements under the machinery established by E.O. 12291 and E.O. 12498. It also placed restrictions and reduced the flexibility of agency heads appointed by the president in the reauthorization of some key environmental laws. The federal judiciary, while recognizing a legitimate role for presidents in regulatory policy, reversed some decisions by agency heads appointed by Reagan when they disregarded statutory requirements in promoting regulatory relief. Thus, Congress and the courts corrected some of the omissions and excesses of the centralized review system, but the basic framework of the centralized review system, established by Reagan's executive orders, remained intact without a successfully mounted constitutional challenge. OIRA's influence declined, however, and Reagan's administrative presidency strategy left his successor a legacy of mistrust and suspicion of White House motives concerning regulatory policy and environmental policy.

As a pragmatic "Tory" conservative, President Bush has attempted to balance and placate environmental and economic development interests as well as Republican moderates and conservative ideologues in his administrative presidency. He restored presidential support for environmental policies in the Republican Party after the Reagan era, but his overall record on environmental and natural resources issues has disappointed the environmental community. In the 1988 election the president and his advisers were aware of the significant and sustained level of public support for environmental protection. However, they are also acutely aware that the political incentives for a president's election and reelection and his overall high public approval rating are primarily related to the public's perception of the effectiveness of presidential leadership in economic matters. Presidential priorities are conditioned by the fact that the American presidency operates in a political economy that has not yet adequately taken into account the environmental costs associated with the goals of economic growth and well-being.

Major research sources for this book include OMB's reports and other presidential documents, congressional hearings and reports and studies by research arms of Congress, federal court decisions, and interviews with environmental agency personnel and environmental organization officials.

Chapter 1 serves as an introduction to an analysis of some of the advantages and limitations of using the administrative resources of the presidency as instruments of presidential influence. It is supplemented by a discussion of the significance of presidential executive orders in Chapter 3. An examination of the presidency of Theodore Roosevelt in promoting conservation policy objectives and Franklin Roosevelt's presidency in advancing conservation and water pollution control policies records their achievements as well as their problems with Congress in using presidential administrative powers. Carter's trusteeship conception of the presidency and his use of administrative presidency resources to promote environmental goals are also analyzed and compared with President Reagan's administrative presidency strategy.

Chapter 2 examines the Reagan Administration's efforts to control the flow of agency information requests and the gathering of statistics as an integral part of its strategy to curb the ability of agencies to issue and justify proposed new regulations. This chapter reviews the background for the adoption of the Paperwork Reduction Act of 1980, the Carter Administration's initial implementation of PRA's Information Collection Budget, the Reagan Administration's interpretation of the law, and the Office of Information and Regulatory Affairs procedures in reviewing agency information requests. The impacts of OIRA's review system upon environmental agency requests and the limitations of OIRA in evaluating complex scientific agency information requests are analyzed. This is augmented by an examination of the influence of the Reagan administrative presidency strategy through appointments, reorganization, and budgets on statistical policy, particularly with regard to EPA and OSHA.

Chapter 3 seeks to evaluate the significance of the presidential executive order in environmental policy. This chapter presents all presidential orders from the high point of the environmental movement in 1970 to the Bush Administration and includes all of President Richard Nixon's and President Carter's executive orders promoting environmental policy. Chapter 3 also includes all of President Reagan's orders, including his key E.O. 12291 and E.O. 12498 dealing with regulatory policy, his "takings" executive order, and orders promoting the Administration's New Federalism. Some selected executive orders are analyzed in more detail in which a president promoted environmental objectives or constrained them to determine if they brought about changes in the substantive or procedural aspects of environmental policy. Where possible, policy outputs are recorded, such as the number of environmental impact statements issued, as well as the number of proposed agency regulations withdrawn or revised in compliance with presidential executive orders.

Chapter 4 contrasts the different perspectives of the Carter and Reagan Administrations on risk assessment and documents OMB's increased involvement in risk assessment as part of the Reagan administrative presidency strategy. Differences between regulatory agencies and OMB in assessing environmental and health risks and in calculating the costs and benefits of reducing such risks are discussed, along with a special analysis of OMB's review of EPA's proposed cancer risk guidelines in the Reagan Administration. The views of critics of the role of OMB and its limitations in reviewing risk assessments are presented, along with the perspective that OMB can have an appropriate role in a pluralistic system of risk management.

Chapter 5 traces the impact of the Reagan administrative presidency strategy on EPA's enforcement activities under the Burford regime and the restoration of EPA's enforcement credibility as "rule-following policeman" under Ruckelshaus's leadership as EPA administrator. The politics of enforcement of some environmental programs under Reagan's New Federalism are also examined. The Surface Mining and Reclamation Act and the Office of Surface Mining (OSM) were prime targets of the Reagan Administration to obtain regulatory relief. A case study of the OSM's role and enforcement policies describes the struggle between the Reagan Administration and congressional oversight committees and between the Administration and environmental groups in federal courts. The case study documents the outcome and political costs borne by the agency. A comparison of enforcement activity of EPA and OSM suggests that agencies may differ in their ability to offer greater resistance to presidential influence.

Chapter 6 traces the counterreaction of Congress and the federal judiciary to Reagan's administrative presidency initiatives and the Reagan legacy inherited by the Bush Administration. President Bush's pragmatic selective use of the administrative presidency resources in appointments and budgetary policy is analyzed as a means of balancing environmental and development interests. Bush's record to fulfill his commitment to be an environmentalist president is examined, along with his assignment of the President's Council on Competitiveness to monitor the costs of proposed social and environmental regulations, his efforts to extend presidential influence, through OMB, over agency risk assessments, and his maintenance of centralized review of agency regulations and their agendas. The controversies surrounding the Bush Administration's national energy strategy and its policies on wetland protection and protection of the spotted owl and ancient forests are probed as examples of the Administration's difficulties in working out compromises between environmental and economic interests.

Chapter 7 concludes that an administrative presidency strategy, exemplified by the Reagan Administration, is counterproductive both in its long-term risks for presidential influence in environmental policy and in its impacts on environmental policy. Some significant gains in conservation policy and environmental protection were realized through tapping the presidential administrative powers in several administrations. But the record indicates there is either the risk of congressional retaliation or the probability that other political incentives and competing policy claims may eventually undercut a president's environmental commitment. The potential for using a president's administrative resources to provide national and international leadership in environmental policy is addressed, as well as some of the problematic aspects of obtaining such leadership in the American political system and political economy.

1

Presidential Administrative Influence: From Conservation Policy to Environmental Policy

The presidency plays a vital role in environmental policy, even though it has not been the dominant branch in forging most of the key environmental laws. The president's role is critical in supporting or in opposing environmental legislation, and presidential administrative powers can also be significant in affecting the course of environmental policy. Recently, there has been more scholarly attention to the administrative or managerial dimensions of the presidency as they impact on public policy and the federal bureaucracy. This study seeks to extend the understanding of the politics and impacts of the administrative presidency, particularly in the field of environmental policy.[1]

One model of the modern administrative state envisions the president as the only nationally elected leader and chief executive with broad electoral support and broad executive power in the Constitution, which justifies significant presidential authority to direct and shape the execution of the laws and to supervise and coordinate the sometimes conflicting activities of the federal bureaucracy. Such a broad interpretation of authority acknowledges that the president is prohibited from acting contrary to the law, but it risks interbranch conflict with congressional prerogatives, especially when congressional priorities are spelled out in statutory provisions, legislative histories, and oversight hearings.

Another model of the administrative state contends that Congress, too, has electoral support and represents constituencies and has valid longstanding prerogatives and constitutional powers to control the bureaucracy. According to this model, federal agencies are directed by statutes and congressional oversight, rather than by hierarchical presidential direction. Agencies are located in the executive branch, but they also are considered arms of Congress, since administrative rule making is seen as an extension of the lawmaking power. Furthermore, the fact that presidents are obliged to take care that the laws are faithfully executed does not mean that presidents or their subordinates should execute the laws themselves. Rather, they are obliged to provide oversight in making sure that those who are statutorily delegated to execute the laws in fact fulfill their responsibility.[2]

These conflicting interpretations have long-standing roots. In fact, from the republic's birth, the Constitution presented an invitation for an inter-branch struggle for control and direction of the infant bureaucracy.

As a source of executive-legislative friction, it would be difficult to select an issue more deep-rooted than control of the bureaucracy. For almost two centuries Congress and the President have competed with one another for the power to regulate the activity of departments and the agencies. Both branches while operating with limits have legitimate claims to a supervisory power.[3]

The legal basis for the administrative presidency rests upon the several powers granted the president in the Constitution's Article II, Sections 1–3;[4] implied powers derived from this article, such as executive privilege, executive orders, and presidential proclamations; statutes that have authorized, expanded, or constricted a president's administrative powers; and Supreme Court decisions that have broadly or narrowly interpreted the chief executive's powers or those of Congress relative to the administrative process.

Congress and the president have significant expressed and implied constitutional powers relating to the direction and control of the administrative state.[5] Much has been left to the play of political forces in the competitive system of separate institutions sharing control over the executive branch. When activist presidents or their subordinates are perceived to be overreaching or poaching on congressional territorial prerogatives, particularly when there is divided party control in the two branches, Congress has curbed administrative presidency initiatives or retaliated in other ways.

The constrained interpretation of presidential power in domestic policy throughout most of the nineteenth century limited broad use of presidential administrative powers. These powers grew eventually by congressional authorization and presidential initiatives in the first part of the twentieth century as a large, complex bureaucracy was constructed to cope with problems of an increasingly urban, industrialized society.

The definition of the administrative presidency in this study refers to an approach in which presidents may use two or more of their powers implied or granted by the Constitution or delegated by Congress to promote change in the goals and priorities of federal agencies at the administrative level, rather than modifying policy through the passage of legislation. The administrative presidency method may be preferred as an alternative to pursuing statutory changes because presidents may be unable or unwilling to effect change in their role as legislative leader.

The instruments of the administrative presidency include those of appointment and removal of federal agency officials, the executive budget process, administrative reorganization of federal agencies, delegation of authority to the states, and presidential executive orders and presidential proclamations. The administrative presidency may also encompass a multilayered central clearance system of agency initiatives and operations through the Office of Management and Budget (OMB). This central clearance system now includes OMB review of agency budget requests, new and revised regulations, agency information collection requests, and annual agency regulatory agendas. OMB also reviews agency proposals for legislation and executive orders to be issued by the president. More recently, it increased its role in risk assessment review of proposed agency regulations.

At first sight, these appear to be a formidable array of presidential administrative tools to influence appointed and career agency officials to supplement a president's priorities. However, Congress shares power with the president in the budget and appointment process and must approve administrative reorganizations and program delegations to the states.

The president's budget power is an important lever in enhancing an administration's power to manage federal agency operations. The executive budget establishes an administration's priorities in expanding or cutting agency programs and activities and sets much of the legislative agenda for a given year. OMB's central clearance of agency budget requests promotes considerable direction and control. During the Reagan Administration, budget decisions became more centralized in OMB and the White House. However, Congress can and has reasserted its power in the budget process and diminished presidential effectiveness. For most of the course of the modern presidency, the executive budget served as an authoritative guide for congressional consideration and action. Presidential requests were given serious examination and appropriations approved by Congress were close to the president's requests. In recent years budget expert Allen Shick notes that the budget has changed from an authoritative instrument into an opening move in a laborious year-long bargaining process. Furthermore, he sees the president's once-formidable budget power weakened due to congressional reassertiveness and presidential unwillingness to protect his stakes.[6]

Some congressional reassertiveness is attributable to President Nixon's administrative action in attempting to impose budget and spending restraints through the impoundment of appropriated funds. Congress retaliated by establishing restrictions on presidential deferrals and recissions of appropriated funds in passing the Budget and Impoundment Control Act of 1974. President Reagan also was blocked by federal courts and the Congress when he sought large-scale deferrals of appropriated funds to promote his domestic policy objectives. His deferrals were overruled in both district and circuit courts and Congress added further checks when it terminated presidential power to make policy-type deferrals in the Gramm–Rudman–Hollings law (P.L. 100–119, Section 1013(b) of the Budget and Impoundment Control Act as amended).[7]

Congress also reasserted itself in playing a stronger role in the reconciliation process provided in the 1974 Budget Act after President Reagan won his powerful budget victory in 1981. However, by 1983 Congress regrouped and shaped the reconciliation process more in line with its priorities, rather than the president's, for the remainder of the Reagan presidency.

The president's power of appointment constitutes another important vehicle for an incoming administration to promote a president's policy goals. Too often, however, presidents constructed a balanced cabinet by accommodating various factions within the president's party or recognizing important constituencies within the president's coalition, instead of selecting individuals who shared their policy objectives or values.

The powers of appointment and removal have been placed in service of a president's claim of a popular mandate to govern and implement policies that were presented in his victorious campaign and election. Even though there are serious doubts that such a policy mandate is attained on many specific issues, public and congressional expectations call for a central presidential leadership role in policy development.8 Furthermore, the considerable discretion granted agency heads in administering many laws provides additional leverage and incentives for presidents to influence public policy and bureaucratic activity through the appointment of political executives who share the president's goals and values. The appointment of loyal agency heads offers a means of overcoming bureaucratic inertia and resistance to presidential priorities, witnessed by both Republican and Democratic presidents. Richard Nathan in *The Administrative Presidency* advanced a vigorous administrative presidency strategy along these lines to provide greater direction and coordination of the administrative state.[9]

Presidential appointees can exert significant influence on an agency's operations through personnel management, such as transfers and staff reductions, through agency reorganizations that do not require congressional approval, and through managerial controls over approval of grants and budget apportionment within the agency. They also can craft an agency's enforcement strategy and approve regulations and proposed studies of their respective agencies.

President Reagan appointed a number of loyalists at the cabinet and subcabinet levels in environmental and natural resources agencies who shared his conservative values. Other presidents with a less integrated administrative presidency strategy appointed department heads who shared their perspective favoring an activist federal government role. Secretaries of the Interior James Garfield, Harold Ickes, Stewart Udall, and Cecil Andrus reflected the more activist values, respectively, of Presidents Theodore Roosevelt, Franklin Roosevelt, Lyndon Johnson, and Jimmy Carter.

The appointment power is a potent lever for change, but there are checks on its use in promoting a president's policy goals. A number of officials in independent regulatory agencies have fixed terms of office, and the White House must wait until an occupant retires or his or her term is completed before an appointment can be made. Although the Senate usually confirms appointments of the president that are required by the Constitution or by statute, key senators of the opposing party have held hostage a presidential appointment in order to indicate their displeasure and to exact concessions from the White House. Furthermore, all appointed agency officials must undertake actions required by law, which may not be in accord with the preferences of an administration. When Congress is concerned that agency heads have strained legislative intent in their discretionary power to implement a law, it can retaliate in various ways, including tightening restrictions on an agency head's discretion, imposing "hammer" time deadlines on the reauthorization of programs, and cutting an agency's appropriations.

There are other limitations on the appointment power in furthering a president's goals. The high level of mobility of many appointed political executives, their lack of governmental managerial skills, unfamiliarity with the Washington political system, and lack of policy-related experience and training have been long-term problems. Clearly, these factors present serious obstacles for a president to find and appoint a large number of qualified, experienced, and loyal political executives to work with career agency personnel in implementing his political goals. On a more limited basis, however, some programs considered successful in implementing an administration's goals through the appointment process involved cooperative, constructive support and participation by agency career personnel working with political executives.[10]

The administrative presidency has been associated recently with Ronald Reagan's neglect of environmental and natural resources policy. However, the tools of the administrative presidency have also been used to advance environmental protection and conservation policy. President Theodore Roosevelt used a vigorous administrative presidency approach with considerable success in conservation policy with the limited tools available to him in the beginning of the administrative state. Franklin Roosevelt relied heavily on his budget powers and his popular leadership to advance conservation and water pollution control policies in the emergence of the administrative state.

A generation later, presidents focused greater attention upon the more complex problems of environmental policy and environmental protection, involving a broader public and a greater constellation of interests, with the emergence of the environmental movement.[11] Jimmy Carter, for example, used administrative powers without the rhetorical and political skills of the two Roosevelts in efforts to balance environmental protection with his Administration's energy and economic policies at another evolutionary stage of the administrative state. Each of these three presidents realized some environmentally related gains, along with problematic consequences, in his application of the administrative presidency.

Theodore Roosevelt came to personify the modern presidency, particularly as popular leader, in his relations with the press and in his efforts to build a more professional federal bureaucracy. Roosevelt is considered to be a founder of the rhetorical presidency, using popular appeals over the heads of Congress and leaders of his party to attain his policy goals.[12] He was also the first twentieth-century president to resourcefully exploit the resources of the administrative presidency. "Roosevelt pushed executive prerogatives to their limits. Nurturing the development of substantive administrative powers, he drove a wedge into the institutional relationships established among parties, courts, Congress and the states."[13]

Roosevelt developed a new presidential concept along Hamiltonian lines, the stewardship theory of the presidency. In domestic policy it was implemented largely within the context of conservation and natural resources policy. He declared that it was not only a president's right "but his duty to do anything that the needs of the nation demanded unless such action was forbidden by the Constitution or by the laws."[14]

One of the most controversial aspects of Roosevelt's implementation of his stewardship theory was his expansive interpretation of presidential withdrawal powers of lands in the public domain. He made extensive, controversial withdrawals of coal lands and land for power sites and watershed control. Without specific statutory authorization, Roosevelt issued an executive order directing the secretary of the interior to withdraw from all entry millions of acres of valuable coal lands. He expanded the application of presidential withdrawal powers in order to prevent the transference of coal lands into private hands. In defense of Roosevelt's withdrawal orders, Secretary of the Interior James Garfield declared:

> From the earliest days the Executive has found it necessary in the public interest to take action concerning the public lands by withdrawing areas from entry. There was no specific provision of law for many of these withdrawals, and yet they were made unhesitatingly by the Executive as steward and were approved by Congress in acts granting land for the purpose for which it was withdrawn.[15]

In implementing his stewardship theory, Roosevelt anticipated the modern administrative presidency in his activist, resourceful, and expansive use of presidential power. Roosevelt's administrative presidency was characterized by the appointment, support, and advancement of skilled, loyal subordinates who shared the president's views on broad executive authority and conservation and natural resources policy. He also appointed four Blue Ribbon study commissions dealing with public lands, inland waterways, national conservation, and rural problems to gather facts, mobilize opinion, and prod Congress on natural resources problems. Facing a more conservative Congress dominated by oligarchs of his own party, he forged "an executive-professional reform coalition through support of a small cadre of ambitious young bureaucrats."[16] His presidency was marked by a liberal construction of existing statutes by himself and by his subordinates. Roosevelt attempted to push his broader reform agenda, avoiding clashes with Congress or bypassing it for much of his presidency, except for the last months of his term of office.

Theodore Roosevelt's expansive application of presidential withdrawal powers and his proposed reform of the land laws eventually met vigorous opposition in affected Western states. Some Western senators appended a rider to an appropriation bill providing that no forest reserves or additions to existing reserves could be created in the timber states of Oregon, Washington, Montana, Idaho, and Wyoming, unless by act of Congress. Roosevelt was forced to sign the appropriation bill but, before affixing his signature, he and Gifford Pinchot outmaneuvered the opposition by proclaiming the addition of twenty-one forest reserves including sixteen million acres of new forests in the same five states. These orders created an uproar. Although none of the reserves was eliminated by Congress, congressional opponents found other means of retaliation by cutting funds for some of Roosevelt's study commissions and by rejecting some of his other policy recommendations.

Roosevelt's administrative record on conservation has been unrivaled by any other president. In fact, he deemed his conservation policies the most important domestic achievements in his presidency.[17] He employed a broad construction of the Antiquities Act of 1906—an act empowering presidents to create national monuments for the preservation of historic landmarks and other objects of historic or scientific interest. The president proclaimed more than eight hundred thousand acres of the Grand Canyon a national monument, protecting much of the area from development until Congress created the Grand Canyon National Park in 1919. In this action he set a precedent for creating vast national monument areas and created eighteen national monuments, the greatest number by any president, including four monuments so large that Congress later declared them national parks.

In spite of his broad interpretation of his statutory and constitutional powers, Roosevelt could not claim preponderant influence, as compared to Congress, in the passage of any major conservation or natural resources legislation.[18] The role of president as legislative leader did not become firmly rooted until the modern institutionalized presidency was launched in Franklin Roosevelt's presidency. Second, Theodore Roosevelt's stewardship theory clashed with a circumscribed presidential tradition that had only been successfully broken by Jackson and Lincoln in the nineteenth century. Moreover, his activist presidency clashed with long-standing congressional prerogatives and interests in natural resources politics and the public domain. Powerful Western senators who controlled key committees dealing with natural resources measures also opposed the policies of Roosevelt and Pinchot. From a political perspective, although the Republican Party controlled Congress and the presidency, Roosevelt had to deal with congressional leaders such as Speaker of the House Joseph Cannon and Senate Majority Leader Nelson Aldrich, who had little interest in national resources matters. Lastly, Roosevelt lacked the power to draw up and submit the budget to Congress, a power Congress later granted the presidency in 1921.

Roosevelt's administrative presidency and his broad construction of executive power eventually brought about party revolt and retaliation from the Congress. The Administration's effort to redistribute prerogatives from the Congress and the courts toward the bureaucracy and the chief executive was checked by Congress and by the erosion of support of members of Roosevelt's own party. The relations between Congress and Roosevelt had become so bitter and frayed concerning administrative reform and other actions of the president that Speaker Cannon and Republican Senate Majority Leader Aldrich were among the leaders considering formal censure of Roosevelt.[19]

With the development of the modern institutionalized presidency, more than a generation later, the role of the president as legislative leader had finally become rooted. Congress granted the presidency powers to reorganize the executive branch as well as budgetary powers, which Franklin D. Roosevelt and subsequent presidents of both parties used to enhance their roles as legislative leader and managerial chief of the executive branch.

The Roosevelt Administration's approach was unique in the magnitude and number of public works investments, in the variety of agencies created by Congress, and tasks undertaken in natural resources and in other fields. The Administration was the first to allocate a significant portion of budgeted funds to redress the water pollution problem. The New Deal addressed the water pollution problem indirectly and incidentally in provisions of other major legislation, in budget allocations providing grant-in-aid and technical assistance to the states in allocated funds for sewage treatment facilities under the National Industrial Recovery Act, and in other emergency work relief and public works programs. In these programs the federal government encouraged local and regional planning efforts for pollution control. The National Industrial Recovery Act included a provision for a comprehensive $3.3 billion program of public works, encompassing conservation and development of natural resources; development of water power; flood control; construction of river and harbor improvements; prevention of soil and coastal erosion; and utilization, control, and purification of water.

Roosevelt and his aides tied Keynesian economics to the older conservation ethos. The Public Works Administration (PWA) spent more than $4 billion on more than 34,000 projects, including flood control, Boulder Dam construction, reclamation, recreation, and water pollution abatement. More than two-thirds of all new sewage treatment plants constructed nationwide between 1933 and 1939 were PWA projects. Public works allotments were distributed for 1,527 sewage systems, of which $325 million were for 873 sewage treatment works. PWA gave preference to those projects that adhered to local and regional planning, and it assisted localities in such planning. Roosevelt also directed PWA to refuse applications for the construction of sewage systems that might allow untreated sewage to increase overall pollution in any lake or stream. The Works Progress Administration (WPA) also provided work for thousands of unemployed in building small dams for flood control and irrigation and for the construction of more than two million sanitary privies in rural and suburban areas. WPA funds were also expended to curb water pollution caused by seepage from abandoned mines. In cooperation with state officials, more than four thousand mine units were sealed, resulting in the reduction of sulphuric acid in rivers and streams.[20]

Congress passed the first inland water pollution control bill in 1938, establishing a division of water pollution in the Public Health Service and providing grants-in-aid to states and municipalities for sewage treatment facilities. F.D.R. clearly approved of the establishment of a division of water pollution control, but he vetoed the bill on the grounds that appropriations for such projects should be based upon estimates submitted in the budget. The president and Budget Director Harold Smith were not going to permit a breach in the president's budget powers.

During the evolution of the Administration's controversial national planning advisory system from 1933 to 1943, which F.D.R. promoted through his administrative powers, an effort was made to lay the groundwork for a comprehensive, long-range national policy for conservation and for the development of the country's natural resources. Long-range goals for land use and conservation and a national water policy were planned. Studies and reports were produced on regional planning, energy resources, river basins, and water pollution, including the status of water pollution in the nation and problems in its abatement. Water pollution abatement was to be considered an integral part of river basin planning, even though the Corps of Engineers and key congressional committees were still reluctant to do so. Secretary of War George Dern and the Corps of Engineers, for example, believed that flood control and stream pollution were special problems, each of which should be dealt with by special groups of experts, and the coordination of unrelated activities could prove disruptive rather than beneficial.

Roosevelt sought to strengthen presidential influence in public works and water resources planning by requiring the National Resources Planning Board to submit yearly recommendations to Congress, including a priority list of public works and rivers and harbors improvements for congressional consideration. Congress and the Corps perceived this innovation as a challenge to the venerable pork-barrel distributist system. They successfully resisted White House efforts in public works planning.

Eventually, Congress killed the National Resources Planning Board by cutting its funds, and the Administration regrouped its efforts to achieve a semblance of planning by requiring agencies to submit public works proposals and rivers and harbors projects to the Bureau of the Budget for review. Roosevelt was more successful in doubling the acreage of national forests and setting aside eleven national monuments by presidential proclamation and protecting wildlife on federal lands.

A generation later, President Johnson, who recalled F.D.R.'s achievements, included conservation and environmental initiatives as part of his Great Society program and supported preservationist goals in conservation policy advocated by Secretary of the Interior Stewart Udall.[21] Recognizing the power of the environmental movement, President Nixon appointed competent environmental officials, signed landmark legislation, and issued executive orders promoting environmental protection, including a reorganization plan establishing the Environmental Protection Agency (EPA). However, within two years Nixon moved on to other policy concerns, after placing institutional constraints on EPA and environmental regulations.

Presidents Nixon, Ford, and Carter became increasingly preoccupied with energy policy questions as American domestic oil production declined and the country depended more on imported oil from the volatile Middle East. They faced tradeoff questions between environmental protection and energy supply policies, as well as concerns about a faltering economy and the increasing costs of environmental and safety regulations required by regulatory policies adopted in the 1960s and early 1970s.

President Jimmy Carter presented an ambitious policy agenda, matching America's most activist presidents, but without the rhetorical skills, political experience, and popular leadership needed to move the American people and Congress, and under political conditions in the post–Watergate period unfavorable for vigorous presidential leadership. He was convinced that the United States could have economic and energy development and adequate environmental protection, but did not fully appreciate the potential conflicts and problems in pursuing such objectives. He campaigned on an environmentalist platform but also committed his Administration to addressing the nation's energy problems to the point of supporting some energy policies that were considered environmentally disruptive. He approved a number of environmental laws, adding to the growth and cost of the administrative state. Yet at the same time, he pledged his Administration to regulatory reform, efficiency in government, administrative reorganization, and a balanced budget. As the country's problems grew by mid-term, he strengthened his administrative presidency machinery to analyze inflationary impacts of new regulations, including environmental, health, and safety regulations.[22] Edward Fuchs pointed out that, on the one hand, Carter endorsed competition and deregulation as the solution to some regulatory problems and, on the other hand, he favored regulation that was costly—for example, environmental and safety regulations—in the public interest. In favoring both liberal and conservative positions in regulatory policy, which he characterized as a common sense, flexible approach, he added some confusion concerning his priorities.[23]

Carter portrayed himself as a programmatic liberal in environmental protection and civil rights and a fiscal conservative in economic affairs.[24] However, Carter's policy agenda plate was so loaded that he was criticized for failing to clearly target his priorities for Congress and the public. To fulfill Carter's commitment to environmental protection, the White House appointed a large number of activists from environmental and public interest organizations and former governmental officials to cabinet, agency head, and subcabinet posts. At the same time, officials were appointed to key economic positions who reflected the president's more conservative fiscal views and interest in deregulation and regulatory reform.

The divergent perspectives of environmental officials and conservative economists that Carter appointed led inevitably to some policy conflicts in which agency heads refused to accede to White House pressure to reduce proposed regulatory standards. Rather than selecting cabinet officials and subcabinet officials who shared the president's values, the Carter White House endorsed granting cabinet officials significant discretion in selecting their subordinates. This was part of the president's commitment to grant greater cabinet department autonomy in order to avoid overcentralized White House control and direction. The cabinet system approach proved unworkable, and cabinet and subcabinet members were accused of pursuing their own agendas. The White House was forced to exert greater control over agency political executives, and in 1979 the cabinet was reorganized following the resignation of four department heads as well as a number of subcabinet officials.

Carter's trusteeship conception of the presidency and presidential policy making involved laying out a comprehensive analysis of a policy issue, leading to the "right choice" on behalf of the public interest, but with limited participation and consultation with members of Congress.[25] His trusteeship approach, his commitment to environmental values and economic efficiency, and his reformist bent were demonstrated in one of his first official acts with the proposed elimination of a number of water projects authorized by Congress. Carter's decision challenged some egregious examples of pork-barrel water and dam building projects.

Eventually, Congress reluctantly agreed to eliminate nine of the eighteen dams and water projects and to modify five others on Carter's final "hit list" in 1977. Over the next two years the president used the veto and threat of the veto to oppose congressional efforts to reinstate some of the originally deleted projects. Carter wanted more presidential oversight and uniform procedures in cost–benefit analysis of water projects. Toward that end, he proposed that the Water Resources Council staff be expanded to conduct independent reviews of preconstruction plans of the Corps of Engineers, the Bureau of Reclamation, and the Soil Conservation Service.

The council survived a House of Representatives vote to abolish it and transfer its functions to the Department of the Interior (DOI). Carter issued an executive order authorizing the council to review all projects before they were submitted to the Congress, but Congress cut the council's funding and refused to appropriate funds for that purpose. Although Carter managed to eliminate some of the most wasteful pork-barrel projects and raised the issue of reforming the system, he failed to bring about more fundamental long-term reforms. Carter later admitted that the water projects battle "left deep scars" and "caused the deepest breach between me and the Democratic leadership."[26] The incoming Reagan Administration promptly canceled Carter's executive order and by 1983 achieved its goal of eliminating the council when Congress denied it any funds.

Carter also applied his trusteeship approach in the Administration's major effort to adopt a comprehensive national energy policy. His commitment to submit a complex energy package, within a rigid ninety-day deadline, produced a National Energy Plan "formulated with no significant substantive consultation" with key members of Congress, officials of established federal agencies, and affected interest groups. The views of interest groups and the public were solicited but with only pro forma participation in the planning process.[27] The president's plan had a strong conservation component that was warmly supported by environmental groups. However, essential parts of the energy package were considerably amended, particularly by the Senate over an eighteen-month period, before energy legislation was signed by Carter. From an environmental and energy conservation perspective, the result was disappointing. The gas guzzler tax on automobiles was considered innocuous, but there were modest tax credits for energy efficiency in buildings and incentives for the installation of solar heating.[28]

However, adoption of elements of the Administration's energy plan did not prevent skyrocketing increases in imported oil prices, and the White House in desperation approved the establishment of two new agencies. The Energy Security Corporation, renamed the Synthetic Fuels Corporation, opposed by environmentalists, was approved in a scaled-down version by Congress. However, the Energy Mobilization Board, with authority to break regulatory barriers in promoting "fast-track" energy projects, was defeated in Congress, aided by the continued combined forces of environmentalists and states rights supporters. Environmentalists were pleased with Carter's proposed windfall profits tax on oil companies, with tax revenues to be placed in an energy trust fund to finance alternative fuels to assist the poor and aid mass transit. However, in approving the tax, Congress chose instead to place the tax revenues in the general fund, setting its guidelines for the same objectives.

Opponents of nuclear power praised Carter for his opposition to funding the completion of the Clinch River Breeder Reactor Demonstration Project. The president vetoed an appropriations bill providing funds for the project on the grounds that it was unnecessarily expensive and could lead to the greater availability of plutonium for nuclear weapons proliferation. The Administration only supported funds for the termination of the project and offered as a compromise fiscal support for the development of alternative breeder reactors that would not produce plutonium. Congress accepted neither proposal and managed to keep the Clinch River Project alive throughout the Carter presidency. Opponents of nuclear power were less pleased with the Administration's proposals to streamline the licensing process for new reactors with proper safeguards from the average of twelve years to six years. After the Three Mile Island accident, a presidentially appointed commission favored replacing the Nuclear Regulatory Commission (NRC) with an agency headed by a single administrator. Carter, however, rejected the commission's abolition and supported granting the NRC chairman more authority.

Carter used his budget authority to support environmental and natural resources programs without drastic cuts in spite of a worsening economic situation by mid-term.[29] Budget requests for renewable energy and conservation programs were also raised significantly during the Carter presidency. Carter was especially committed to administrative reorganization and management reforms. In the areas of energy and environmental and natural resources policies, he obtained approval for a new Department of Energy but abandoned cabinet reorganization plans and a proposed Department of Natural Resources in the face of agency and clientele groups opposition. He also rejected his advisers' reorganization plan recommending disbanding the President's Council on Environmental Quality (CEQ) and allocating its functions to other environmental agencies.

The Carter Administration used presidential executive orders and presidential proclamations as major tools in advancing environmental and natural resources objectives. Executive orders were issued (1) to empower CEQ to issue regulations to promote federal agency compliance with the 1970 National Environmental Policy Act (NEPA), (2) to require federal agency environmental assessments of their actions having extraterritorial impacts, and (3) to protect flood plains and wetlands. Presidential proclamations were also issued to protect Alaska lands from mineral entry and development. The background of these and other executive orders and proclamations is more fully examined in Chapter 3. Some proved useful policy instruments in advancing the president's environmental and natural resources goals. However, their use illustrated the complex, protracted interagency negotiations needed to forge some executive orders, as well as problems in obtaining compliance. Moreover, Carter faced the wrath of members of Congress with his executive order providing greater presidential oversight of water projects. Finally, executive orders may become transient policy instruments that can be revoked or revised by a president's successor. President Reagan, for example, promptly revoked almost all of Carter's executive orders relating to environmental and natural resources policies.

The Carter White House was tentative in its approach to regulatory affairs in its first year, but by 1978 the president's environmental regulations and the actions of the Regulatory Analysis Review Group (RARG) were criticized by the environmental community for benefiting the business community at the expense of the broader public. Carter then established a Regulatory Council, with EPA Administrator Douglas Costle as head, to provide some input of regulatory agencies and some balance in the regulatory process. The Administration's regulatory machinery depended on the active involvement and interest of the president, who served as a final court of appeals in major regulatory disputes. Carter's direct intervention to pressure the Occupational Health and Safety Administration (OSHA) to relax maximum permissible levels of cotton dust led to vigorous protests by environmental and public health groups. After the rupture, Carter withdrew as a major actor and the RARG system floundered. While the Carter Administration's presidential oversight in regulatory policy was stronger than in the Nixon and Ford Administrations, the results were mixed. There were claims that agencies gave more attention to cost-effective considerations in order to avoid RARG reviews, but there were no serious penalties that could be imposed on agencies for noncompliance.[30]

In addition to their misgivings about some of Carter's initiatives in energy policy, environmentalists criticized the Administration for pressuring Congress to extend the auto emission standards for two years with tighter limits for 1980, 1981, and 1982. They also found fault with the Administration's Roadless Area Review Evaluation (RARE II) proposals and vigorously opposed Secretary of the Interior Andrus's proposals to lease over twenty-three million acres of the offshore continental shelf for oil and gas exploration, including acreage proximate to the George's Bank fishing grounds in New England. On the other hand, they praised Secretary Andrus and President Carter for their leadership and support in the passage of the Alaska National Interest Lands Conservation Act of 1980. In the closing days of the Carter presidency, Andrus added five California rivers, including 1,235 miles, to the nation's preserve under the Wild and Scenic Rivers Act. Carter could also claim credit for approving the Clean Air Amendments of 1977, the Superfund law, and the Surface Mining and Reclamation Act (SMRCA), which President Ford had vetoed two times.

One of the Carter Administration's major legislative achievements, the Civil Service Reform Act of 1978, expanded presidential power over the bureaucracy, permitting the White House to transfer members of a newly created Senior Executive Service between and within agencies. Carter also strongly supported the Paperwork Reduction Act of 1980, which created an Office of Information and Regulatory Affairs in OMB to review agency information requests. The Reagan Administration was to use these two laws to better advantage in its administrative presidency strategy in influencing the bureaucracy to fulfill its goals.

Modern presidents must be concerned with a broad number of policy issues and with competing claims for their attention and support, but the bulk of their time and energies is usually taken up with economic issues and foreign policy and national security problems. According to one observer, even those presidents who start out with strong pledges for environmental protection, like Carter, "come more and more to seek what they call 'balance' and their critics decry as leniency."[31] Carter's belief that adequate environmental protection could be maintained along with energy development and economic growth constituted a formidable challenge for any president, especially since the 1970s. In Carter's case, however, the challenge proved exceptionally difficult because his trusteeship conception of presidential leadership, for example, in energy policy, led to a widespread belief that he was a conscientious but ineffective leader. However, although energy and economic priorities prevailed many times at the expense of environmental goals, there were some environmental and natural resources gains achieved by working with Congress and by a selective use of the tools of the administrative presidency.

The Carter Administration increased the size and scope of the administrative state, while attempting to pressure agencies to consider the costs and paperwork burden of regulations on the private sector. The Reagan Administration, by contrast, used the tools of the administrative presidency to reduce the size and influence of the administrative state in social regulation.

The Reagan administrative presidency strategy's impact on environmental policies was, for the most part, shaped indirectly relative to the Reagan Administration's approach to economic policy and to the reduced role of the federal government and federal regulation of the private sector. The Reagan Administration's approach to governance in general included a short policy agenda; centralized executive decision making for economic and budget decisions in the Executive Office of the President (EOP) and the White House; an elaborate framework for regulatory clearance and review; improved political mobilization, at least in the first term, aimed at Congress and the public; and heavy reliance upon an administrative presidency strategy for some other policy areas, such as environmental policy.[32] Legislative strategy focused on budget and tax matters, while the Administration counted upon ideologically motivated political appointees, particularly at the subcabinet level, to implement the Administration's goals via administrative means.

Reagan's approach was considered an example of an administrative presidency strategy in which presidents as nationally elected leaders were urged to penetrate federal agency operations to ensure that their values were reflected in the execution of laws as well as in their passage.[33] In his first term, Reagan's political appointees did, in fact, penetrate agency operations in EPA, in the Department of the Interior, and other agencies through personnel management, including transfers, reductions in force, and resignations; through internal agency reorganizations that did not require congressional approval; and through enforcement strategies that reinterpreted environmental laws in line with Reagan's agenda. The Administration also sought to reduce the federal government's role by expediting the devolution of programs to state governments for implementation under existing laws. It initiated a short-lived Cabinet Council system, including a Cabinet Council on Natural Resources and Environment headed by James Watt, in order to achieve greater White House coordination and control of agencies and their programs.

The Reagan administrative strategy centered on the budget process, curbing budget requests through Reagan loyalist agency heads and OMB. The Administration pressured Congress to approve drastic budget cuts in the Omnibus Reconciliation Act of 1981 and additional budget cuts in 1981–82. These budget cuts, approved by Congress, had a drastic impact on environmental and natural resources agencies. EPA's operating budget was slashed by more than a third, adjusting for inflation, but even after

Congress restored some of its cuts, the agency's real operating budget, excluding funding for sewage construction and Superfund operations, stayed at pre-1980 levels.[34] The president's strategy wreaked considerable damage upon EPA's personnel resources and its key operating and research programs. After 1983 the tide turned; top-level officials at EPA were fired or resigned. The White House abandoned the Cabinet Council system and disbanded the President's Task Force on Regulatory Relief. Congressional investigations and oversight hearings and lawsuits filed by environmental groups placed the Administration increasingly on the defensive. EPA Administrator William Ruckelshaus and his successor Lee Thomas steered a more independent course for the agency from undue White House pressure for the remainder of the Reagan presidency.

In Reagan's second term some key environmental laws were reauthorized over White House opposition, including the Clean Water Act, which Reagan vetoed, and the Superfund law. The principal restriction on the revival of environmental and other domestic policy programs remained the deficit problem, which the Administration and Congress had drastically enlarged in Reagan's first term. In 1985 the White House expanded its regulatory oversight system with E.O. 12498, requiring agencies to submit their proposed annual regulatory agendas in line with presidential priorities when permitted by law. Congress finally managed to make the regulatory oversight system established under E.O. 12291 more open to public view.

During the waning years of the Reagan presidency, however, the Administration's centralized clearance and review of agency information requests under the Paperwork Reduction Act of 1980 and E.O. 12291, requiring cost–benefit procedures for proposed agency regulations, still exercised significant influence over environmental agencies. The following chapter traces the evolution of the centralized review system of agency information requests under the Paperwork Reduction Act from the Carter to the Reagan Administration. It also examines the impact of the Reagan administrative presidency strategy on agency information collection and statistical policy, with special reference to environmentally related programs.

NOTES

1. Perceptive studies that examine environmental politics and the administrative presidency include: Norman J. Vig and Michael E. Kraft, eds., *Environmental Policy in the 1980s: Reagan's New Agenda* (Washington, D.C.: CQ Press, 1984); Norman J. Vig and Michael E. Kraft, eds., *Environmental Policy in the 1990s: Toward a New Agenda* (Washington, D.C.: CQ Press, 1990); Walter A. Rosenbaum, *Environmental Politics and*

Policy, 2d ed. (Washington, D.C.: CQ Press, 1990); James P. Lester, ed., *Environmental Politics and Policy Theories and Evidence* (Durham, N.C.: Duke University Press, 1989); and Richard W. Waterman, *Presidential Influence and the Administrative State* (Knoxville: University of Tennessee Press, 1989).

2. National Academy of Public Administration, *Presidential Management of Rulemaking in Regulatory Agencies* (Washington, D.C., 1987), 15–16.

3. Louis Fisher, *The Politics of Shared Powers: Congress and Executive*, 2d ed. (Washington, D.C.: CQ Press, 1987), 121.

4. The Constitution's provisions authorizing presidential administrative prerogatives include: presidential appointment power with Senate confirmation in Article II, Sec. 2; presidential authority to "require the opinion in writing of the principal officers in each of the Executive Departments upon any subject relating to the duties of their respective offices"; presidential responsibility to take care that the laws are faithfully executed, Article II, Sec. 3; and the vesting clause, "The Executive power shall be vested in a President of the United States," Article II, Sec. 1.

5. Congress's constitutional powers include: law making, which it shares with the president, Article I, Sec. 7; congressional appropriations and fiscal powers, Article I, Sec. 8; appointment powers and Senate confirmation power of presidential appointments, Article II, Sec. 2; and Congress's broad power "to make all laws which shall be necessary and proper for carrying out executive powers vested in the government of the United States or in any Department or office thereof," Article I, Sec. 8.

6. Allen Shick, *The Capacity to Budget* (Washington, D.C.: Urban Institute Press, 1990), 162.

7. *New Haven v. United States*, 634 F. Supp. 1449, 1458 (D.D.C. 1986).

8. Francis Rourke, "Presidentializing the Bureaucracy: From Kennedy to Reagan," in *The Managerial Presidency*, ed. James P. Pfiffner (Pacific Grove, Calif.: Brooks/Cole, 1991), 125.

9. Richard P. Nathan, *The Administrative Presidency* (New York: John Wiley and Sons, 1983), 88.

10. Waterman, *Presidential Influence and the Administrative State*, 87; and Patricia W. Ingraham, "Political Direction and Policy Change in Three Federal Agencies," in *The Managerial Presidency*, 192–93.

11. Henry P. Caulfield, "The Conservation and Environmental Movements," in *Environmental Politics and Policy*, 49–52.

12. Jeffrey K. Tulis, *The Rhetorical Presidency* (Princeton, N.J.: Princeton University Press, 1987), 19.

13. Stephen Skowronek, *Building a New American State: The Expansion of National Administrative Capacities, 1879–1920* (New York: Cambridge University Press, 1982), 172.

14. Theodore Roosevelt, *Theodore Roosevelt: An Autobiography* (New York: Charles Scribner, 1922), 357.

15. *Annual Report of the Department of the Interior* 12 (1908), 25.

16. Skowronek, *Building a New American State*, 172.

17. Paul Russell Cartright, *Theodore Roosevelt: The Making of a Conservationist* (Urbana: University of Illinois Press, 1985), 223–24.

18. Lawrence H. Chamberlain, *The President, Congress and Legislation* (New York: Columbia University Press, 1946), 457.

19. Skowronek, *Building a New American State*, 172.

20. Robert A. Shanley, "Franklin D. Roosevelt and Water Pollution Control Policy," *Presidential Studies Quarterly* 18, no. 2 (Spring 1988): 321.

21. Martin V. Melosi, "Lyndon Johnson and Environmental Policy," in *The Johnson Years*, vol. 2, *Vietnam, the Environment, and Science*, ed. Robert A. Divine (Lawrence: University of Kansas Press, 1987), 122–23.

22. Marc Landy, Marc J. Roberts, and Stephen R. Thomas, *The Environmental Protection Agency: Asking the Wrong Questions* (New York: Oxford University Press, 1990), 51, 172.

23. Edward Paul Fuchs, *Presidents, Management and Regulation* (Englewood Cliffs, N.J.: Prentice-Hall, 1988), 47–48.

24. Jimmy Carter, *Keeping Faith: Memoirs of a President* (New York: Bantam Books, 1982), 74.

25. Charles O. Jones, *The Trusteeship Presidency: Jimmy Carter and the United States Congress* (Baton Rouge: Louisiana State University Press, 1988), 210.

26. Jimmy Carter, *Keeping Faith*, 78–79.

27. John E. Chubb, *Interest Groups and the Bureaucracy: The Politics of Energy* (Stanford, Calif.: Stanford University Press, 1983), 230.

28. Richard H. K. Vietor, *Energy Policy in America since 1945: A Study of Business–Government Relations* (Cambridge, Mass.: Cambridge University Press, 1984), 344.

29. See Appendix 3, Budget of Selected Environmental and Natural Resources Agencies, in *Environmental Policy in the 1990s*, ed. Norman J. Vig and Michael E. Kraft (Washington, D.C.: CQ Press, 1990).

30. Fuchs, *Presidents, Management and Regulation*, 67, 79.

31. R. Shep Melnick, *Regulation and the Courts: The Case of the Clean Air Act* (Washington, D.C.: Brookings Institution, 1983), 34–35.

32. Lester M. Salomen and Alan J. Abramson, "Governance: The Politics of Retrenchment," in *The Reagan Record: An Assessment of America's Changing Priorities*, ed. John L. Palmer and Isabel V. Sawhill (Lexington, Mass.: Ballinger Books, 1984), 40–41.

33. Richard Nathan, *The Administrative Presidency*, 13.

34. Norman J. Vig, "Presidential Leadership: From the Reagan to the Bush Administrations," in *Environmental Policy in the 1990s*, 38. See also the excellent examination of Reagan's impact on environmental policy in Norman J. Vig, "The President and the Environment: Revolution or Retreat?" in *Environmental Policy in the 1980s*.

2

The Administrative Presidency: Information Collection, Statistical Policy, and Environmental Policy

Information control—collecting and disseminating information and reports—whether by the federal government or by the private sector, confers extraordinary power in modern society. Information Resources Management, a key management concept promoted by the Commission on Federal Paperwork in 1977, deals with a variety of legal, economic, technological, social, and economic issues. This chapter focuses more narrowly on a sector of information resources management dealing with the processes of collecting and disseminating government information and government publications. The aim here is to explore the power of the administrative presidency to shape the processes of information collection and information dissemination, through government documents, so as to further the political goals and criteria of the White House.

Agencies collect information, propose research, and amass statistics relative to their missions. This activity serves as the basis for proposing new or revised regulations. Without such information and statistics, considerable difficulty is posed in proposing regulations or justifying them in court challenges.

This chapter examines the background for the adoption of the Paperwork Reduction Act of 1980 (PRA) and the Carter Administration's establishment of the Information Collection Budget system. It also analyzes the Reagan Administration's controversial, centralized review system of agency information requests and its approach to statistical policy with particular reference to environmentally related programs. This analysis views the Reagan Administration's approach to agency information collection and statistical policy as part of its strategy of regulatory relief and a reduced federal government presence in American society.

INFORMATION COLLECTION POLICY

Congress and the presidency have long-standing interests in the field of records management and government publications. Congress first became interested in records management in 1810 and established the Government Printing Office in 1860. Since then, and particularly in the twentieth century, a variety of committees and commissions have attempted to cope with the information revolution and paperwork associated with the federal government. The Taft Commission (1910–13), the First Hoover Commission (1948–49), the Second Hoover Commission (1955), "The Paperwork Jungle" Hearings (1967), the Kaysen Committee (1969), and the Commission on Federal Paperwork (1975–77) sought to examine the paperwork management problem. Profound technological developments in data collection and in records management, and the exploding costs of federal government record keeping from the Hoover Commission's estimate of $27 million in 1948 to the Paperwork Commission's estimate of $100 billion in 1977, have forced Congress as well as the presidency to revise their thinking and the federal role in information resources management.[1]

Congress initially gave the Bureau of the Budget some powers in 1922 to exert internal management controls over the numbers and types of federal reports and documents. However, the burden of reporting requirements on individuals and business in the private sector was not addressed until the middle of World War II, when the Federal Reports Act (1942) established more formal machinery to review and approve agency reporting requirements. The Reports Act sought to eliminate the duplication of records, and to encourage information sharing in the collection of data by federal agencies with a minimum load upon businesses and individuals and at a minimum cost to the federal government. The Bureau of the Budget was empowered to investigate collection-gathering methods of agencies and to coordinate an information-collecting system. But the law permitted significant reporting exceptions, and later exemptions were added by Congress, so that by the 1970s the Bureau of the Budget (transformed into the Office of Management and Budget, OMB) had oversight over less than a third of federal government paperwork and shared its monitoring activity with three other agencies. The revision of the federal tax code and the adoption of new social legislation in the Great Society and later in the environmental movement led to the creation of more than a dozen new agencies, including the EPA, the Occupational Safety and Health Administration (OSHA), and the Consumer Product Safety Commission (CPSC), that produced new forms and reporting requirements. The growth of new regulations and forms stirred a greater public reaction from individuals and businesses, as well as state and local officials concerned about the mounting pile of forms, red tape, and costs involved.

Congress responded by creating a Commission on Federal Paperwork in 1974, which eventually presented over eight hundred recommendations to the executive branch and to Congress. The commission's recommendations went far beyond the paperwork problem and favored a buildup of OMB's responsibilities in procurement, the development of a Federal Information Locator System, consolidation of automatic Data Processing Standards, greater central clearance by OMB of agency information requests, federal–state cooperation, and the development of an information management system. The law that created the Paperwork Commission also mandated reports by OMB to the president and Congress concerning the status of implementation of the commission's recommendations.

President Carter implemented some recommendations of the Paperwork Commission in E.O. 12044, including a stipulation that an estimate must be made of a regulation's anticipated paperwork burden before it is approved by the head of an agency. "To prepare for a new system of information management," OMB unified the separate responsibilities of its Regulatory Policy Branch and its Reports Management Branch "into a single 'burden analyst' function," so that individual staff members were charged with both regulatory and oversight duties for departments. The reorganization was deemed a more efficient use of OMB's resources, since the source of paperwork grievances "is actually the regulatory requirements."[2]

Carter, who had campaigned in 1976 against red tape and the federal paperwork glut, considered paperwork reduction an important initiative of his Administration's goal of restoring confidence in government along with regulatory reform, efficiency, administrative reorganization, and civil service reform.[3] The president's E.O. 12174 provided for a "sunset" review of forms on requests for information, an annual paperwork calendar in the *Federal Register*, and an annual paperwork collection budget system.

The Information Collection Budget (ICB) was the centerpiece of the Carter Administration's program, the result of its experience of dealing with the paperwork problem from 1977 to 1979, and the Paperwork Commission's study and recommendations. The ICB, patterned after the fiscal budget process, sought to establish a paperwork budget requirement for all executive agencies, whether or not their reports were subject to the Federal Reports Act review system. Using its budgetary powers over the executive branch and citing the authority of the Federal Reports Act, OMB required agencies to draw up a list, along with an estimated time required to complete the forms that were to be used in the following fiscal year. Agency officials could defend their information requests at OMB hearings, where OMB could impose cuts. The information budget approach could allocate burden ceilings for each agency, requiring agencies to make judgments about eliminating or paring forms or information requests. OMB's measurement of the paperwork burden was calculated by estimating the number of respondents, the average amount of time needed to complete a given form, and the number of times annually a form had to be filled out. OMB officials in the Carter Administration acknowledged the limitations of their paperwork burden criteria; the problematical estimates of average time for reporting by institutions compared to individuals; and the understating of difficulty, cost, and trouble for many individuals in filling out forms. Lastly, OMB's own studies of burden measurement indicated that the time reporting estimates of several agencies were largely judgmental.[4]

The Carter Administration claimed that it implemented a number of recommendations of the Paperwork Commission and realized a net reduction of nearly fifty million hours in time required to fill out federal forms and reports. However, a report by the General Accounting Office found that OMB made inaccurate claims and overstated its accomplishments in implementing the recommendations of the Commission on Federal Paperwork.[5]

Congress also sought to implement many of the commission's recommendations. After four hearings over several years, it passed the Paperwork Reduction Act of 1980. Some prophetic opponents of the bill feared that the rule-making and regulatory aspects would smother the paperwork and information responsibilities if they were combined in the same office. President Carter, who had supported paperwork legislation under consideration, ignored the last-minute effort of opponents in EPA and the Treasury and Labor Departments who sought a presidential veto. EPA and the Department of Labor believed the new law would curb their ability to manage their programs. EPA endorsed the general intent of the PRA in clarifying accountability within the executive branch, but it filed several reservations, including the suggestion that, rather than undertaking a *de novo* review of each reporting requirement, OMB should provide a more flexible system of periodic reviews.[6] Carter signed the bill, declaring, "We've addressed the bureaucrats and we've won."[7]

The title "Paperwork Reduction Act" sounded bland and politically innocuous. But its mandate encompassed much more than the reduction of burdensome paperwork requirements and red tape. It authorized a new information management system, extending the power of OMB in federal information policy. The statute authorized the creation of the Office of Information and Regulatory Affairs (OIRA) to serve as principal adviser on federal information policy. OIRA's director was charged with developing and implementing federal information policies and was specifically empowered to "provide direction and oversee the review of information collection requests, the reduction of the paperwork burden, Federal statistical activities, records management activities, privacy of records, interagency sharing of information, and acquisition and use of automatic data processing telecommunication and other technology for managing information resources."[8] OIRA was also charged with setting goals for the reduction of the paperwork burden by 25 percent and with designing and operating a Federal Information Locator System, including a directory of information resources and an information referral service. Proregulation forces managed to insert a provision permitting an override of OIRA's disapproval of a collection request by an independent regulatory agency. They also obtained an amendment submitted by Senator Edward Kennedy that declared, "Nothing in this chapter shall be interpreted as increasing or decreasing the authority of the President, the Office of Management and Budget or the Director . . . with respect to the substantive policies and programs of departments, agencies and offices, including the substantive authority of any Federal agency to enforce the civil rights laws."[9]

President Carter signed the Paperwork Reduction Act, but President Reagan became its beneficiary. At the outset the Reagan Administration created a Task Force on Regulatory Relief and mobilized the newly created Office of Information and Regulatory Affairs toward the goals of regulatory oversight under the machinery established in Reagan's E.O. 12291. President Reagan also announced the suspension and review of almost two hundred proposed and final rules published by the Carter Administration.

Not only were rules affected in the presidential transition but also government publications. One information specialist noted: "The changing philosophy of presidential administrations can affect the accessibility of publications at any point in the process. Though government publication seems immutable, policy decisions made by the president can have dramatic effects on the quantity, cost, format, and control of publications issued."[10] President Reagan demonstrated this power by declaring a moratorium on the publication and procurement of new periodicals, pamphlets, and audiovisual material. OMB immediately issued a bulletin confirming the moratorium and ordered government departments to undertake a comprehensive review of existing and planned publications in order to eliminate or reduce

duplicative, wasteful, and otherwise "unnecessary" activity unessen-
tial to the achievement of agency missions. Each agency was required
to develop a publication control system to be approved by OMB. Upon
the completion of OMB's review and the installation of OMB-sanc-
tioned control systems, the moratorium was to be lifted.

Most agencies were not sure about the cost and the actual number of
publications they produced. And some departments had published
pamphlets without determining how the document related to their overall
mission. There was confusion and resistance on the part of agencies, due
in part to the unclear definition of the term *periodical* in the U.S. code.
OMB claimed, "Some agencies may have interpreted this definition so as
to exclude most of their periodicals from the OMB clearance process
specified in [OMB] Circular A–3."[11] In its cost-cutting goals OMB sought
to narrow agency discretion in the publication area, stating:

> Fewer than 10 percent of the publications were listed as "required by
> statute." . . . We suspect that many of the titles listed as *required* by
> statute are, in fact, *authorized* but not required. Over 10 percent were
> "deemed essential by agencies." Therefore, most agencies probably
> have greater latitude in changing or even terminating most of their
> publications than is readily acknowledged.[12]

OMB issued a series of circulars aimed to extend its control over
recurring publications and to obtain a more comprehensive identification,
description, and evaluation of more than 12,000 federal publications.
Departmental inventory and reduction proposals were reviewed by the
budget examiner for each agency and new review boards were established
by agencies to produce departmentwide recommendations for further
elimination and reduction of publications.

Inescapably, however, some critics charged that the substantive political
biases of the Reagan White House filtered through the process. Valerie
Florance, editor of MEDOC, noted:

> At HHS [Department of Health and Human Services] Reagan appoin-
> tees at the top form a panel with final say on all publication requests,
> a responsibility which was previously assigned to a career public
> employee. This "political" review board can (and does) manipulate
> both the number and subject matter of departmental publications. In
> this way, the president can be sure that publications issued during his
> term of office reflect his official position on a subject. Thus, we see
> an increase in publications from HHS which deal with personal

responsibility for disease and a decrease in those which detail environmental and occupational hazards.[13]

The discontinued publications at HHS included bibliographies of asbestos and health, *Cancer Information in the Workplace*, *Working in Confined Spaces*, *Smoking and Health*, *Research on Smoking*, *Health Resources Statistics*, and the *Poison Control Center Bulletin*. Along with the reduction of individual free copies, the distribution and prices of publications were geared to reflect the Reagan Administration's philosophy on government publications. This resulted in an 82 percent price rise for HHS publications from 1981 to 1983, including a 192 percent increase in the price for its *Registry of Toxic Effects*.[14]

The Reagan Administration's preference for market forces in the development of energy resources led to budget cuts in research and development and the axing of some publications on environmentally benign sources of energy, such as wind power, solar energy, and other sources of renewable energy. Five solar energy publications, including the *Solar Law Reporter* and *Solar Research in Review* were discontinued. Also, six wind energy publications, as well as Geothermal and Ocean Energy Research publications, *Oil Pollution Abstracts*, *Battelle News Quarterly*, *Argonne Bulletin*, and *Laser Fusion Quarterly* were discontinued. The EPA also terminated the publication of *Pesticide Abstracts* and the *Pesticide Monitoring Journal*, and other publications that presented information about the agency and summaries of laws, developments, and problems in the environmental field in layman's terms. Other discontinued publications included a booklet on brown-lung disease and the Department of Transportation's popular publication, *The Car Book*.

The paperwork clearance process requires OMB review of all activities of federal agencies in the collection of information from ten or more individuals. The clearance process encompasses a variety of agency activities, including forms, surveys, questionnaires, and applications, as well as reporting or record-keeping requirements. In order for an agency to undertake an information collection, it must prove to OMB's satisfaction that the collection is the least burdensome approach for the agency to comply with legal requirements and to realize the program's objectives, that it is of "practical utility," and is not duplicative of information that otherwise might be accessible. If OMB approves the collection proposal, an OMB control number is provided that is valid for no more than three years.

The Information Collection Budget was expanded and refined by the Reagan Administration under its interpretation of the PRA. Although not specifically sanctioned in the act, the information budget became institutionalized as an annual review process by the Reagan Administration and was carried beyond the overall mandatory paperwork reduction burden of 25 percent from 1980 levels. OMB continued to review information budget reports from agencies and provided each with an information collection budget allowance each year. Although there was no statutory mandated burden reduction target from 1982 until 1986 when PRA was reauthorized, OMB continued its efforts to achieve paperwork reduction goals without statutory authorization until the 1986 reauthorization of PRA provided a mandatory 5 percent reduction each year of the three-year reauthorization. OMB claimed that in the first three years of the Reagan Administration, the ICB process resulted in a reduction of 400 million burden hours, or 32 percent, of all federal paperwork.[15] It also reported that one out of every four federal publications had been eliminated since the beginning of the Reagan Administration.[16] OMB also claimed an additional reduction of over 85 million burden hours in the 1985 fiscal year. Anticipating a lower percentage reduction in fiscal year 1986, OMB Director James Miller declared, "Our efforts must be directed toward restructuring the paperwork imposed by statutory or regulatory changes."[17]

The ICB process was opposed on several counts. First, by allocating a certain number of paperwork reduction hours for each agency, the paperwork budget requires "a wholesale rather than retail approach to paperwork reduction." The Public Citizen Litigation Group maintains that, with this approach, OMB does not simply offer suggestions; it also makes allocations along the same lines that it does with fiscal budgets. Furthermore, Public Citizen stated, "There is no standard by which OMB is to assign 'burdens' between agencies. Is Defense entitled to more or less hours than EPA, and on what basis are the precise allocations to be made?"[18]

OMB is required to report on the disposition of agency information requests. While relatively few information requests have been rejected outright, the public interest group OMB Watch maintained that the overall acceptance record may be misleading since OMB may shape the scope of an agency's proposal before it is approved. Furthermore, when OIRA is displeased with an agency's request, it may grant a short-term approval, sometimes from three to six months, which serves to put added pressure on the agency to comply with OIRA's priorities. OMB Watch claimed that OIRA may also arbitrarily inform agencies that their proposal is too burdensome, or duplicative of other collection activities, over the strong protests of agency experts. The watchdog group also claimed that the "practical utility" criterion may be a catchall means of rejection employed by OIRA for disapproving proposals that do not square with the Administration's policies and priorities.[19] In a number of disapprovals of information requests, agencies have made changes along the lines suggested by OIRA and their requests have eventually been accepted.

One possible indication of disagreement between OIRA and an agency is the length of time that OIRA may grant for the information collection request. According to OMB Watch, a short-term approval may indicate that OIRA has plans to phase out the paperwork. It may also be used to shape proposed regulations, and it can be employed to obtain more detailed agency justifications before OIRA determines whether it should veto the agency collection activity. Because of the range of OMB's informal powers and influence, OMB Watch has maintained that "it is impossible to know the extent to which OMB can pressure agencies into withdrawing their submissions."[20]

Prior to 1986 most criticisms of the information collection process were based on legal grounds and on scattered anecdotal information. There had been no systematic analysis of the OIRA's handling of agency information collection requests, as they impacted on the substantive dimensions of public policy. The most comprehensive and detailed study of OIRA's review of agency collection submissions was undertaken by research staff from the Harvard School of Public Health and Mount Sinai's School of Medicine, at the request of a House oversight subcommittee. The study examined six major Centers for Disease Control (CDC) research requests that had been delayed, altered, or entirely disapproved by OMB. The research team analyzed OIRA's review of six CDC submissions where three studies received conditional acceptance and three were rejected, despite the fact that all had obtained peer review approval. It also undertook a statistical evaluation of OIRA's acceptances and rejections of the CDC research study requests over more than two years, in order to determine if OIRA was selectively applying its information collection powers.

The Harvard–Mount Sinai team found, for example, that, despite peer review analysis of a dioxin study over three years, OMB rejected the study proposal on the grounds that it "would add little, if any, further intelligence." The study group declared that

OMB's conclusions show little awareness of the nature of the scientific literature on dioxin and specifically of the need for exposure-related data that would be provided by the study. Second, OMB's assertion that the dioxin registry data should be adequate indicates a failure to understand the difference between morbidity (disease-related) and mortality (death-related). . . . These gross misconstructions of the basic science involved in the study suggest serious deficiencies in the OMB review process.[21]

Under pressure by the Senate Committee on Appropriations, OMB worked out a conditional acceptance of the dioxin study. But the Harvard–Mount Sinai study group still was critical of OIRA's role. "The history of the dioxin study is highly inspective in indicating the effects of the paperwork review process in the research arena. In this case the impact of OMB's interference has been substantial. OMB's activities have not only delayed the development of important public health information, they also have diverted Federal dollars from productive research."[22] The study methodology imposed by OMB was estimated to have added at least $270,000 to the contract costs of the dioxin study.

In another proposed CDC study, which OIRA rejected, concerning the carcinogenic risk of the chemical MBOCA, the Harvard–Mount Sinai team concluded that OIRA weakened the research design and "OMB officials and their technical consultants appeared to lack basic familiarity with the occupational medicine and public health issues addressed by the study."[23] This and other CDC studies might have been canceled were it not for the combined efforts of agency personnel, medical community pressure, and congressional action.

The Harvard–Mount Sinai research group also performed a statistical analysis of fifty-one research projects submitted by the CDC to determine if OMB's rejections fell disproportionately on certain kinds of studies. The review group concluded:

Statistically reviewing the patterns of OMB rejection, we found that OMB was seven times more likely to reject studies with an environmental or occupational health focus than to reject studies that focused on issues such as infectious diseases or other conventional diseases. Studies with a reproductive focus, such as birth defects or venereal disease, also were more likely to be rejected by OMB.[24]

"A demonstrable bias" was found in the OIRA's application of PRA's information clearance process, as well as a clearcut case of the agency's interference with substantive research matters. The Harvard–Mount Sinai team acknowledged that OIRA's reviewers would be less likely to consider public health information as important as the public health community would. But the study team declared:

It is possible that OMB's bias represents an intentional effort to block occupational, environmental, or reproductive studies that ultimately might lead to additional Federal regulations. Although its Paperwork Reduction Act does not vest OMB with the authority to interfere with proposed research on policy grounds, the increased rejection rates for occupational, environmental, and reproductive studies raises the possibility that such political interference has occurred.[25]

The redirection and delay of research in this complex policy area are illustrative of the broader problem that occurs when OIRA generalists, seeking to coordinate information requests and to reflect presidential priorities, in this case, regulatory relief, may at the same time short-circuit the regulatory process because of inadequate scientific background or training and insufficient data, thus hampering informed decision making. Critics maintained that OIRA's second-guessing of agency officials adversely affected the research agendas, data gathering for policy decisions, and the development and enforcement of regulations by federal agencies.

OMB's summary of the disposition of agency requests for paperwork clearance indicated that the number of requests declined over two terms of the Reagan Administration. There were 1,250 fewer requests from 1981 to 1983 as compared to between 1985 and 1987. A higher percentage of information requests were approved, 96.7 percent from 1985 to 1987, compared to 91.6 percent from 1981 to 1983, and a lower number and rate of agency information requests were disapproved, 3.2 percent from 1985 to 1987, compared to 6.5 percent from 1981 to 1983.[26] This does not include the number of information requests withdrawn by agencies. The lower number of disapprovals of agency paperwork requests from 751 from 1981 to 1983 to 205 from 1985 to 1987 was not dramatic, but it would appear that OIRA succeeded in lowering the overall number of agency information requests, as well as the number and rate of disapprovals, thus meeting some of the goals of the PRA as well as some of the Reagan Administration objectives.

OIRA was inclined to use its veto power of information collection requests more for blocking new information collection proposals than for revisions or reinstatements of existing collections. For example, approximately 65 percent of all OIRA disapprovals for information collections and approximately 50 percent of all agency withdrawals of information collection requests were new information collection submissions in 1987. In addition, some agencies, particularly in the social and environmental policy fields, had the largest number of information collection requests disapproved or withdrawn. The Departments of the Interior, Health and Human Services, and Energy, as well as EPA, ranked among the highest in information requests withdrawn or disapproved by OIRA in 1987. The Commerce Department led the list of proposals rejected, withdrawn, or approved for less than six months at 30 percent, with the Energy Department and EPA ranking 23 and 17 percent in the same categories.[27] Even after the termination of the Burford regime, EPA had the second highest number of information collection requests disapproved by OIRA. EPA also had one of the highest percentages of information collection requests disapproved and withdrawn by an agency as a percentage of an agency's total requests.[28] In 1987 EPA also had the highest percentage of information collection requests disapproved by OIRA. This would appear to lend credence to the finding of the Harvard–Mount Sinai research team that there was a selective bias against CDC research proposals of an environmental and occupational health nature. And it would appear to confirm the claim that OIRA and the administrative presidency strategy had another vantage point in selectively shaping the regulatory process dealing with environmental and social policies through its information collection responsibilities under the Paperwork Reduction Act.

Some of the criticisms of OMB that had been previously registered by congressional oversight committees and other congressional committees in hearings and reports and in studies of private groups were verified and were more fully documented in a comprehensive study by the General Accounting Office (GAO) published in 1989. The study had been requested by the chairman of the House Committee on Science, Space, and Technology at the end of Reagan's second term and was, in part, a longitudinal study of agency information requests submitted to OMB over Reagan's presidency from 1982 to 1987.

After almost a decade of operation, the first systematic analysis of OIRA's information collection process was finally realized. The GAO study used four data collection methods, including (1) a longitudinal data base of information requests, submitted to OMB by agencies between 1982 and 1987, a base that included approval and disapproval rates, modification of requests, and duration of OMB's review; (2) in-depth interviews of nineteen OMB officials responsible for thirty-eight of the fifty agencies of the study's sample, to ascertain the formal and informal procedures and criteria in evaluating data collection requests as well as training required for such work; (3) a detailed examination of OMB review processes in seventeen cases, representing a sample of research, evaluation, and statistical information requests that OMB received and disposed of in one year, 1987; and (4) an evaluation of the technical adequacy of OMB's review of submissions by an outside panel of nationally recognized experts, with the experts' views and analyses of case examples chosen by GAO, compared with the results of OMB's review of the same agency submissions.

The GAO study found inconsistent applications of OMB's policies by OIRA's office staff, reporting that some agency submissions that were approved were deemed technically inadequate by the outside panel and some submissions considered technically satisfactory by the panel were disapproved by OMB. The inconsistent applications of the OMB's policies were attributed, in part, to inadequate on-the-job training for new personnel, their minimal training, in most cases, in fields needed to evaluate the technical aspects of information collection requests, and a serious turnover of OIRA's staff.

OMB offices and agency heads acknowledged that turnover of desk officers affected the review process. For example, in GAO's sample of fifty agencies, more than two-thirds of the agencies had three or more primary reviewers over the period from 1982 to 1987. In addition, in GAO's case studies, in thirteen out of seventeen cases examined, turnover occurred either before or after action on the case. The study also found that a small number of agencies had persistent problems in obtaining OMB's approval to collect information and with new collection requests, particularly new submissions involving research, evaluation, or statistical data collection. These new submissions were much more likely to be withdrawn or vetoed than were other kinds of agency submissions. Regulatory agencies with low approval rates by OMB lowered their research-oriented submissions by 41 percent and their non-research-type requests by 14 percent, reductions that were greater than agencies with high approval rates.[29] It was discovered that some agencies had discontinued collecting some data because of problems encountered in OMB's clearance process. The GAO study stated:

> For these agencies OMB's review has had a chilling effect on likely availability of data. This effect has been pronounced for new information collections and for research oriented collections. Some agencies have predicated their information collection budget constraints have limited them to carrying out collections required by statute, while preventing them from performing program evaluations and collecting new data in problems arising within their areas of authority.[30]

The acting director of OIRA declared the GAO study was "rife with methodological problems." He challenged use of the analysis of three outside experts, employing the Delphic process, as too simplistic for analyzing information collection decisions. He noted that the experts' insights were quite useful but that the arithmetic mean of their quality ranking of decisions was not. He also criticized the arbitrary definition of high and low approval rates and took particular exception to the GAO's description of the chilling effect of OMB's review process upon agency information requests. He termed the description pejorative and claimed that the review process "*should* have a chilling effect on poor design, poor planning, duplications, excessive burden and unnecessary collections."[31] GAO responded by defending its multiple-type methodology and answered the major criticisms, underscoring the technical weaknesses at OMB and the limited technical expertise and lack of on-the-job training of OIRA's staff. The assistant comptroller general concluded that "OMB, in fact, has approved data collections with technical flaws of such dimensions that they are both unnecessarily costly and could render the information collected useless or seriously misleading."[32]

Members of the library and academic community, congressmen, and federal agency officials also provided some recommendations and criticisms of an OMB draft proposal of a circular to implement the PRA. Some recommendations were incorporated in the final circular. Some draft proposal provisions, although strongly criticized, were not eliminated or were only slightly altered. Despite assurances by OMB, some reviewers of the draft and final circulars were apprehensive about the agency's rationale of sound information resources management, particularly its emphasis on user fees for information services; its encouragement of maximum feasible reliance on the private sector in the dissemination of agency services and products; and its introduction of the cost–benefit concept in information resources management.

OMB circular A–130 stipulated that in disseminating information, products, or service agencies are required to act in the most cost-effective manner "including maximum feasible reliance on the private sector." Although certain functions were recognized as inherently governmental in nature and related to protection of the public interest, OMB declared the "government should look first to private sources, where available, to provide the services needed by the government to act in the public's behalf."[33] In its analysis and explanation of key sections of the circular, OMB declared that the general policy of relying upon the private sector in no way was intended to abrogate inherent governmental functions.[34]

Another one of OMB's basic assumptions and considerations in the circular dealt with the cost–benefit criterion. "In order to minimize the cost and maximize the usefulness of government activities, the expected public and private benefits derived from government information, insofar as they are calculable, should exceed the public and private costs of the information."[35] OMB defended this provision against the reaction of commentators who objected to the application of cost–benefit analysis to government information activities.

> Many stated that the benefits of government information cannot be easily calculated and that such information holds more benefits than simply economic ones. Recalling that the statement is an assumption underlying policy, not itself a policy prescription, OMB notes that the statement does not preclude the existence of benefits other than economic ones (some of which are enumerated in Statement 7b). Nor does it necessarily presuppose that benefits can easily be calculated. The statement has been revised to incorporate by reference the purposes of the Paperwork Reduction Act in the preceding statement, ensuring that benefits exceed costs, insofar as they are calculable as a means to minimizing burdens and costs and maximizing usefulness.[36]

Critics of the circular maintained that maximum feasible reliance on the private sector for information dissemination could narrow the gap of available public information, since private businesses are not under obligation to provide governmental information at an affordable price or to keep such information readily accessible and easily available. Even though OMB, in response to criticisms, affirmed in the final circular the value of information and its uninterrupted flow from the government to critics in a free society, the American Library Association and some public interest groups, aware of the Administration's efforts to broaden exemptions of the Freedom of Information Act and to raise fees in its use, counseled vigilant oversight over the implementation of OMB's circular. OMB was also criticized for its emphasis on privatization and for neglecting its responsibilities to deal with governmental statistics mandated by PRA. Critics in Congress, including some who originally cosponsored PRA, maintained that the Reagan Administration had aggravated problems in the acquisition and handling of governmental statistics, in its overemphasis on regulatory review, and in monitoring the agency information collection process.

THE PLIGHT OF STATISTICAL POLICY

The United States has the most decentralized federal statistical system among the world's developed nations, with many of its government departments generating their own data relating to their overall missions. Since the emergence of the modern presidency more than fifty years ago, except for a brief period from 1977 to 1980 in the Carter Administration, the administrative and political fortunes of centralized statistical policy have been tied with the Bureau of the Budget, later reorganized as OMB.

The Carter Administration transferred the statistical policy function from OMB to the Department of Commerce, reducing the size of OMB as part of a broader reorganization of the Executive Office of the President (EOP). Apparently the Carter Administration had second thoughts about the wisdom of this transfer, since it soon commissioned a Statistical Reorganization Project whose purpose was to recommend the best location for a statistical policy office, to examine contemporary problems of statistical policy, and to recommend a more coordinated system of federal statistical policy. The Project finally recommended the creation of a separate statistical policy office in the EOP, rejecting the return of the statistical function to OMB on the grounds that

> OMB's primary function . . . presidential budget development and oversight involves immediate, often crisis-driven, decisions of great political and economical significance which dominate OMB's internal agenda and resource priorities. Statistical policy was not perceived as important in such an environment, was not understood, and slowly eroded in personnel and institutional strength.[37]

During congressional hearings, which eventually led to the adoption of PRA, an OMB spokesman opposed the return of statistical policy functions to OMB. He maintained that the statistical policy function required sufficient independence and should not be absorbed in an organization charged with paperwork reduction and information resources management. Combining these functions would produce an incompatible arrangement that would submerge either statistical policy or other functions.[38]

The Carter Administration eventually supported legislation for a separate statistical office in the EOP, but the views of key committees of Congress prevailed when the statistical policy function was returned to OMB in a new Office of Information and Regulatory Affairs (OIRA) created by PRA. That act was enthusiastically signed by President Carter, but James Bonnen, head of Carter's Statistical Reorganization Project, declaimed the outcome for statistical policy.

> Statistical policy was then returned to OMB by Congress without any thought for institutional safeguards and embedded in a regulatory

environment run by political appointees with little or no under-standing of statistical policy or its necessity. Congress shares the responsibility for this failure. It threw into OMB a set of "information management" functions with a clear directive to improve its perfor-mance, but without any recognition of the great differences between these functions and without insisting that an adequate staff be recruited for that purpose.[39]

Without adequate safeguards for the preservation of the integrity of the statistical policy function, the incoming Reagan Administration was able to shape the PRA and OIRA toward its goals of regulatory relief and regulatory review at the expense of statistical policy and other PRA requirements. President Reagan issued E.O. 12291, which harnessed OIRA's staff to work toward the goals of regulatory policy on a scale that was not envisioned in PRA's legislative history. Within a relatively short period of time, the interagency statistical policy committee was disbanded, the separate statistical branch of OIRA was abolished, and the statistical function was eventually merged with regulatory activity after a series of reorganizations, retirements, and reassignments. Fifty-eight data series were eliminated and staff reductions were implemented in some of the major statistical agencies, including more than three hundred personnel fired and five hundred reassigned or downgraded in the Census Bureau, along with staff reductions in the Energy Information Administration.

The Reagan Administration's selective implementation of PRA, its widespread cuts in statistical programs, its elimination of the Statistical Policy Branch within OMB, and its neglect of statistical policy coor-dination in favor of regulatory review activity prompted a response from several congressional committees. A GAO study revealed that OIRA was having difficulties in meeting the extensive requirements of the PRA, including its statistical policy obligations. Comptroller General Charles Bowsher noted, "A substantial portion of OIRA's resources have been devoted to regulatory review activities under Executive Order 12291, activities [that are] unrelated to the purposes for which OIRA was established."[40]

The reorganization of OIRA, which eliminated a separate statistical division, was defended by the Administration as a means of strengthening the agency's statistical potential because four major statistical agencies were monitored by statisticians-turned-desk-officers. A congressional sub-committee report questioned the reorganization on the grounds that there were no statisticians giving full-time attention to other major statistical agencies and to dozens of minor statistical programs in other agencies.

Although there were some improvements, a congressionally funded study found that in several cases statistical activities were disapproved by desk officers without conferring with statistical policy staff. Desk officers also mandated long-range plans without contacting statistical policy personnel. Furthermore, budget examiners were undertaking budget and program decisions pertinent to statistical activities without bringing in statistical policy staff. The congressional report concluded:

> The role of the statistical policy staff in internal activities, such as budget review, is minimal. There is relatively little interaction between statistical policy staff and the budget examiners. Other groups in OMB, such as the budget examiners and OIRA desk officers, influence statistical policy issues.[41]

Another specialist in statistical policy found there were insufficient personnel to monitor specific substantive areas, such as health and labor, which cut across statistical items, and that staff assignments were made less logically to specific projects as needed.[42] These staff arrangements made it more difficult to coordinate and monitor the activities of more than eighty federal agencies and $1.5 billion involved in the gathering, processing, dissemination, and analysis of statistics.

The budgets of eight major statistical agencies, including the Census Bureau and the Bureau of Labor Statistics (BLS), declined from 1978 to 1982. And although spending increased for most, if not all, of the eight agencies, the 1984 budget level was still below that of 1980, before the Reagan Administration came to power. Some statistical budgets were also reduced in other cabinet departments, in independent regulatory agencies, and in regulatory agencies such as EPA.

EPA relies on statistical personnel and findings in its analysis of water and air samples and in its surveys of exposure to pesticides and hazardous and toxic substances. According to sources in EPA and OMB, it is difficult to obtain an accurate reading of EPA's statistical expenditures because statistical activity cannot be easily separated from the agency's programmatic work, and it is deemed impossible to obtain a true account of the expenditure of EPA's grant funds on statistical work. Yet some comparative measure of the agency's fiscal commitment can be gauged by examining EPA's annual budget obligations for statistical activity from fiscal years 1980 through 1984. The agency's budgetary commitment declined each year from a high point in 1980, both in current and in constant 1980 dollars. Statistical budgets for the Forest Service, Soil Conservation Service, and in almost all categories of energy statistics were also reduced over the same period in real, adjusted 1980 dollars.[43] In many instances, Congress prevented deeper budget cuts by raising budget commitments above presidential requests.

The Reagan White House was also able to influence the gathering of statistical information by appointing political loyalists, such as OSHA Administrator Thorne Auchter, who sought to implement the president's policy views on regulatory relief. The Reagan Administration compounded the problem of industry underreporting of illnesses and injuries in the workplace when Auchter instituted a new OSHA inspection and reporting program. The new program allowed manufacturing industries with a lost-workday injury rate below the national private sector average to be exempted from general schedule safety inspections. In addition, under the new program instituted by Auchter, a firm could also be spared an on-site inspection if the company's records had shown a workday injury rate below the national private sector average in these manufacturing sectors over the past two years. "As a result of the reviewed inspection policy Auchter decided that those exempted should not have to keep records since they could not be reviewed by OSHA officials."[44]

Critics of OSHA's more flexible inspection policy pointed out that the methodology that BLS used and upon which OSHA relied in determining work injury rates left out valuable information regarding the individual worker, the nature of the illness or injury and its causes, and the medical treatment provided. Equally important, studies confirmed a pattern of employers underreporting illnesses and injuries. This situation led to severe criticisms of the system of reporting by specialists in occupational health and safety. Eric Frumin, a specialist in the field of occupational health and safety, declared: "Every epidemiological study in the workplace shows that the OSHA-required recordkeeping system grossly understates the injury rates, and so the BLS annual survey on injuries and the OSHA exemption policy to exempt workplaces from inspections based on injury data is a house of cards. It is built on a foundation of statistical fraud."[45]

Critics blamed the Reagan Administration for relying on flawed injury rates in its cost–benefit analyses, which gauge risks and benefits faced by workers who might be covered by a proposed OSHA standard. Because of the problems of employer underreporting of injury rates and other limitations in the BLS data, risks to workers may be underestimated and, consequently, a proposed standard's benefits may also be underestimated. Furthermore, critics charged that the Administration placed a lower estimate on the risks involved for an individual worker, as well as a lower dollar value for each of the lives that could be estimated to be saved.[46]

Criticisms of OSHA's exemption programs led to some modest changes in the agency's inspection system. BLS revised its 1978 Recordkeeping Guidelines for occupational injuries and illnesses to include broader definitions and some improvements in coverage. Under congressional prodding for a full-scale examination of the accuracy and quality of occupational health and safety statistics, the Labor Department requested the National Academy of Sciences (NAS) to examine the quality of injury and illness data and the disease latency factors in the collection of reliable data. Critics approved of these changes, but they maintained that the occupational safety and health statute gave OSHA and the National Institute for Occupational Safety and Health the power to command whatever records they chose in the reporting of injuries and illnesses, and all that the BLS had to do was ask what medical information they needed.

In energy policy statistics, the Reagan Administration terminated the Environmental Information Administration's long-term analysis of the supply and demand for coal, oil, gas, nuclear energy, and alternative fuels. It also eliminated the Industrial Sector Survey, which produced data on industry's conservation efforts, as part of the Administration's broader goal of relying on market forces in energy policy.

The Reagan Administration's goals of deregulation, New Federalism, and reduced federal spending on domestic social programs inevitably promoted a more limited federal role in the provision of domestic policy statistics. The Administration's enormous military budgets and federal deficits provided additional pressure on Congress to accede to the Administration's preference for privatization of the collection of domestic social data. Congress, however, managed to support some incremental changes in OIRA's approach to statistical matters in PRA's reauthorization in 1986. The act required OIRA to hire a trained chief statistician, to integrate statistical functions with other responsibilities in information resources management, and to periodically renew budget, planning, and statistical activities.

NOTES

1. *Information Resources Management. A Report of the Commission on Federal Paperwork* (Washington, D.C.: U.S. Government Printing Office, 1977), 19–20.

2. OMB, *Paperwork and Red Tape—New Perspectives—New Directions* (Washington, D.C.: U.S. Government Printing Office, 1979), 22–23.

3. Federal Paperwork Reduction, Message to Congress, 30 November 1979, *Public Papers of the Presidents of the United States, Jimmy Carter* (Washington, D.C.: U.S. Government Printing Office, 1980).

4. *Paperwork and Red Tape*, 25.

5. *Program to Follow Up Federal Paperwork Commission Recommendations is in Trouble*, General Accounting Office, 14 March 1980, GGD–80–36, iv.

6. Edward J. Hanley, Environmental Protection Agency, *The Paperwork Reduction Act of 1980*. Hearings on H.R. 6410 before the Subcommittee, Legislation and National Security, House Committee on Government Operations, 96th Cong., 2d sess., 1980, 348.

7. Richard M. Neustadt, "Taming the Paperwork Tiger: An Experiment in Regulatory Management," *Regulation* (January/February 1981): 32.

8. Paperwork Reduction Act of 1980, P.L. 96–511, 44 U.S. Code sec. 3504 (1988).

9. P.L. 96–511, 44 U.S. Code, sec. 3518 (e).

10. Valerie Florance, "The Reagan Administration and Health Information: A Summary of Trends," *Government Publication Review* 11 (1984): 72.

11. U.S. Office of Management and Budget, *Report on Eliminations, Consolidations, and Cost Reductions of Government Publications* (Washington, D.C., n.d.), 6.

12. Ibid.

13. Florance, "The Reagan Administration," 73.

14. Ibid.

15. "Government Information Policy," *OMB Watch* (November 1984): 5.

16. *Washington Post*, 6 January 1984, B5.

17. James C. Miller, Introduction, *Information Collection Budget of the U.S. Government*, Fiscal Year 1986, OMB, 1986, n.p.

18. Statement of Alan B. Morrison, Director, Public Citizen Litigation Group, *Paperwork Reduction Act Amendments of 1984*, Senate Hearing 98–888, Subcommittee on Information Management and Regulatory Affairs, Senate Committee on Governmental Affairs, 98th Cong., 2d sess., 1984, 234.

19. "Paperwork Reduction the Quick Fix of 1986," *OMB Watch* (November 1986): 15.

20. "OMB Control of Government Information," *OMB Watch* (27 January 1986): 4.

21. Subcommittee on Oversight and Investigation, House Committee on Energy and Commerce, *OMB Review of CDC Research, Impact of the Paperwork Reduction Act*, 99th Cong., 2d sess., 1986, 24.

22. Ibid., 26.

23. Ibid., 33.

24. Ibid., 3.

25. Ibid., 20.

26. OMB, *Managing Federal Information Resources, 6th Annual Report under the Paperwork Reduction Act of 1980*, July 1988, 4.

27. "OIRA Paperwork Decisions in 1987," Appendix 2, Monthly Review, *OMB Watch* (31 January 1988): 1–2.

28. Ibid.

29. U.S. General Accounting Office, *Paperwork Reduction Mixed Effects on Agency Decision Processes and Data Availability*, 1989, 24–25.

30. Ibid., 56, 64.

31. Letter of James B. MacCrae, Jr., Acting Administrator, Deputy Administrator of OIRA, to Eleanor Chelimsky, Assistant Comptroller General, GAO, 15 November 1989, in *Reauthorization of OMB's Office of Information and Regulatory Affairs*, Senate Committee on Government Affairs, S. 1742, Senate Hearing 101–588, 101st Cong., 2d sess., 1990, 164–65.

32. Letter of Eleanor Chelimsky, Assistant Comptroller General, GAO, to James B. MacCrae, Jr., Acting Director, OIRA, 8 January 1990, in ibid., 261.

33. OMB, Circular NO–A–130, "Management of Federal Information Resources," *Federal Register* 50, no. 247 (24 December 1985): 52, 736.

34. Ibid., 52, 748. *The Paperwork Reduction Act of 1980*, House Report 96–835, 96th Cong., 2d sess., 12–13.

35. Ibid.

36. Section by section analysis. Ibid., p. 52, 732. In the analysis of another key section of the circular, OMB declared that basic management controls for agency information systems should ensure "periodic cost–benefit evaluation of overall information resources management in light of agency missions," 52, 747.

37. James T. Bonnen et al., "Improving the Federal Statistical System," *Statistical Reporter* 80 (May 1980): 197–212.

38. 96th Cong., 2d sess., H.R. Rep. No. 96–835, 12–13.

39. James T. Bonnen, "Federal Statistical Coordination Today: A Disaster or a Disgrace?" in *Federal Government Statistics and Statistical Policy*. Hearings before the Subcommittee on Legislation and National Security, House Committee on Government Operations, 97th Cong., 2d sess., 1982, 377.

40. U.S. Congress, House Committee on Government Operations, *Implementation of the Paperwork Reduction Act of 1980*. Hearings before the House Subcommittee on Legislation and National Security, 97th Cong., 1st sess., October 1981, 4.

41. Study by Baseline Data Corporation for House Committee on Government Operations, *The Federal Statistical System, 1980 to 1985*, 98th Cong., 2d sess., 1984, 53–54, 64, 65.

42. Jeanne E. Griffith, "Oversight of Statistical Policy," in *Office of Management and Budget: Evolving Roles and Future Issues*, Congressional Research Service, 99th Cong., 2d sess., 1986, 249.

43. OIRA, Statistical Policy Office, *Federal Statistics: A Special Report on the Statistical Programs and Activities of the U.S. Government, Fiscal Year 1986*, June 1985, 46–48; and *The Federal Statistical System, 1980–1985*, 280–81.

44. John Shepard, "Working in the Dark: Reagan and the 'Right to Know' about Occupational Hazards," *Public Citizen* 5 (January/February 1986): 36.

45. Eric Frumin, *OSHA Injuries and Illness Information System*. Hearing, Subcommittee on Manpower and Housing, Committee on Government Operations, 98th Cong., 2d sess., 1984, 180.

46. Shepard, "Working in the Dark," 14–15.

3

Presidential Executive Orders and Environmental Policy

More attention has been paid to the legal and constitutional aspects of executive orders than to their political and public-policy dimensions. This study examines the uses of executive orders in the administrative presidency from the high point of environmental concern in the Nixon Administration to the Bush Administration. The focus is upon a handful of executive orders in which presidents exercised a discretionary role, either issuing orders dealing with environmental problems or, as in President Reagan's case, impacting on environmental concerns. Executive orders are also analyzed as an integral part of the Reagan administrative presidency strategy. For the most part, the executive orders analyzed are "twilight zone" cases in which no clear jurisdictional mandates for either the president or the Congress are charted by the Constitution. Some of the interacting political and legal factors that appeared to shape presidential decisions to issue orders are discussed. The problems of implementation of several executive orders are examined. Where possible, policy outputs are traced, such as the numbers of environmental impact statements and agency regulations filed in compliance with these presidential directives. Lastly, selected executive orders are analyzed to determine if there have been any important changes in the substantive or procedural aspects of environmental policy.

The Constitution contains no specific provisions for presidential authority to issue executive orders. They are generally issued to direct actions of governmental officials but may indirectly affect private individuals and groups. Orders have the force of law and the presumption of validity when issued under a valid claim of authority. But increasingly, orders have been promulgated under unclear claims of authority. Even when there may be a specific citation of statutory or constitutional authority, it is exceptional for an administration to provide prior notice and solicit widespread public comment or input. There are some constraints in case law, but traditionally the courts have accorded presidents a wide berth and deference in issuing executive orders. Furthermore, there are significant problems in obtaining judicial review of executive orders.

Presidential use of executive orders may also present problems for congressional input and congressional oversight, especially if important procedural impacts and substantive implications are involved. Executive orders can also pose a variety of conflicts with the principles of administrative law. "Administrative law provides a structure based on statutory and constitutional elements for administrative adjudication. Executive orders and proclamations are not well suited to that structure and are seemingly used without it."[1] Thus, it is argued that there should be presidential restraint in issuing executive orders as well as improved procedures in their issuance and implementation.

With the exception of the field of civil rights, the greatest number of case studies have examined executive orders dealing with foreign policy and national security issues. In the civil rights field, Morgan analyzed the determining factors that led Presidents Franklin Roosevelt, Truman, Eisenhower, Kennedy, and Johnson to issue executive orders, as well as the orders' constitutionality and effectiveness. Factors that shaped presidential decision making included the president's personal values and his conception of the office, the pressure of interest groups and federal agencies, the unwillingness or inability of Congress to act, and partisan electoral factors—the estimation that presidential action or inaction might help or hinder a president's chances for reelection. Some civil rights executive orders were effectively realized in certain areas, while other less-effective orders were judged incrementally instrumental in laying the foundation for later legislation. The choice between recommending legislation and issuing an executive order depended on the priority of the president's goals, the opportunities for legislative enactment, the degree to which his program could be realized administratively, and the impact that the presidential initiative might have on other White House programs being considered by Congress. Morgan concluded that, in controversial policy areas, the president must weigh the possibility of congressional reprisal or defeat of his programs. Each president, in choosing the legislative or executive order route, must balance a multiplicity of considerations in a political cost–benefit analysis before undertaking action.[2]

Historically, the overwhelming majority of executive orders deal with routine, noncontroversial matters.[3] The executive order is not customarily viewed as a viable tool for major policy initiatives. Usually orders are considered vehicles for pragmatic, short-term solutions to a problem offering only a limited, temporary alternative for policy proposals when it is impossible or difficult to move legislation through Congress. Though presidents may be able to achieve some of their policy goals through administrative means, legislation is the preferred route—the political currency that politicians and bureaucrats respect most highly.[4] Faced with difficulties in achieving their legislative agendas, Kennedy and Nixon, in the initial stages of their administrations, chose the executive order route— Kennedy in civil rights and Nixon in environmental protection.

Adequate and prompt implementation of executive orders can also present problems. Although the federal bureaucracy has been cooperative in implementing some executive orders, noncompliance does occur. An exploratory study of Nixon's directives, including executive orders, requests, and commands issued during 1969 and 1970 suggests there may have been widespread noncompliance.[5] The judicial and administrative enforcement of some executive orders can be protracted and burdensome, as demonstrated in the Carter Administration; and the preferred enforcement tool is persuasion.[6] However, the executive order can be an integral part of an administrative presidency strategy, as illustrated in the Reagan Administration's use of executive orders dealing with regulation policy and environmental and natural resources policies.

EXECUTIVE ORDERS AND ENVIRONMENTAL PROTECTION: FROM NIXON TO CARTER

Leadership in environmental policy, generally, has been acceded to Congress rather than to the presidency, particularly in the areas of air and water pollution, land use, stripmining, and the development of the National Environmental Policy Act of 1970 (NEPA). Although Presidents Truman, Eisenhower, Kennedy, and Johnson were involved in the formulation of pollution control legislation, the innovative thrust for pollution control came largely from Congress. When public pressure for environmental protection mounted in the late 1960s, President Nixon, who had previously taken little interest in environmental matters, began to shift his priorities. Initially, he opposed the NEPA, which had been nurtured by political rivals Senators Henry Jackson and Edmund Muskie. With an eye on the 1970 congressional elections and an anticipated contest with Senator Muskie in the 1972 presidential election, Nixon and his aides submitted numerous environmental initiatives to Congress, including a legislative package of environmental proposals. Nixon included environmental requests in presidential messages, and issued executive orders and reorganization plans that created the Environmental Protection Agency and the National Oceanic and Atmospheric Administration.[7] Aided by the Council of Environmental Quality (CEQ) and others, the president issued a battery of executive orders, most of them in the first eighteen months of his Administration. They dealt with the implementation of the NEPA (E.O. 11514);[8] the prevention and abatement of pollution in federal government properties and facilities (E.O. 11752);[9] increased protection of historic and culturally important sites (E.O. 11593);[10] the banning of federal contracts, grants, and loans to businesses convicted of Clean Air Act and Water Act violations (E.O. 11738);[11] the regulation of the use of off-road vehicles on public lands (E.O. 11644);[12] provision of environmental safeguards for animal damage control on federal lands (E.O. 11643);[13] delegation of authority to the OMB director to implement provisions of the Water Resources Planning Act (E.O. 11747);[14] delegation of authority to the OMB relative to the Rivers and Harbors Act of 1970 (E.O. 11592);[15] creation of the National Industrial Pollution Control Council in the Department of Commerce (E.O. 11523);[16] and the establishment of a permit program for water quality control (E.O. 11574).[17]

Most of Nixon's executive orders were approved by environmental groups. But his creation of the National Industrial Control Council, made up entirely of industrial executives, was criticized for providing special access in policy making to those companies and industries that were the most vulnerable targets of environmental regulations. In effect, polluting firms on this presidential advisory council were able to examine and press for modification of any proposal for an environmental or health regulation before it was made public. In the case of the National Industrial Control Council, the Nixon Administration sought to balance its environmental initiatives with assurances to industry, particularly the powerful industrial polluting concerns. After the first eighteen months of the Nixon Administration, the CEQ met White House resistance to some of the executive orders that it proposed as the Administration weighed the input of affected industries with environmental concerns.

One of Nixon's most effective executive orders from an environmental and implementation perspective was E.O. 11574. Prodded by conservation groups, the CEQ, and Representative Henry Reuss, the Nixon Administration issued an order that converted the 1899 Refuse Act's permit system into one of the federal government's principal enforcement tools in water pollution abatement.[18] Adopted originally to prevent obstacles to navigation, the 1899 Refuse Act prohibited discharge of refuse into navigable waters without a permit or in violation of permit requirements. Nixon's order made the EPA responsible for establishing the permit program's criteria and the Corps of Engineers continued to issue permits. The Refuse Act program was short-lived, however, lasting about a year-and-a-half. But during that time EPA submitted 371 enforcement actions to the Justice Department. One hundred and sixty-nine were criminal actions; 106 were civil actions; and 96 companies were cited for neglecting to apply for a permit. Criminal actions were filed against some of America's largest corporations, including Gulf Oil, Mobil Oil, Texaco, U.S. Steel, Cities Service, Republic Steel, Allied Chemical Corporation, Jones and Laughlin Steel, and Minnesota Mining and Manufacturing. In many cases, necessary remedial steps were negotiated. In other instances, fines were levied, although the maximum fine was $2,500 for any single violation.[19] The permit program was invalidated by two court decisions. In *Kalur v. Resor*, a federal court declared that an environmental impact statement had to be included with each permit, fulfilling NEPA's mandate.[20] In *U.S. v. Pennsylvania Industrial Chemical Corporation*, a circuit court of appeals decided that a corporation could not be held criminally liable for effluent discharges until the permit program was completely operative.[21] The permit program established by executive order was brief, failing to meet the scrutiny of the courts. But there were a significant number of enforcement actions, and valuable experience was gained by EPA in administering the permit system. The interruption proved to be temporary, because the permit program was soon incorporated in the 1972 amendments to the Water Pollution Control Act.

Another important Nixon Administration executive order reaffirmed, extended, and strengthened the CEQ's authority in implementing NEPA provisions. Nixon's E.O. 11514 implemented many of NEPA's provisions, but it also required a broader oversight responsibility for CEQ, authorizing it to coordinate federal programs relating to environmental quality, to issue guidelines relating to the preparation of detailed impact statements, to conduct public hearings on matters of environmental significance, and to request information from other agencies in order to fulfill its responsibilities. By directing federal agency heads to hold public hearings, to obtain the views of interested parties, and to provide information on alternative courses of action to the public, the executive order helped citizens and environmental advocates to use the leverage of favorable federal court rulings to force recalcitrant federal agencies to comply with environmental impact requirements. As an advisory agency, however, the CEQ had to rely on low-key persuasion and its own interim and revised guidelines in effecting compliance without much additional political support from the White House in implementing the president's order.

In interpreting CEQ's authority and its guidelines, some initial court rulings held that the guidelines were advisory and that the agency had no regulatory powers.[22] However, within five years after NEPA's adoption, several courts held that the council's interpretation of NEPA should be accorded greater deference and its guidelines afforded greater consideration, since the council was entrusted with the responsibility of developing and recommending national environmental policies.[23] Although federal agency compliance with environmental assessment and environmental impact statement guidelines gradually improved, some agencies were recalcitrant, others lax. Environmental impact statements were of encyclopedic proportions, and some observers saw only cosmetic changes in federal decision-making processes. Congress was not particularly interested in strengthening NEPA; in fact, environmentally oriented congressmen were called upon to protect the law from crippling amendments and exceptions to its mandates.

With this background of criticism and recommended changes, President Carter issued E.O. 11911 in 1977, empowering CEQ to issue regulations and requiring federal agencies to abide by its directives. Carter cited his authority in fulfilling the policies of NEPA, the Environmental Quality Improvement Act, and Section 309 of the Clean Air Act. The Supreme Court, in *Andrus* v. *Sierra Club*, did not question the constitutionality of Carter's order granting regulatory authority to CEQ. It declared that the president had ordered CEQ to issue regulations for the implementation of procedural provisions of NEPA, stating that CEQ's interpretation of NEPA was "entitled to substantial deference." It stated further that NEPA created CEQ, charging it with the task of making recommendations to the president and of reviewing and appraising programs and activities of the federal government relating to the policy established by NEPA.[24]

The council published its detailed and lengthy set of regulations in 1978, and they took legal effect on July 30, 1979. Each federal agency was given eight months to adopt procedures to supplement CEQ regulations. CEQ published ten progress reports on federal agency compliance in implementing E.O. 11911 during the remaining months of the Carter Administration. But federal agency compliance with Carter's order and CEQ's deadline was slow. By 1981 eleven agencies, including the Navy Department, the Farmers Home Administration, and the National Highway Traffic Safety Commission, had still not submitted their proposed procedures to the *Federal Register* for publication, and sixteen agencies or divisions of cabinet departments had published their procedures in the *Register* but did not as yet have them formally accepted by the CEQ. These agencies included the Nuclear Regulatory Commission, the Civil

Aeronautics Board, the Air Force, the Federal Energy Regulatory Commission, the Federal Communications Commission, and the Federal Trade Commission.[25] For more than two years, through coaxing, prodding, and persuasion, CEQ sought compliance with its regulations mandated by E.O. 11911.

Federal agencies involved in international affairs, commerce, and national security were concerned that a more powerful supervisory role for the CEQ would interfere in their functional spheres of influence. On a number of occasions, starting in 1970, CEQ urged all agencies to recognize the worldwide and long-range character of environmental problems. The council's Legal Advisory Committee, the council's 1973 Guidelines, and a 1976 memorandum from CEQ Chairman Russell Peterson served as a basis for CEQ's claim that federal agencies must use Environmental Impact Statement (EIS) requirements for proposed major agency actions abroad.[26] CEQ Chairman Peterson cited statements from congressional leaders, congressional hearings, and court cases in buttressing his claim that Congress intended that NEPA cover environmental impacts of federal agencies beyond American borders.

The question of NEPA's application to federal agency actions abroad not only concerned the council, but it also plagued some federal agencies, the courts, environmentalists, and occasionally some congressional committees for almost a decade. Proponents and opponents of the law's applicability to extraterritorial matters seized different sections of the law to justify their positions. The legislative history of NEPA was ambiguous, and those who hoped that Congress would clarify the issue by amending NEPA waited in vain. While some agencies, such as the National Aeronautics and Space Administration (NASA), the Coast Guard, and the Arms Control and Disarmament Agency, voluntarily adopted their own procedures in compliance with NEPA, other important agencies, such as the Nuclear Regulatory Commission, the State Department, the Agency for International Development, and the Export-Import Bank of the United States either refused to comply or adopted minimal procedures. In at least ten litigated cases, the question of NEPA's application to federal agency actions beyond American borders was raised.

Although the Senate Committee on Environment and Public Works appeared willing to take up the issue, it was left to the executive branch, specifically to CEQ, to consult with other federal agencies on drafting regulations to assess extraterritorial environmental impacts. Detailed and extended negotiations between the CEQ and the State Department eventually produced a draft executive order that attempted to reconcile environmental goals consistent with foreign and national security policies. Some of the compromises were reflected in President Carter's E.O. 12114.[27] Rather than citing the NEPA as one of its sources of authority, the order cited a source of "independent authority," which presumably meant the president's constitutional authority as chief executive, and inferentially his role as the nation's principal organ in foreign relations. Although NEPA was not cited as a source of legal authority, the order claimed to further the purpose of the law. In disclaiming NEPA as an authoritative source, the order sought to foreclose judicial review of agency compliance with the order, precluding environmental and private suits. The provision foreclosing judicial review clearly reflected the State Department view, to the dismay of environmentalists, the CEQ, and Senator Edmund Muskie.

The executive order stipulated environmental assessment for four separate categories having extraterritorial impacts: (1) federal actions affecting the global commons; (2) federal actions in the environment of countries participating with the United States in bilateral agreements; (3) federal actions impacting on third-party "innocent bystander" nations; and (4) the effects of federal actions on resources of global importance, unique resources not included in the global commons. The executive order required that a full environmental impact statement be utilized by all federal agencies, solely as a vehicle for evaluating those actions affecting the global commons. Less rigorous procedures and more options were allowed in the other categories. The executive order provided for seven listed exemptions for certain actions for environmental review, including actions taken by the president; presidential and cabinet-level activities dealing with national security; governmental actions related to private commercial exports; votes and other actions by U.S. authorities in international conferences and organizations; and disaster and emergency relief activities. Other exemptions or exclusions were permitted agencies if they related to sensitive foreign policy or national security considerations.

Some environmentalists roundly criticized President Carter's executive order as a patchwork compromise and as a setback in American environmental policy. Critics denounced the order for the following reasons: (1) the possibility of federal agency manipulation of the order's multiple exemptions; (2) the failure to provide public review of draft statements; (3) the limitation on requirements for submitting EISs; and (4) the omission of judicial review and any viable enforcement mechanisms for lax or recalcitrant agencies.[28] The order did not provide any means of enforcing NEPA's policies or the provision of the order itself. If agencies used their procedures to avoid their environmental obligations under the order, the State Department and CEQ were supposed to assume the responsibility for resolving the situation by persuasion. If their efforts failed, the only recourse was to present the controversy to the White House staff and the president. Parenthetically, only six agencies (the Departments of State, Defense, Agriculture; the Export-Import Bank; the EPA; and NASA) established internal procedures in compliance with E.O. 12114 in Carter's presidency,[29] and only one final environmental impact statement was filed in compliance with this executive order.[30]

Carter issued E.O. 12264, relating to foreign relations, in the closing days of the Administration after extensive negotiations concerning the exports of dangerous toxic chemicals. It ended up simply requiring American vendors to notify importing nations of the risks of the hazardous imported products. The order proved short-lived and was rescinded by another executive order by President Reagan.

In terms of the number of environmental impact statements filed, the Carter Administration was more successful with its E.O. 11990, dealing with the protection of wetlands, and with E.O. 11988, protecting floodplains.[31] The purpose of these orders was to avoid long- and short-term adverse effects associated with the modification and destruction of floodplains and wetlands. E.O. 11990, for example, sought to avert new construction in wetlands "whenever there is a practicable alternative." In 1979 six draft and five final environmental impact statements were submitted, and in 1980 twenty-five draft and seventeen final impact statements were filed in compliance with this wetlands order.[32] In compliance with the Carter Administration's floodplains order, fourteen draft and eight final statements were submitted in 1979, and twenty-eight draft and eighteen final environmental impact statements were filed in 1980.[33]

Carter Administration environmental executive orders were shaped by varied sources. A few executive orders, such as E.O. 12113, providing technical review and tighter standards in submitting water projects, appeared to bear the imprint of Carter's activist conception of his office, his commitment to environmental values, and his willingness to battle Congress to the point of jeopardizing other Administration programs. More commonly, the executive order was used for administrative purposes to foster coordination and oversight. Although the Carter Administration sought the adoption of a comprehensive energy policy, sometimes to the dismay of environmentalists, President Carter signed several key environmental bills and issued two environmental messages that introduced one hundred legislative proposals, executive orders, directives, and policy reforms.[34]

President Carter and Interior Secretary Cecil Andrus also acted to protect Alaskan lands from mineral entry and development. When Congress was unable to reach agreement on the designation of more than 100 million acres to be placed in the National Forest, Park, Wildlife Refuge, and Wild and Scenic Rivers systems, Andrus withdrew from state selection 110 acres of Alaskan land and President Carter designated 56 million acres as seventeen national monuments, in a series of presidential proclamations under the Antiquities Act of 1906. These actions prevented commercial development in these areas until Congress and the president approved a new Alaskan lands law in the closing days of the Carter Administration.[35]

EXECUTIVE ORDERS: OTHER APPLICATIONS IN ENVIRONMENTAL PROBLEMS

Executive orders have been issued for administrative, oversight, intergovernmental, political, and symbolic purposes in environmental and other policy areas. Orders have established temporary study commissions and were issued for symbolic purposes, as in Nixon's creation of the Citizen's Advisory Committee on Environmental Quality (E.O. 11472).[36] They have served as administrative instruments in fulfilling international treaties and executive agreements, delegating to the secretary of state responsibilities for their implementation (for example, E.O. 11629, Convention between the United States and Mexico on Migrating Birds and Animals).[37] Intergovernmental commissions whose membership includes federal and state agency officials have also been established by executive order. Five river basin commissions and two lake basin commissions were formed by executive orders in the Johnson and Nixon Administrations; later almost all of these commissions were deactivated by President Reagan's executive order.

As the nation's chief problem solvers, presidents have established federal interagency committees or commissions to investigate complex, urgent problems; to coordinate federal activity toward their resolution; or to provide an oversight role in federal agency compliance. Carter set up the Radiation Policy Council, constituting fourteen federal agencies (E.O. 12194)[38] and the State Planning Council on Radioactive Waste Management (E.O. 12192).[39] Nixon's Cabinet Committee on the Environment (E.O. 11472)[40] and the nine-member Lake Tahoe Federal Coordinating Committee created by Carter (E.O. 12247)[41] are other examples of federal interagency committees created by executive orders. President Reagan established the machinery of Federal Regional Councils (E.O. 12314), including eight cabinet agencies and the EPA. The purpose of this interagency committee was to promote reforms in federal government administrative practices and regulations, explaining the Reagan Administration's philosophy to state, local, and tribal officials.[42] A federal oversight committee was established by President Carter (E.O. 12202)[43] to advise the president on the progress of federal and state authorities and the nuclear power industry in improving the safety of nuclear power, monitoring the rate of implementation of recommendations of the President's Commission on Three Mile Island. The Nuclear Oversight Committee's mission was to evaluate the recommendations of the Nuclear Regulatory Commission's chairman and the NRC in instituting procedural, management, and substantive reforms to improve safety.

Executive orders may reflect a president's political and administrative priorities. After the 1980 presidential election, the Reagan Administration revoked President Carter's E.O. 12113, which had sought to move Congress away from the fragmented pork-barrel allocation of water projects toward a more coherent national water resources management system within the executive branch.[44] Carter's directive aimed to obtain a technical review of preauthorization reports or proposals for federal water and land resources projects. All such projects were to be submitted to the Water Resources Council (WRC) and required (1) consideration of water conservation measures and an evaluation of alternative plans, such as nonstructural approaches; (2) evidence that the public and state and local officials were involved in the planning process; and (3) consideration of the relationship of the proposal to approved water resources management plans. WRC was directed to develop a planning manual so that each agency in calculating benefits and costs would apply such standards more consistently. The order also sought to provide a longer lead time for WRC's consideration of projects, requiring agencies to submit their reports to WRC at least ninety days before their filing dates with OMB. In its place, President Reagan issued E.O. 12322, requiring all federal agencies to submit federal water and related land resources plans to the director of the OMB.[45] Under the new centralized system, the OMB director would advise an agency of the relationship of its proposal with the programs and priorities of the president as well as its relationship to principles and standards of water resources planning.

EXECUTIVE ORDERS AND FEDERAL REGULATIONS

Probably the most important recent use of executive orders impacting environmental policy has been in managing the burgeoning output of federal regulations. Seven new regulatory agencies were created in the early 1970s and at least twenty-nine major regulatory statutes were enacted. Congress passed almost forty new laws calling for the economic impact of regulations proposed in the fields of health, education, transportation, housing, environment, and agriculture. It adopted almost ninety bills, sometimes despite presidential disapproval, with legislative veto provisions, many requiring agencies to submit regulations to the Congress for approval before their formal implementation.

The expansion of social regulation activity in the 1970s extended the reach of the administrative state. Prior to that movement for social regulation, the traditional paradigm of the separation of politics and administration and the concept of neutral competence were being supplanted by competing approaches in regulatory policy. One perspective called for strengthened congressional oversight of regulatory policy, while another characterized administrative policy making as a pluralistic enterprise involving many competing interests and players. But the perspective that gathered the most support envisioned the president as a chief policy maker as well as a manager and chief executive. Proponents of this viewpoint argued that the president, rather than the Congress, which reflects more narrow interests, represents a broader national constituency with a broader perspective of the public interest. There are also greater pressures on the presidency and greater incentives to coordinate competing and conflicting elements in the federal bureaucracy. This perspective gathered momentum as presidents became involved in the oversight of regulatory policy through increasingly powerful executive orders in the Ford, Carter, and Reagan Administrations.

Taking a leaf from the Environmental Impact Statement (EIS) process established in the National Environmental Policy Act of 1970 (NEPA), President Ford initiated an Inflation Impact Statement Program (E.O. 11821) applicable to all executive agencies, with the exception of independent regulatory commissions.[46] OMB established a threshold of $100 million or more to identify major regulations needing an Inflation Impact Statement. Later in 1976 Ford changed its title to Economic Impact Statement Program, with the purpose of estimating inflationary and broader economic impacts of major proposed regulations and legislative recommendations of federal agencies. The Economic Impact Statement approach sought only to encompass major federal programs having a significant economic impact. It applied only to executive branch agencies; independent regulatory agencies were legally exempt from complying with the executive order. All of the independent regulatory agencies were urged to cooperate with the program, but all stipulated their right not to be bound by the order. Approximately half of the economic impact statements filed in the first two-and-a-half years of operation related to environmental, health, and safety regulations and were submitted by EPA, OSHA, the Food and Drug Administration, and the Department of Agriculture.

President Carter extended and strengthened the economic impact program by E.O. 12044 in 1978.[47] His order stipulated that, in submitting major regulations, federal agencies were required to file a statement containing a succinct description of the problem requiring federal attention, the major means of dealing with the problem, an evaluation of the economic effects of the proposed regulation, and of alternative ways considered as well as a statement justifying the method selected. The order also provided for advance notice, public hearings, and a two-month period for public comments on any major proposed regulation.

Coordination, review, and implementation of the economic impact analysis activities were parceled out to OMB, the Regulatory Advisory Review Group (RARG), and the Regulatory Council. Carter's order gave OMB the responsibility of ensuring that analyses were performed by federal agencies. A more detailed selective oversight of the content of the analyses was undertaken by RARG of no more than a score of those regulations with inflationary or potentially inflationary impacts of more than $100 million a year on affected industries or on other levels of government. Although Carter's regulatory management system was a fragmented arrangement, he hoped to exert greater dominance over the regulatory actions of diverse agencies.

While the RARG system depended on the interest and sustained support of the president, opponents questioned the constitutionality of the president's role in regulatory management; and he faced political risks if he personally intervened in regulatory matters. This was demonstrated when President Carter intervened along with RARG members in an effort to persuade OSHA to lower standards of a cotton dust regulation in order to save industry regulatory costs. Secretary of Labor Ray Marshall opposed lowering the standard, and a federal court eventually decided in favor of OSHA and Secretary Marshall to the political embarrassment of the president. The court did not address the question of presidential intervention, but in a 1981 case the Carter Administration regulatory analysis and review program was not only upheld, but also the presidency was provided with a more expansive definition of executive power in regulatory management.[48]

THE REAGAN ADMINISTRATIVE PRESIDENCY STRATEGY AND EXECUTIVE ORDERS

Executive Order 12291: Presidential Management and Regulatory Review

Congress began to examine the merits of cost–benefit analysis directed by the presidency in the Ford Administration and continued the debate during the Carter Administration. Members of Congress were generally supportive of the idea that executive branch agencies should be obliged to analyze proposed major regulations on a cost–benefit basis, but they remained reluctant to grant an expansion of presidential control over regulatory policy. President Reagan and his lieutenants, buoyed by their 1980 victory and by an American Bar Association (ABA) report that favored a stronger presidential role in regulatory management, decided to forgo the risk of a long legislative struggle and opted for swift establishment of presidential power in regulatory oversight by issuing E.O. 12291. In some respects the order built incrementally upon prior executive orders of Presidents Ford and Carter, but it departed substantially from them in its scope, structure, and impact. It became one of the most important executive orders in domestic policy since the development of the administrative state and the institutional presidency. It has also been termed the most important governmental initiative in the field of regulatory policy since the adoption of the Administrative Procedure Act, and "the most detailed, comprehensive, and mandatory regulatory agency activity review instituted by a president."[49] However, by the end of the Reagan Administration, the theory and practice of OMB review of regulations in institutionalizing the primacy of politics was adjudged to provide evidence of deep and continuing strains between presidential power and the principles of a republic, the rule of law, and neutral competence in the federal bureaucracy.[50]

The new order instituted a centralized system for presidential coordination and management of agency rule making, providing OMB with significant authority to intervene and influence all stages of the processes of regulation.[51] The order stipulated that all regulatory actions should not be undertaken unless net aggregate social benefits were furthered, taking into consideration the state of a particular regulated industrial sector, the condition of the national economy, and the potential impact of the proposed rule on existing or pending regulations. It also mandated all executive agencies, except independent regulatory agencies and those prohibited by statute, to undertake a Regulatory Impact Analysis (RIA), including a strict cost–benefit analysis for all preliminary and final drafts of major regulations, which would eventually be submitted to the Office of Information and Regulatory Affairs (OIRA) within OMB for evaluation. Responsibility for establishing standards and guidelines for RIAs and for monitoring agency rule making was also assigned to OIRA. Those exemptions to the RIA process for major regulations included rules mandated by statutory deadline, judicial orders, and those required by emergencies. But the OMB director could also exempt any class or category of regulations from requirements of the order, at his discretion, in accordance with Administration objectives. Categories of exemptions included non-regulatory rules and regulations delegating authority to the states. Although, in fact, relatively few exemptions were issued, there were criticisms that OMB granted blanket exceptions to those types of regulations that relaxed or deferred regulatory requirements or those that delegated regulatory responsibilities to the states. As applied, this meant that for approval of state plans dealing with mining reclamation and solid waste management an RIA was not needed. Critics charged that deregulatory as well as devolutionary objectives of the Reagan Administration were advanced in the implementation of these exemption procedures. OMB granted twenty-nine exemptions to eight agencies, with the largest number applicable to EPA.

E.O. 12291 allowed OIRA to overrule an agency's determination of a major regulation and to designate any regulation as major, even though it did not meet the formal definition. According to OIRA Administrator James Miller, "authority to designate rules as major keeps agencies on their toes and allows us to identify especially burdensome or controversial regulations for review, even if ordinarily they would not qualify as major."[52] In addition, the regulatory review process permitted OIRA to delay publication of the notice of a proposed regulation until the agency replied to its criticisms of the draft regulatory impact analysis. Even though agency heads were legally permitted discretion in issuing regulations, and were legally charged with the identification of major regulations, OMB's criteria and its considerable power exerted considerable influence in determining what might constitute a major regulation.

The executive order allowed a measure of administrative flexibility to waive the regulatory analysis and review for some proposed major regulations in order to prevent administrative overloads. Environmental groups opposed the waiver arrangement on the grounds that the rule-making process might be undermined by a politicization of the decision-making process.[53] In fact, a critic of the OMB regulatory review process in Reagan's first term noted, "A close look at OMB's use of exemptions and waivers demonstrates that if an EPA action relaxes a standard, there is likely to be no effort on OMB's part to assess the costs and benefits of the action."[54] Public interest and environmental groups were also concerned that the explicit requirements for early and meaningful public participation in regulatory review in the Carter Administration's E.O. 12044 were omitted in the new order. The Reagan system prevented public filing of proposed discussions between OIRA and an agency, as well as other comments by reviewing agencies, thereby preventing public and environmental groups from learning how the judgments of reviewing agencies might have differed from the perspective of the agency proposing the regulation.

Reagan's executive order mandated the controversial economic policy approach of cost–benefit analysis into most areas of social regulation. Critics of the order, particularly those concerned with the fate of environmental, health, and safety programs, claimed that, although the cost–benefit approach had some appeal as an objective policy analysis approach, in fact it served as a justification for further deregulation. They cited familiar criticisms of cost–benefit analysis, its neglect of ethical and moral choices, and its inapplicability to the value of human life. According to Lester Lave:

> The executive order overstates the possible contribution of benefit cost analysis and ignores factors that benefit cost analysis does not treat, such as equity issues involving who pays and who benefits. For virtually all of the relevant regulatory decisions, there is important uncertainty concerning the magnitude of effects. . . . Often the decision makers can be given no more than a clear statement of the uncertainties and their implications. By insisting that benefits must exceed costs and that the alternative chosen be the one that imposes the least cost on society, the executive order ignores these uncertainties and requires the tool to be something which cannot be done with confidence.[55]

The legal basis for executive orders rested primarily on a broad interpretation of the Constitution's Article II, Section 1, on executive power, and particularly on Section 3, charging the president "to take care that the laws be faithfully executed," and on selected parts of Chief Justice Taft's reasoning in *Myers* v. *United States*. The imposition of the order led to a number of law journal articles, both challenging and supporting the constitutional and legal basis of the order. One influential proponent, in support of the president's role in regulatory management, maintained that the framers of the Constitution were mainly concerned about maintaining a balance of power between Congress and the president and that they created a unitary executive and elected head of the federal government to serve as a counterweight to the anticipated dominance of Congress. Although it is acknowledged that Congress empowers and structures agencies within the executive branch, the president must serve as coordinating authority in the executive branch, and Congress must refrain from interfering in day-to-day operations and must observe "a principle of parity" with the presidency in political control of agency actions.[56] This interpretation strengthened the position of those who favored the president as chief policy maker, as a more likely representative of the public, as a leader of a national constituency, and a more appropriate interpreter of the public interest than the Congress. The presidency, it was argued, is the only institution that can coordinate and exert needed controls within the Administration to counter the centrifugal pull of subgovernment forces. Congress, on the other hand, was perceived as having little interest in coordinating the federal bureaucracy activities and was seen instead as a better representative of local constituencies and special interests.

Another commentator saw ample constitutional and legal justification for the order in textual analysis and broad interpretation of Article II, Sections 1–3; in structural analysis of the executive and legislative branches; in historical precedents of presidential efforts to control or influence federal agencies; in pragmatic arguments in favor of a single source of executive autonomy; and in some rulings of the Supreme Court and federal courts. Although the Supreme Court placed some constraints on the president in several of its decisions, in *Humphrey's Executor* v. *United States*, *Weiner* v. *United States*, and *Youngstown Company* v. *Sawyer*, more recent cases that were decided after the executive order was issued were cited as bolstering the Court's recognition of rule making as a legitimate province of the president's authority.[57] In addition, a lower-court ruling (*Sierra* v. *Costle*), handed down after the order, was widely cited in support of an expanded role of presidential management in rule making.

Opponents of expanded presidential control of regulatory activity argued that Article II, Sections 1–3, should be interpreted more narrowly in accord with the intent of the Constitution's framers, who envisioned the president as a managerial arm of Congress rather than an independent actor in domestic policy making. According to Morton Rosenberg this perspective has long-term roots, evidenced in the initial creation of agencies by Congress and in administrative practice established in the nineteenth century, lasting into the early part of the twentieth century. The take-care clause was seen not simply as a requirement that the president must faithfully execute the laws, but also that he has the responsibility to execute laws passed by Congress.[58] Rosenberg charged that, by empowering OMB to adopt and enforce substantively oriented procedures, the order aimed to control the process of informal rule making and jeopardized congressional intent in the adoption of the Administrative Procedure Act and particularly Section 533 of that act. Even though Reagan's order claimed that only heads of agencies had legal authority to issue regulations, the discretionary power of agency heads might be totally displaced because of the enforcement powers given OMB in the order, and therefore the result could be a violation of congressional delegation of rule-making authority.

On a broader level of criticism, two other critics noted:

> Little justification exists for any wholesale or comprehensive equa-
> tion of the presidency and the public interest. The Madisonian prin-
> ciples that underlie the balanced and overlapping distribution of
> power and function in the American political system assume that the
> public interest emerges out of a process of decision-making, not out
> of a superior wisdom or virtue of a particular branch or office. And
> rightly so, because all constituency principles distort as well as
> represent. The presidency thus has failings as well as strengths as a
> representative of the nation. . . . The interests it [Congress] represents
> are national as well as local in scope because the interests of its
> constituents are not limited to the geographical boundaries of their
> districts.[59]

The order triggered a considerable number of congressional investigations and reports and court cases that documented OMB's pattern of
interference into agency regulatory activity.

> Congress and investigation and court litigation have brought to light
> instances of arbitrary delays in the OMB review process forcing
> violations of statutorily prescribed or Court-ordered deadlines; the
> modification or complete displacement of technical, scientific and
> policy judgments of agency officials as a result of OMB pressure;
> OMB imposition of cost–benefit criteria in agency rule making in
> contravention of specific congressional mandates; OMB substitution
> of political considerations for the economic analysis required by the
> Order; secret meetings between OMB officials and affected industry
> representatives; OMB transmission of industry views to agency
> decision-makers without identification; and failure to record OMB
> input in the public docket of an agency rule making.[60]

OIRA was able to avoid administrative procedural rules limiting ex parte
contacts and record-keeping guidelines in the Administrative Procedure
Act because these guidelines applied only to formal rule making. OIRA's
refusal to log its activity, for example, was considered legally permissible
since neither the courts nor Congress required documentation of such
"informal" activity. OIRA resisted congressional inquiries and criticisms

on the grounds that it was not required to provide information to the public and that logging was an impractical, onerous exercise that might lead to "pointless" court challenges of its activities. OMB also claimed that docketing of oral communications was exempt from disclosure under the Freedom of Information Act.

However, critics charged that OMB often violated the executive order by basing reviews on nonstatutory considerations and conducting reviews in an unduly secret manner, strongly opposing efforts to require it to summarize, log, or docket any oral contacts with outside parties or with an agency. OMB was also criticized as a conduit from industry to EPA, sometimes merely laundering industry positions along the way.[61]

Opponents of President Reagan's regulatory review system continued to press for greater public access. Eventually a bipartisan effort grew in Reagan's second term to ensure that OIRA's activity would conform more closely to standard procedures of administrative behavior, as part of a bargain to guarantee OIRA's continued funding. By mid-1986 OMB was on the defensive and gave ground, agreeing to provide greater disclosure. Upon formal request it agreed to make available copies of all written communications between OIRA and agency heads and drafts of proposed and final agency rules submitted to OIRA for review. These changes appeared to have placated most of the opponents of OIRA on the issue of public access, but some critics still complained that there were too many loopholes allowing communication without public view. Some critics maintained that the agency would make a more rigorous effort to avoid a paper trail that might have to be reported under the new procedures. Prior to this accommodation, EPA developed guidelines for agency and external party contacts issued initially by Administrator Ruckelshaus and renewed by Administrator Lee Thomas in 1985.

After more than a score of congressional hearings, reports, and investigations, several important court cases constraining OIRA, and three unsuccessful reauthorization bills and considerable attention to the regulatory review process by public interest groups and the academic community, OIRA was reauthorized for three years through fiscal year (FY) 1989. None of its new line-item funds could be used for regulatory review, but regulatory review was permissible by drawing from other OMB funds. The regulatory review system survived, along with the required agency agenda planning system under E.O. 12498.

Objective evaluation of the Administration's regulatory review program under E.O. 12291 has proved difficult, due in part to the extensive confidential interactions and discussions of OIRA members with agency officials. Authors of a National Academy of Public Administration

(NAPA) report who favored a strong but congressionally approved presidential role in regulatory review stated, "There is little agreement over whether OMB's regulatory planning and review efforts have actually produced better regulatory decisions."[62] They also noted there has been no comparative study dealing with the quality of regulations formulated before and after the Administration's regulatory review system. But one study of RIAs during the first two years of the Reagan Administration concluded that cost–benefit analysis was not potent enough at that time to handle the complexities of many environmental issues and that "the requirements of E.O. 12291 may force an improvement in benefit cost techniques, but for the moment they add little to the regulatory process."[63]

The process established under the executive order provided some significant information for some high-quality as well as low-quality RIAs. The study also noted that six problems consistently developed in the RIA process—all traditionally related with cost–benefit analysis. They included inadequate consideration of alternatives and distributional issues, problems in coping with uncertainty, technical obstacles in valuation of benefits and costs, and an inability to gauge long-term benefits. The Reagan ideological bias for deregulation was evidenced in a number of RIAs that accented reduced monetary costs for business interests, matched by a virtual neglect of benefits for workers and consumers. In most cases RIAs supported the chosen regulative alternative, but in several cases the final decision differed from RIA's recommendations.

After eight years of operation, analysis of the number of rules submitted for review indicated that the review process had proved to be a significant control vehicle. "The surety of OMB review has increased steadily over time as the fervor for deregulation has declined and more normal patterns of conflict over agency responsibilities and goals have reemerged."[64] Since then designation of minor changes has been omitted, but that revision did not alter the importance of the rise in revisions of submitted regulations. Rules withdrawn by agencies and those returned by OMB to agencies for reconsideration constituted small percentages; those withdrawn by agencies increased from 1.8 percent to 2.8 percent from 1981 to 1986, and those returned for reconsideration increased from 1.3 percent in 1983 to 2.7 percent in 1986. The numbers of those accepted after some revision and of those withdrawn or returned for reconsideration were relatively small. However, the low number may have concealed the significance of individual regulations, especially in the environmental and safety and health fields.

It is difficult to assess accurately the significance of OIRA's regulatory review system in impeding the submission of proposed regulations once major rules are required by statutes. Moreover, the distinction that OIRA made between the designation of a rule as major or minor has been criticized on the grounds that it can designate a minor regulation or group of minor regulations as major. Through its contacts and negotiations with agencies in the review process, suggestions can also be made that may substantively change both minor as well as major regulations.[65]

According to OMB's designation, a very small percentage of the total number of regulations were classified as major from 1981 to 1988. However, it is possible that the review process may have been a factor in the reduction of proposed major regulations by EPA, particularly in the first three years of the Reagan Administration, when there were only three notices of proposed rule making, as compared with 1984 to 1986 when there were seventeen notices of proposed rule making and 1987 to 1989 when there were thirty-three notices of proposed rule making (see Table 3.1).

This was intentional. In fact, the regulatory review process had one of the strongest impacts on proposed environmental regulations. Christopher DeMuth, OIRA's first administrator, from 1981 to 1984, stated that approximately "a fifth to a quarter" of the regulations "we tried to go after" were those submitted by EPA.[66] In fact, EPA realized the greatest percentage decline, 73 percent in the total number of agency regulations submitted from 1981 to 1986. Even under a new regime in President Reagan's second term, EPA was among the highest of all federal agencies in terms of the total number of rules withdrawn by an agency in 1986, and in terms of rules returned by OMB for reconsideration in 1985.[67]

OMB's data and charts on the regulatory review system present a limited perspective on the agency's influence, since they do not indicate OMB's influence in consultation with EPA and other agencies before proposed regulations are submitted for review. They also do not account for a number of other ways in which OMB can indirectly affect the regulatory review through delay, through budget reviews of agency requests, and through OMB's ability to shape agency information requests.

Documentation of OMB's interactions and its interference in agency rule making have been difficult to trace, since OMB has relied largely on oral communications, avoiding a paper trail by limiting its written comments to agencies. Gradually, however, an impressive documented record of OMB's intervention in EPA's rule making was provided in congressional oversight hearings and reports and in lawsuits. The record included OMB's intervention in proposed rules concerning asbestos, drinking water standards, storage of hazardous waste in tanks, and the development of the national priorities list to implement the Superfund law. The congressional oversight reports also documented OMB's interference in EPA's national

Table 3.1
Major Rules Reviewed by OMB and Notice of Proposed Rules under Executive Order 12291 for All Agencies and for the Environmental Protection Agency, 1981–1989

	1981	1982	1983	1984	1985	1986	1987	1988	1989
All Agencies									
Notice of Proposed Rule Making (NPRM)	25	29	22	33	21	25	40	43	32
Final Rules	35	50	41	27	39	48	30	39	47
EPA									
NPRM	1	1	1	7	5	5	12	10	11
Final Rules	1	5	1	0	7	2	7	6	3

Source: OMB Annual Reports on Executive Order 12291 as reported in *Office of Management and Budget Influence on Agency Regulations.* S. Prt. 99–156, 99th Cong., 2d sess., 1986, p. 7; and *Regulatory Program of the United States Government, 1985–1986,* p. 573; *Regulatory Program of the United States Government, 1986–1987,* p. 555; *Regulatory Program of the United States Government, 1987–88,* pp. 624, 626; *Regulatory Program of the United States Government, 1988–1989,* p. 548; *Regulatory Program of the United States Government, 1990–1991,* pp. 627–29; all published by the Office of Management and Budget.

ambient Air Quality Standards for particulate matter, new source performance standards for air pollution sources, natural ambient Air Quality Standards for particulate matter, a proposed rule for high-level radioactive waste disposal, a final rule for ethylene oxide, and effluent guidelines for iron and steel.[68] Some of the aforementioned EPA rules and guidelines were held for protracted review by OMB, including National Ambient Air Quality Standards for NO_2 (five months); the phasing down of asbestos (six months); high-level radioactive waste disposal (one year); and iron and steel guidelines (one year). In a number of instances, the length of OMB's review of proposed EPA regulations, which critics claimed was a way of slowing the regulatory process and softening agency resolve, extended far beyond fixed time schedules mandated by Congress for the issuance of regulations. In Reagan's first term, almost half of EPA regulations submitted to OMB with federal or statutory deadlines were held beyond acceptable time limits permitted under the extensions order.[69] In *Environmental Defense Fund* v. *Thomas* the court ruled that OMB caused delay in the issuance of regulations by pressuring for substantive changes.

The use of E.O. 12291 to create delays and to impose substantive changes raises some constitutional concerns. . . . Under E.O. 12291, if used improperly, OMB could withhold approval until the acceptance of certain content in the promulgation of any new EPA regulation, thereby encroaching upon the independence and expertise of EPA. Further, unsuccessful executive lobbying on Capitol Hill can still be pursued administratively by delaying the enactment of regulations beyond the date of a statutory deadline. This is incompatible with the will of Congress and could not be sustained as a valid exercise of the President's Article II powers.[70]

Although the constitutionality of the executive order system was raised once in federal courts, the District of Columbia Court of Appeals avoided the constitutional issue. The courts have focused on narrower issues of statutory interpretation concerning OMB's exercise of power in regulatory oversight. While the Supreme Court placed some constraints on executive power in several past cases, more recent decisions in *Buckley* v. *Valeo*, *Immigration and Naturalization Service* v. *Chadha*, and *Bowsher* v. *Synar* have been cited as an acknowledgment of rule making as a legitimate aspect of presidential authority.[71] Historically, the Supreme Court and federal courts have given the president considerable deference in the issuance of executive orders and presidential proclamations. Thus, a long-term remedy for purported presidential incursions in regulatory oversight is perceived to be a bill passed by Congress, subject to a presidential veto, rather than a judicial remedy. However, more short-term, effective accommodations can also be negotiated without legislation between the respective claimants of the White House and in the Congress.

Executive Order 12498: Presidential Oversight over Agency Regulatory Agendas

E.O. 12498, issued in 1985 after Reagan's landslide reelection, became the capstone of the Administration's centralized process for regulatory oversight. It was potentially a powerful executive order to ensure the engrafting of an Administration's substantive political priorities in the regulatory process. The objectives of the order were

> to create a coordinated process for developing on an annual basis the Administration's Regulatory Program, establish Administration regulatory priorities, increase the accountability of agency heads for the regulatory actions of their agencies, provide for Presidential oversight of the regulatory process, reduce the burdens of existing and future regulations, and enhance public and Congressional understanding of the Administration's regulatory priorities.[72]

The order provided an early warning system through which OMB could determine the acceptability of significant regulatory actions relative to the Administration's policies and priorities. It expanded Reagan's oversight function far beyond the requirement that agencies apply a cost–benefit test to all major regulations, to a broadly interpreted test for all proposed agency actions, which might eventually lead to a proposed rule. By requiring an annual regulatory program to be submitted to OMB, the order added additional presidential controls over agency information policy, augmenting the presidency's power over agency information collection in the Paperwork Reduction Act. E.O. 12498 was initially feared as the "thought control" order by some EPA officials, and as might be expected it was considered by congressional liberals to be another powerful invasion of congressional terrain in regulatory policy. In fact, one commentator noted with the addition of the order, "The Reagan centralized control strategy had established a presidential regulatory veto within the executive branch."[73]

The legal and constitutional basis of the order rested on the same provisions of the Constitution and court decisions as were submitted by the Justice Department in support of E.O. 12291.[74] Proponents cited the

Sierra v. *Costle* ruling, which recognized "the basic need of the President and his White House staff to monitor the consistency of executive agency regulations with Administration policy"[75] and the position of the American Bar Association (ABA), which supported the order as a legitimate exercise of presidential power. However, an ABA report, noting possible abuses, declared, "The distinction between activating a political process for agenda and priority setting, and taking over an agency's ultimate authority, is a subtle one, yet one wants assurance that it will be observed."[76]

The opposing position maintained that the order as well as the predecessor, E.O. 12291, constituted an incursion upon congressional prerogatives.

> The emergent pattern of OMB intervention in agency rule-making under the purported authority of Executive Orders 12291 and 12498 is argued to violate congressional intent in three ways: it effectively displaces those agency officials Congress has explicitly designated as administrative decision-makers; it prevents meaningful public participation in and effective judicial review of the rule-making process as prescribed by the Administrative Procedure Act and other statutes; and it causes the application of statutorily impermissible substantive criteria. Such interference with a proper exercise of congressionally delegated rule-making authority cannot be justified as a valid application of executive power under Article II of the Constitution. It is instead a usurpation of Congress' legislative prerogatives.[77]

Another commentator argued that the Reagan Administration's Justice Department did not demonstrate how the authority claimed under E.O. 12498 was functionally implicit in Article II.

> The executive order does not demonstrate the requisite nexus between the authority asserted and the president's constitutional obligations. The order does not show how the power to supervise and guide agency discretion for the purpose of imposing the administration's regulatory agenda is functionally incident to the president's duty to execute the laws.[78]

Furthermore, it was charged that the authority under the executive order did not square with a checking and balancing test used by the Supreme Court to measure the claims of executive authority against other competing constitutional claims. This test requires that the exercise of one branch's authority must not harm the ability of another branch to exercise its essential function or perform its procedural check within the constitutional system.[79] Two cases involving President Nixon were cited as examples demonstrating this balancing test exercised by the Supreme Court.[80]

E.O. 12498 attempted to influence the regulatory process at the earliest stage of pre–rule making, not simply at the final stage of the regulatory process under E.O. 12291.

> Developing a governmental rule often involves years of studies, hearings, and intermediate decisions before even a proposed rule is issued for public comment. Frequently, senior agency officials are involved only after these earlier activities have greatly narrowed the options for final action and precluded effective policy review.[81]

Under the executive order, agencies designated by OMB are required to submit an annual regulatory agenda for OMB review. Submitted agendas must explain how they are consistent with the Administration's regulatory principles enunciated by the President's Task Force on Regulatory Relief. If a proposed agency action is deemed inconsistent with the Administration's principles, it may not be pursued unless it is required by statute or a court order. If an agency seeks to undertake an activity that is not part of its previously approved regulatory agenda, it must request OMB's approval. Each agency's regulatory program must specify all significant regulatory activity, planned or ongoing, "including the development of documents that may influence, anticipate, or could lead to the commencement of rule-making proceedings."[82]

The scope of agency rule-making activity was defined broadly to include requests for public comment, development of strategy statements, and other documents "that may influence, anticipate, or could lead to the commencement of rule-making proceedings at a later date."[83] According to OMB, "the decision to create an agency task force to evaluate the need for a regulation that, if proposed, would be a 'significant regulatory action,' or to undertake a study to assess an economic problem related to possible regulatory action that would be 'significant,' or to analyze health and safety risks concerning the regulation of which could be 'significant,' should all be considered as significant rule-making activities."[84] This broad definition of pre–rule making activity was provided not only to promote agency planning and coordination, but also to discourage lower-level career officials from initiating activities and plans without the approval of OMB and the agency political executive appointed by the president.

Each agency head is required to submit a critical analysis to OMB justifying each proposed significant regulatory action. Critical analysis requires the agency to evaluate the need for regulatory action relative to several criteria. The analysis must explain why the private sector or state and local governments cannot satisfactorily address the problem. The agency official must indicate those who are likely to obtain the benefit or sustain the costs of the proposed activity. Other federal regulatory options and alternative solutions to regulation, such as marketable rights, must also be considered; and the agency director must discuss why market failure may have created a need for a regulatory approach.[85]

E.O. 12498 provides considerable additional managerial powers to OMB in the form of regulatory clearance. It empowers the OMB director to return all or part of a proposed regulatory agenda that may be inconsistent with the Administration's policies and priorities, and permits the director to recommend changes including further regulatory or deregulatory actions that may be necessary to achieve consistency. By requiring significant regulatory actions to conform with criteria in E.O. 12291 and with policy guidelines developed in the 1983 Report of the Presidential Task Force on Regulatory Relief, the scope of E.O. 12498 became more than an information and planning tool. It reached into policy formation. An authority on regulatory policy noted, "The actual practice of presidential control under the most recent executive orders indicates that this structural tool is being used as much to advance particular substantive ends as to eliminate duplication and overlap."[86]

Despite its significance, in comparison with E.O. 12291, comparatively little has been written about the constitutional and legal aspects of E.O. 12498, and almost nothing about the politics of implementation of the regulatory agenda system. Congressional oversight and hearings have focused on the regulatory review process under E.O. 12291, gathering information and examining abuses and proposed changes in that system, and have paid much less attention to the regulatory agenda system. Partially as a response to congressional pressure and as an effort to document the results of its regulatory relief objectives, OMB published annual summaries, classification by agency, and detailed descriptions of each significant regulatory action. After considerable congressional pressure, OMB agreed to release agency draft agendas, after the publication of the final regulatory agenda, but it successfully resisted the provision of other detailed information concerning OMB's negotiations with agencies. Thus, much is unknown about OMB's influence in the possible revision, rejection, and delay of proposed regulatory actions in the agenda system. The information about the politics of the regulatory agenda system is largely anecdotal, and as yet there has been no systematic analysis of agency draft regulatory agendas to discern the influence of OMB.

In the initial political struggle over that system, the House leadership, the House Government Operations Committee, the Senate Governmental Affairs Committee, and the Senate Environmental and Public Works Committee took issue with OMB's claims of necessary secrecy concerning the release of draft regulatory plans submitted to OMB. Congressmen John Dingell and Ted Weiss sought to have draft regulatory agendas of agencies under their jurisdiction submitted to their respective oversight subcommittees, so that the draft programs could be analyzed and compared with the final published programs, in order to determine the influence of OMB. At first, OMB denied these oversight requests on the grounds that predecisional documents must be protected by executive privilege. Congressional Republicans were divided on the issue; some supported and others opposed the Administration's claim, while others on key House and Senate committees hoped for an informal accommodation between Congress and the Administration. When it appeared that the issue was more than partisan and could develop into another confrontation between the two branches, OMB Director David Stockman issued a memorandum informing agencies that it was acceptable to release their draft agendas in 1985, since some agencies had already done so and because of the unique situation in the first year of the program.[87]

Most agencies refused to release draft materials for their regulatory programs, but the Departments of Agriculture and Health and Human Services released some information. Ten proposed significant regulatory actions in Agriculture's draft program and sixty-seven Health and Human Services draft proposals did not appear in their respective final program approved and published by OMB.[88] A leak to the *New York Times* in the same year revealed that OMB disapproved a Public Health Service study to examine the relationship between infant mortality rates and cuts in federal funding.[89] Before the issuance of E.O. 12498, OMB could disapprove such a study, but first a notice had to be placed in the *Federal Register* indicating the Public Health Service's intent to submit the study for OMB's approval under PRA provisions.

Initially the executive order created some concern and confusion in the ranks of federal agencies. Some agencies attempted to negotiate agreements with OMB to obtain exemptions of some rules on the grounds that they were too technical for OMB's staff to review. There was also some evidence of "overstacking"; that is, sending a batch of proposals so as to get more acceptances from OMB.[90] Initially some EPA staff members perceived E.O. 12498 as a "thought control" order, consolidating OMB's power to curb EPA's regulatory planning activity and obstruct its ability to collect information to sustain regulatory activity. The first year of the

Administration's regulatory planning system was termed "one of the most incredibly mismanaged programs in the Federal Government" by one EPA official.[91] EPA officials thought they had obtained fundamental agreement with OMB, but three months later it posed five additional major questions. Some people in EPA thought that it made sense for an agency to evaluate itself and to have an annual planning agenda. But by the end of 1986 one EPA official stated, "No one takes it seriously; it is another hoop to jump through rather than a creative program." This negative reaction was not attributed to OMB's "deep-sixing" of regulatory proposals. Instead, delay was the principal cause, not so much a part of a grand design, but more the result of overburdened, sometimes arrogant desk officers, and a lack of communication and coordination within OMB itself.[92]

In examining compliance with the order, it is difficult to determine the extent of "overstacking" in the first year after the adoption of the executive order. But there was a reduction of pre–rule making proposals by EPA from thirty in 1985 to twenty in 1986, including the repeat of nine proposals from the prior year, to seventeen pre–rule making proposals in 1987, including ten submitted again from the two previous years. This amounted to a slight reduction of new pre–rule making proposals from 1986 to 1987.[93]

By 1986 OMB faced concerted pressure from both House and Senate oversight committees to provide more information and more checks on the regulatory review system. With mounting pressure by key House committee leaders to defund OIRA, Senators David Durenberger and Carl Levins negotiated a settlement that resulted in concessions mostly in the regulatory review system. But the settlement also provided that annual agency draft regulatory agendas would be available for public review after the final regulatory program was published. Some advocates of greater public disclosure found as a practical matter that the final program was published much later, sometimes five months after the regulatory program officially began each year, and that OMB had provided no timetable to comply with written requests for agency draft submissions.

According to critics, the concessions made by OMB did not eliminate all the conflicts between the OMB review system and standards of due process. Since OMB's disapproval of proposed pre–rule making activity is not fully documented, no judicial review is possible. OMB's decisions do not involve discussion by outside groups, and congressional oversight is also hampered. Advocates of greater public access and disclosure are critical on the grounds that a summary of oral communications and disclosure of written communications between OMB and agency officials are not made available in the regulatory agenda process.

Some reformers proposed that Congress adopt a centralized regulatory review system, whereby the president would be required to submit a list of major proposed regulations to Congress. A new regulatory review committee in each house would then hold hearings and eventually would propose a regulatory calendar for enactment. This and another proposal to create a Joint Committee on Regulatory Affairs to approve or disapprove regulations by concurrent resolution have failed to gain adequate support. A centralized congressional regulatory review and management system has been opposed on the grounds that additional delay and difficulty would be heaped upon the regulatory review process and added burdens would be placed on an overloaded congressional agenda. Instead, it is argued that the president should formally submit the regulatory program to Congress without formal congressional approval and review of the regulatory program.

E.O. 12498 added significant power in the continuing trend toward politicization and centralization of the administrative presidency. Subsequent administrations may revise Reagan's executive orders on regulatory review and the regulatory planning agenda, but so far President Bush has retained these orders in full force. Although authorities recommended that Congress establish by law the basic ingredients of the regulatory management system,[94] congressional reluctance to deal with the problem and to structure the process and grant presidential authority in regulatory oversight has been aggravated by the aggressive tactics of the Reagan presidency. There are a number of modest incremental ways in which mutual suspicion can be reduced between the two branches so that the groundwork can be rebuilt for a more permanent resolution of the problem. A law should grant presidential authority in regulatory management with adequate protection in accordance with the Administrative Procedure Act.

Executive Order 12630: The "Takings" Executive Order

In its final year the Reagan Administration sought to extend its philosophy of minimizing the intrusion of federal regulations upon private interests by adopting E.O. 12630. The order purportedly was a response to two key Supreme Court decisions and attempted to deal with the issue of whether a federal regulatory action affecting private property might result in a taking or increased condemnation subject to the Fifth Amendment's just-compensation clause. The order sought to ensure that federal agency actions were in accord with the Fifth Amendment's protection and to reduce the risk of inadvertent or undue burdens on the public treasury that might be produced from agency actions.

Characterized as a response to two Supreme Court decisions in 1987,[95] the order included three principal problematic features: the Takings Information Assessment (TIA) requirement, the substantially advance criterion, and the proportionality test. All three features restructured and complicated the regulatory process for agencies. Under the order, agencies must prepare and submit to OMB documents that might incorporate a taking of private property. The proportionality requirement stipulates that any regulation of any use of private property may not be "disproportionate" to that use's contribution to the overall problem that the regulation is crafted to remedy. Moreover, the order requires that no action be undertaken to regulate private property unless the restriction that is required will "substantially advance" the same governmental objective as a clearcut governmental ban of the use of the same activity.

The TIA provision requires federal agencies to consider the takings implication of proposed rules, actions, policies, and legislation that may affect the use of private property or interests in private property. The TIA process augments and is similar to Regulatory Impact Analysis mandated by President Reagan's E.O. 12291, in that every proposed rule and legislative program must be submitted to OMB along with a completed TIA. Thus, the TIA requirement gives OMB additional control over regulations and policy decisions, augmenting other OMB powers in regulatory clearance and information policy, including the RIA requirements, information clearance under the Paperwork Reduction Act, agency regulatory calendar requirements under E.O. 12498, as well as OMB budgetary and other powers. The TIA process constitutes another hurdle that agencies encounter in the regulatory process, slowing that process and requiring added agency staff and validation techniques.

Guidelines provided by the Justice Department called for the alternative that can meet the statutory objective and present "the least risk" to private interests.[96] The TIA must also include a dollar estimate of the potential liability of the federal government—no easy task—in case the regulatory action or legislation is determined to be a taking. Critics anticipated that dollar estimates and the creation of TIA documents in the rule-making record could lead to more litigation challenging regulations and other governmental actions.

In imposing the "substantially advance" criterion, the executive order attempted to place some constraints on officials in public health, welfare, and safety agencies.

Before undertaking any proposed action regulating private property use for the protection of public health and safety, the Executive

Department or agency involved shall . . . establish that such proposed action shall substantially advance the purpose of protecting public health and safety against the specially identified risk.[97]

One critic noted that

the Executive Order expressly directs agency decision makers that "any" permit conditions must "substantially advance," not merely advance the government's purpose. This is not required by the Supreme Court decisions. Indeed to the contrary, the courts give substantial deference to agency expertise in setting permit conditions in matters of public health and safety.[98]

Under the Supreme Court's recent takings decisions, the substantiality criterion is only one consideration in determining whether a regulatory approach overreaches. The fact that the order makes the substantiality test determinative in the agency's regulatory choice may preclude other important agency actions or decisions that are not takings. The "substantiality" test was deemed to go beyond Supreme Court requirements in the *Nollan* v. *California Coastal Commission* decision and, in fact, many regulatory and permitting actions may be crafted for other secondary purposes. This approach has been attributed "to a political philosophy of regulation [more] than to a neutral understanding of takings jurisprudence."[99]

The executive order's "proportionality" requirement states that government agencies shall not overburden a property owner when a proposed action places a restriction on a use of private property. The order states: "The restriction imposed on the use shall not be disproportionate to the extent to which the use contributes to the overall problem that the restriction is imposed to redress."[100] Critics maintained that this language is "not premised in any recognizable principle yet established in takings law,"[101] and that it clearly contradicts another Supreme Court ruling on the takings issue.[102] Furthermore, the proportionality approach has furnished no guidance or standards in the determination of a taking. The order was criticized as running counter "to virtually every form of police power regulation of property," since governmental regulation includes many other factors besides proportionality or fairness in the protection of public health, welfare, and safety.[103]

Environmentalist critics charged that the order could have a crippling effect upon enforcement, with potential application to any situation where federal regulations could require industry to incur additional costs. The order raised special concern and uncertainty as to its impact on EPA programs, particularly the wetlands program. The chief of EPA's Office of General Counsel complained to his counterpart in OMB that the order's language was "hopelessly vague, dangerously overbroad," maintaining that "the proposed order is at best unnecessary and wasteful and at worst counterproductive."[104] It was seen as an invitation to developers to raise challenges in the permitting process, forcing possible reconsideration of permit denials that constituted takings by EPA and Army Corps of Engineers officials. Other EPA officials and other observers were more sanguine about their agency's ability to cope with the executive order, particularly since it was issued in the closing months of the Reagan Administration and was perceived by some as more of a political statement than a well-constructed legal requirement.

Another objective of the order, to reduce the burden on the public treasury as the result of agency takings actions, did not appear warranted by the evidence. The order's requirement of an annual itemized list of all takings compensation made against rules and regulations, including awards made in fiscal years 1985, 1986, and 1987, indicated (based on a Freedom of Information Act request) that there were no regulatory takings awards against the government during those fiscal years. A critic of the executive order declared:

> There is no substantial record of takings by permit or regulation. Thus, the rationale of protecting the treasury through the Executive Order is unsupported by the data or recent judicial experience.
>
> Therefore, it is difficult to understand why the order has been issued at all, except as a statement of regulatory philosophy—or as a technical means of slowing the pace of regulation.[105]

Whether the order was another legal stratagem to slow regulation or primarily a restatement of Reagan's conservative beliefs, the Reagan Administration was criticized for inventing a new takings law supplanting the role of the Supreme Court. In addition, two environmental lawyers stated:

> Rather than helping the agencies to preserve as many regulatory options as possible notwithstanding the threat of a takings finding, the Executive Order and the guidelines do just the opposite. Takings law is expanded and regulatory options are narrowed. This approach appears effectively to usurp the respective roles of Congress and the Supreme Court, to the extent the takings issue influences agency

decisions, by precluding regulatory action that would have been taken in the absence of the executive order.[106]

The use of executive orders was also an integral part of the Reagan administrative presidency strategy in promoting the President's New Federalism objectives. In Reagan's first term, executive orders promoting the New Federalism included the creation of the President's Advisory Commission on Federalism, E.O. 12303;[107] the formation of Federal Regional Councils (for devaluation of federal authority and reduction of federal programs), E.O. 12314,[108] which were later revoked by E.O. 12407;[109] the termination of river basin commissions (Pacific Northwest, Great Lakes, New England, Missouri, and Upper Mississippi River Basin Commissions), E.O. 12319;[110] the elimination of the Lake Tahoe Federal Coordinating Council, E.O. 12298;[111] and the replacement of detailed provisions in previous executive orders with E.O. 12342's brief general statement permitting predator controls with environmental safeguards.[112]

E.O. 12372 promoting the Administration's New Federalism sought to encourage intergovernmental cooperation and strengthen federalism by greater communication and reliance on state and local governments for their coordination and review of proposed federal financial and direct federal development. The creation or reauthorization of federally funded planning organizations was discouraged, particularly those that were not accountable to or representative of state and local officials. States were also encouraged to simplify existing federally required state plans and to substitute state plans for federally required state plans when permitted by law and when state budget and planning systems were deemed "sufficient."[113]

Another last restatement of Reagan's conservative and New Federalism principles, enunciated in E.O. 12612, sought "to restore the division of responsibilities between the national government and the states, that was intended by the framers."[114] The objective of the order was to accord greater deference and discretion to state authorities and to promote greater constraints on the scope of federal preemptive actions and national regulatory standards. Only when a statute specifically provided for federal preemption or there was palpable evidence of congressional intent was federal preemption justifiable. And only when there was clear constitutional authority and the problem was national in scope was it acceptable for federal limitations on state functions. When national policies were to be administered by state authorities, as for example in much environmental legislation, maximum discretion was accorded to state officials. For agency policies or regulations that had sufficient federalism implications, another new assessment process had to be prepared and submitted to OMB to implement the order's principles. This New Federalism assessment was also required to indicate the extent to which new regulations or policies might add burdens or costs to the states or affect their traditional functions.

Some environmental and public interest groups were concerned that the executive order might cause delays in the implementation of those environmental laws that provided broad agency discretion, particularly if OMB and EPA disagreed over the original intent of Congress. The order was initially perceived as having the greatest potential impact on Superfund regulations, the Clean Air Act, and the Resource Conservation and Recovery Act. Others saw it as having minimal impact after Administration setbacks and the 1986 elections produced an emboldened Democrat-controlled Congress and stronger resistance within regulatory agencies. The order added still another assessment hurdle for regulatory agencies subject to OMB review. But it was issued rather late in the Reagan Administration to have much practical political effect and appeared largely as a symbolic effort to reaffirm the president's New Federalism principles. In these last executive orders in Reagan's second term, the executive order was used more as a defensive, delaying tactic in efforts to control federal agencies, after Congress had placed constraints on OMB in the regulatory review process and the log jam had been broken in the reauthorization of environmental legislation.

The examination of selected executive orders of a discretionary policy nature in this study indicates that they have led to several significant procedural changes in environmental administration, including (1) wider public participation in the Environmental Impact Statement (EIS) process, (2) more uniformity in federal agency regulations adopted in compliance with NEPA's EIS requirements, and (3) the required application of cost–benefit analysis in submitting major federal regulations, unless prohibited by law.

Since executive orders are seldom used in major policy initiatives, they are rarely struck down by the courts or revoked by Congress. More commonly, they are revised by the presidents who issued them or amended or sometimes revoked by succeeding presidents of different partisan or ideological outlook. Orders are infrequently part of a president's arsenal in policy struggles with Congress, as demonstrated in the Carter and Reagan presidencies. President Carter used executive orders as a major tool in his efforts to change the system of evaluating water projects, but it resulted in congressional retaliation.

The executive order was an integral part of the Reagan administrative presidency strategy in promoting New Federalism principles and in establishing a central system of regulatory policy clearance. That system, established by E.O. 12291 and reinforced by E.O. 12498, authorized OIRA to apply its version of cost–benefit analysis. The centralized clearance system manned by Reagan appointees influenced the substance of regulatory policy in environmental, health, and safety areas. E.O. 12291 became one of the most important orders in domestic policy since the development of the administrative state and the institutionalized presidency. E.O. 12498 ensured that agency rule-making planning squared with market-oriented political priorities of the Reagan Administration unless directed otherwise by statute. Through these two orders the Reagan Administration accelerated and deepened the politicization and centralization of the institutionalized presidency in regulatory review and management, and they remain in effect in the Bush Administration.

However, political costs resulted from the circumvention of Congress regarding its approval of presidential management of regulatory policy: an adverse reaction occurred to the ex parte contacts and to secrecy in the implementation of E.O. 12291. For the Reagan Administration, the advantages of greater politicization and centralization in gaining greater control over the flow and content of regulations were matched by the growing mistrust of OMB and the excesses and flaws in the regulatory review system, documented in congressional oversight reports and hearings and in court litigation.

The Administration benefited in the short term, using the flexibility of an executive order that could be immediately applied to a problem without congressional obstruction or delay. However, it heightened the level of conflict with Congress by its long-standing resistance to greater public access to the processes of regulatory review. More than that, the use of an executive order for such an important objective makes it a controversial and problematic policy instrument, not so much because it can be supplanted by another executive order or statute, but because intrinsic difficulties are inherent in judicial review and in congressional input and oversight. There are also legitimate concerns about the ambiguous citations of constitutional and statutory authority in the use of some executive orders.

NOTES

1. This discussion of the historical and problematic aspects of executive orders is informed by the study of Philip J. Cooper, "By Order of the President, Administration by Executive Order and Proclamation," *Administration and Society* 18 (August 1986): 252.

2. Ruth P. Morgan, *The President and Civil Rights: Policy Making by Executive Orders* (New York: St. Martin's Press, 1970), 78–84.

3. Sarah Slavin Schramm, *The Politics of Executive Orders* (Ph.D. diss., American University, 1981), 153.

4. Paul Charles Light, *The President's Agenda: Domestic Policy Choice from Kennedy to Carter (with notes on Ronald Reagan)* (Baltimore, Md.: Johns Hopkins University Press, 1981), 117.

5. Raymond Chambers, "The Executive Power: A Preliminary Study of the Concept and Efficacy of Presidential Directives," *Presidential Studies Quarterly* 7 (Winter 1977): 31–32.

6. Robert B. Cash, "The President: Use and Enforcement of Executive Orders," *Notre Dame Lawyer* 39 (December 1963): 44–45.

7. Richard N. L. Andrews, *Environmental Policy and Administrative Change: Implementation of the National Environmental Policy Act* (Boston, Mass.: Lexington Books, 1976), 28–29.

8. Executive Order 11514, 3 C.F.R. 902 (1966–1970).

9. Executive Order 11752, 3 C.F.R. 829 (1971–1975).

10. Executive Order 11593, 3 C.F.R. 559 (1971–1975).

11. Executive Order 11738, 3 C.F.R. 799 (1971–1985).

12. Executive Order 11644, 3 C.F.R. 616 (1971–1975).

13. Executive Order 11643, 3 C.F.R. 664 (1971–1975).

14. Executive Order 11747, 3 C.F.R. 821 (1971–1975).

15. Executive Order 11592, 3 C.F.R. 559 (1971–1975).

16. Executive Order 11523, 3 C.F.R. 915 (1966–1970).

17. Executive Order 11574, 3 C.F.R. 986 (1966–1970).

18. J. Clarence Davies and Barbara S. Davies, *The Politics of Pollution*, 2d ed. (Indianapolis, Ind.: Pegasus, 1975), 209.

19. "The First Two Years," *EPA* (February 1973): 8, 19, 68–91.

20. *Kalur v. Resor*, 335 Supp. 1 (D.D.C. 1971).

21. *U.S. v. Pennsylvania Industrial Chemical Corp.*, 93 S. Ct. 1804, 411 U.S. 655 (1973).

22. *National Helium Corp. v. Morton*, 455 F.2d 650 (10 Cir. 1971); *Continental Illinois Bank and Trust v. Kleindienst*, 382 F. Supp. 107 (N.D. Ill. 1973); *Hiram Clarke Civic Club v. Lynn*, 476 F.2d 421 (5th Cir. 1973).

23. *Sierra v. Morton*, 514 F.2d 856 (D.C. Cir. 1975); *Greene County Planning Board v. Federal Power Commission*, 455 Fed. 412 (2d Cir. 1972); *Carolina Action v. Simon*, 389 F. Supp. 1244 (M.D.N.C. 1975).

24. *Andrus v. Sierra Club*, 442 U.S. 357–358 (1979).

25. "Tenth Progress Report on Agency Implementation Procedures under the National Environmental Policy Act," Federal Register 46, no. 88 (7 May 1981): 25502.

26. *CEQ, Annual Report (1970); Report of the State Department Legal Advisory Committee to the CEQ* (December 1971), 13–17; *CEQ Guidelines*, 40 C.F.R. Sec. 1500 (a)(3)(1) (1978); Russell Peterson, Chairman, CEQ, Memorandum to Heads of Agencies on Applying the EIS Requirement to Environmental Impacts Abroad (24 September 1976).

27. Executive Order 12114, 3 C.F.R. 356 (1979).

28. Sue D. Sheridan, "The Extraterritorial Application of NEPA under Executive Order 12114," *Vanderbilt Journal of Transnational Law* 13 (Winter 1980): 214–17;

Sanford Gaines, "Environmental Effects Abroad of Major Federal Actions: An Executive Order Ordains a National Policy," *Harvard Environmental Law Review* 3 (1979): 157–59.

29. C.F.R. 7, 3100 (1990); C.F.R. 12, 409 (1990); C.F.R. 32, 197 (1990); C.F.R. 14, 1216 (1990); C.F.R. 40, 6 (1990); C.F.R. 22, 161.4 (1990).

30. *EIS Cumulative 1980* (Arlington, Va.: Information Resources Press, 1981), 294; *EIS Cumulative 1979* (Arlington, Va.: Information Resources Press, 1980), 409.

31. Executive Order 11990, 3 C.F.R. 121 (1977); Executive Order 11988, 3 C.F.R. 117 (1977).

32. *EIS Cumulative 1980*, 294; *EIS Cumulative 1979*, 409.

33. Ibid.

34. *Environmental Quality 1979*. Tenth Annual Report of Council on Environmental Quality, December 1979, iv.

35. *Environmental Quality 1980*. Eleventh Annual Report of the Council on Environmental Quality, 299–300.

36. Executive Order 11472, 3 C.F.R. 792 (1966–1970).

37. Executive Order 11629, 3 C.F.R. 629 (1971–1975).

38. Executive Order 12194, 3 C.F.R. 142 (1980).

39. Executive Order 12192, 3 C.F.R. 139 (1980).

40. Executive Order 11472, 3 C.F.R. 792 (1966–1970).

41. Executive Order 12247, 3 C.F.R. 387 (1980).

42. Executive Order 12314, 3 C.F.R. 161 (1981).

43. Executive Order 12202, 3 C.F.R. 243 (1980).

44. Executive Order 12113, 3 C.F.R. 354 (1979).

45. Executive Order 12322, 3 C.F.R. 178 (1971).

46. Executive Order 11821, 3 C.F.R. 926 (1971–1975).

47. Executive Order 12044, 3 C.F.R. 152 (1978).

48. *Sierra* v. *Costle*, 657 F.2d 298 (1981).

49. Howard Ball, *Controlling Regulatory Sprawl: Presidential Strategies from Nixon to Reagan* (Westport, Conn.: Greenwood Press, 1984), 71.

50. Joseph Cooper and William F. West, "Presidential Power and Republican Government: The Theory and Practice of OMB Review of Agency Rules," *Journal of Politics* 50 (November 1988): 884–89.

51. Morton Rosenberg, "Presidential Control of Agency Rulemaking," *Arizona Law Review* 23 (1981): 1199.

52. Testimony of James C. Miller, OIRA Administrator. Senate, *Regulatory Reform Act*, S. 1080, Hearing before the Subcommittee on Regulatory Reform, 97th Cong., Senate Committee on Governmental Operations, 1st Sess., May 1981, 138.

53. *Regulatory Reform Act*, Hearing, S. 1080, ibid., 348, 382.

54. Erik Olson, "The Quiet Shift of Power: Office of Management and Budget Supervision of Environmental Protection Agency Rulemaking under Executive Order 12291," *Virginia Journal of Natural Resources Law* 4, no. 1 (Fall 1984): 51.

55. *Regulatory Reform Act*, Hearing, S. 1080, 519.

56. Peter L. Strauss, "The Place of Agencies in Government: Separation of Powers and the Fourth Branch of Government," *Columbia Law Review* 84 (Spring 1984): 160.

57. Frank B. Cross, "Executive Orders 12291 and 12498: A Test Case of Presidential Control of Executive Agencies," *Journal of Law and Politics* 4 (Spring 1988): 516, 518.

58. Morton Rosenberg, "Regulatory Management at OMB," in *Office of Management and Budget: Evolving Roles and Future Issues*, Congressional Research Service, S. Print 99–134, 99th Cong., 2d sess., 1986, 225–26.

59. Cooper and West, "Presidential Power and Republican Government," 885.

60. Subcommittee on Oversight and Investigations, House Committee on Energy and Commerce, *EPA's Asbestos Regulations: A Report on a Case Study on OMB Interference in Agency Rulemaking*, 99th Cong., 1st sess., 1985, Committee Print 99–U, 109.

61. Olson, "The Quiet Shift of Power," 40.

62. *Presidential Management of Rulemaking in Regulatory Agencies* (Washington, D.C.: National Academy of Public Administration, 1987), 7.

63. W. Norton Grubb, Dale Whittington, and Michael Humphries, "The Ambiguities of Benefit–Cost Analysis: An Evaluation of Regulatory Impact Analysis under Executive Order 12291," in *Environmental Policy under Executive Order 12291, the Role of Benefit–Cost Analysis*, ed. V. Kerry Smith (Chapel Hill: University of North Carolina Press, 1987), 154.

64. Cooper and West, "Presidential Power and Republican Government," 875.

65. Senate Committee on Environment and Public Works, *Office of Management and Budget Influence on Agency Regulations*, 98th Cong., 2d sess., S. Print 99–156, 1986, 6.

66. Management Case Study (No. C 96–85–638). Kennedy School of Government, as quoted in *Office of Management and Budget Influence on Agency Regulations*, 4.

67. Office of Management and Budget, *Regulatory Program of the United States Government, 1 April, 1987–31 March, 1988*, 631, 538; and OMB, *Regulatory Program of the United States Government, 1 April, 1986–31 March, 1987*, 1986, 628.

68. *Report on the President's Claim of Executive Privilege over EPA Documents; Abuses in the Superfund Program and Other Matters*, Subcommittee on Oversight and Investigations, House Committee on Energy and Commerce, 1984, Committee Print 98AA, 292–93; and Senate Committee on Environment and Public Works, *Office of Management and Budget Influence on Agency Regulations*, 22–32.

69. *Environmental Defense Fund* v. *Thomas*, F. Supp. 566, 571 (D.D.C. 1986).

70. Ibid. *Buckley* v. *Valeo*, 424, U.S. 1 (1976); *Immigration Naturalization Service* v. *Chadha*, 103 S. Ct. (1983); *Bowsher* v. *Synar*, 106 S. Ct. 3181 (1986).

71. See also Cross, "Executive Orders 12291 and 12498," 516, 518.

72. Executive Order 12498, 3 C.F.R. 323 (1985).

73. Edward Paul Fuchs, *Presidents, Management and Regulation* (Englewood Cliffs, N.J.: Prentice-Hall, 1988), 121.

74. Proposed Executive Order, titled *Regulatory Planning Process, Office of Legal Counsel, Department of Justice*, 21 December 1984.

75. *Sierra* v. *Costle*, 657 F.2d, 298 (D. Cir. 1986), 405–6.

76. Cass R. Sunstein and Peter L. Strauss, Administrative Law Section Report to the House of Delegates, in *OMB Review of EPA Regulations*, Hearing, House Subcommittee on Oversight and Investigations, 99th Cong., 2d sess., 1986, 108.

77. Rosenberg, "Regulatory Management at OMB," 224.

78. Ann Rosenfield, "Note: Presidential Policy Management of Agency Rules under Reagan Order 12498," *Administrative Law Review* 38 (1986), 88.

79. Ibid., 82–83.

80. *United States* v. *Nixon*, 418 U.S. 683 (1974); and *Nixon* v. *Administration of General Services*, 408 F. Supp. 321 (1976).

81. Memorandum for the Heads of Executive Departments and Agencies, Development of Administration's Regulatory Program, from President Ronald Reagan, 4 January 1985. *Public Papers of the Presidents of the United States, Ronald Reagan*, I, 1985 (Washington, D.C.: U.S. Government Printing Office, 1990), 12.

82. E.O. 12498, Sec. 2(a), 3 C.F.R. 324 (1985). Significant regulatory actions include prerule-making actions, notices of proposed rule-making actions, and publications of final rules. The criteria for defining a significant regulatory action include (1) a major rule as defined by E.O. 12291, (2) an action required by statutory or judicial deadline, (3) a priority of an agency director, (4) an activity of unusual interest to other federal agencies or of unusual public interest, (5) an activity likely to set an important new legal or policy precedent, or (6) an activity designated by the OMB director to be reviewed as a significant regulatory action. Thus, the order gives the OMB director wide scope to designate any regulatory activity as significant, even though it may not fall within the other named criteria. *OMB Bulletin* 85–9, 10 January 1985, sec. 5(c).

83. *OMB Bulletin*, 85–9, sec. 5 (a, b).

84. *OMB Bulletin*, 85–9, Attachment 1, Instructions, 2.

85. *OMB Bulletin* 85–9, Attachment 1, sec. 8, 10.

86. Thomas O. McGarity, "Regulatory Reform and the Positive State," *Administrative Law Review* 38, no. 4 (1986): 420.

87. *Inside the Administration* 4, no. 15 (12 April 1985): 4.

88. "A Record of Loss: Agency Proposals that Did Not Survive the OMB Regulatory Planning Process," *OMB Watch* (December 1985): 2–3.

89. *New York Times*, 5 May 1985, 28.

90. Morton Rosenberg, interview, 10 December 1986.

91. Interview, EPA official, 11 December 1986.

92. Interview, EPA official, 10 December 1986.

93. These figures were drawn from: OMB, *Regulatory Program of the United States Government, April 1, 1985–March 31, 1986*, Index I, 599–600, n.d.; OMB, *Regulatory Program of the United States Government, 1 April 1986–31 March 1987*, Index I, 582–83, n.d.; and OMB, *Regulatory Program of the United States Government, April 1, 1987–March 31, 1988*, Index I, 653–54, n.d.

94. *Presidential Management of Rulemaking in Regulatory Agencies*, 40.

95. *First English Evangelical Lutheran Church of Glendale* v. *County of Los Angeles*, 107 S. Ct. 2378 (1987); and *Nollan* v. *California Coastal Commission*, 100 S. Ct. 3141 (1987).

96. "Attorney General Guidelines for the Evaluation of Risk and Avoidance of Unanticipated Takings," *Environmental Law Reporter* 18 (30 June 1988): 35172.

97. Executive Order 12630, 3 C.F.R. 554 (1988).

98. James M. McElfish, Jr., "The Takings Order: Constitutional Jurisprudence or Political Philosophy?" *Environmental Law Reporter* 18 (November 1988): 10476.

99. Ibid.

100. Executive Order 12630, Sec. 4(b), 3 C.F.R. 557 (1988).

101. Jerry Jackson and Lyle D. Albaugh, "A Critique of the Takings Executive Order in the Context of Environmental Regulation," *Environmental Law Reporter* 18 (November 1988): 10469.

102. 107 S. Ct. 1245, n. 21.
103. McElfish, "The Takings Order," 10477.
104. *Inside EPA*, 9, 20 May 1988, 4.
105. McElfish, "The Takings Order," 10478.
106. Jackson and Albaugh, "A Critique of the Takings Executive Order," 10473.
107. Executive Order 12303, 3 C.F.R. 148 (1981).
108. Executive Order 12314, 3 C.F.R. 161 (1981).
109. Executive Order 12407, 3 C.F.R. 154 (1983).
110. Executive Order 12319, 3 C.F.R. 175 (1981).
111. Executive Order 12298, 3 C.F.R. 142 (1981).
112. Executive Order 12342, 3 C.F.R. 127 (1982).
113. Executive Order 12372, 3 C.F.R. 197 (1982).
114. Executive Order 12612, 3 C.F.R. 153–54 (1987).

4

The Administrative Presidency and the Politics of Risk Management

This chapter examines the institutional presidency, particularly the Office of Management and Budget and its interactions with regulatory agencies and congressional oversight committees in the politics of risk assessment and risk management. Risk assessment and risk management operate in a political system that has been characterized as relatively open, competitive, pluralistic, and often confrontational.[1] As one of a number of public and private participants, OMB has a legitimate role to play in the risk management process, reflecting the political concerns and priorities of an administration. Some basic questions relating to that role have involved both the broader struggle to obtain greater political accountability and public access in OIRA's operations and the adequacy of its scientific expertise in reviewing agency risk assessments. Conflict, even a measure of distrust, is inescapable between OMB and congressional oversight committees, as well as between OMB and regulatory agencies, because of their institutional roles and perspectives on risk-related matters. While some progress was achieved by agencies in adopting risk assessment procedures, particularly in the second term of the Reagan Administration, the different perspectives of OMB and some regulatory agencies were complicated by the manner in which OMB dealt with risk-related matters and by the heightened conflict between OMB and Congress over regulatory policy. The Reagan administrative presidency strategy managed to carve out a more important role for OMB in risk management without specific congressional authorization or approval. But this gain was realized at the expense of addressing longer-term complex problems of coordination and cooperation between Congress and the presidency dealing with risk-related problems.

OMB's role in risk assessment became more important during the Reagan Administration for several reasons. Congress, the courts, and the Carter Administration had become more involved in risk-related issues, and there was a growing trend toward politicization and centralization of the institutional presidency in regulatory policy. Furthermore, the Reagan administrative presidency desired a more risk-tolerant approach in regulatory policy; its broader objective was to reduce the output and scope of federal regulations.

Many of the new social regulation statutes adopted in the 1970s provided for a balancing of risks, costs, and benefits in ambiguous provisions calling for the application of reasonable standards. Agency officials were given considerable discretion in rule making in the proliferation of new social and environmental regulations, but the escalating regulatory costs caused a counteraction by affected organized interest groups in the Nixon and Ford Administrations. The Carter Administration, in its turn, sought to balance rising regulatory costs with the Regulatory Analysis Review Group (RARG) machinery, established under E.O. 12044. The assessment of environmental, health, and safety rules by RARG frequently pushed President Carter's economic advisers into the use of risk–benefit analyses. Some agencies, such as OSHA, were cautious about applying the quantification of risk as an integral part of its standard setting under the Occupational Safety and Health Act, but EPA undertook a number of risk assessments of carcinogens in the late 1970s.

Some of President Carter's economic advisers favored risk–benefit analysis, and the president himself intervened in a proposed cotton dust standard to protect workers, favoring a less costly revised regulation supported by the Council of Economic Advisers. Under some pressure by RARG, health, environmental, and safety agency officials took a more unified position to counteract risk assessment arguments and formed the Interagency Regulatory Liaison Group (IRLG). The group, whose membership included EPA, OSHA, the Food and Drug Administration, and the Consumer Product Safety Commission, adopted the position that quantitative risk assessment of cancer-related risks should be only utilized in establishing priorities, with the goal of obtaining rough estimates of the magnitude of risks. It adopted a conservative perspective on risk assessment that implied that if the impact of threshold levels of carcinogens for human beings could not be scientifically established, a proposed regulation should rest on the assumption that any potentially suspected carcinogen constituted a hazard. The final draft of the IRLG group on cancer policy was criticized for not undergoing the rigors of peer review.[2] However, it was the Carter Administration's last major statement on cancer policy reflecting the regulatory perspective of a more liberal, activist, risk-averse Democratic Administration.[3]

Two developments in the 1980s not directly related to the initiatives of the Reagan Administration provided added stimulus to the acceptance of quantitative risk assessment in regulatory decision making. The first was the Supreme Court's ruling invalidating OSHA's benzene standard. The highest court requested the agency to determine by appropriate quantitative methods that there was, in fact, a significant risk at the existing exposure level for workers and that the risk could be cut back by reducing exposure conditions. The second development was the National Academy of Sciences (NAS) report, issued in 1983, drawing a distinction between risk assessment, as the more objective quantitative method of estimating risk, and risk management, as the broader policy-making method, which incorporated economic, social, and scientific considerations. Long before the NAS report was released, however, the quantification of risk was also given a boost by the incoming Reagan Administration. Business and industry groups that had filed lawsuits in the 1970s to require regulating agencies to adopt formal cost–benefit analysis were doubly pleased with both the Supreme Court's ruling in the benzene case and President Reagan's E.O. 12291 requiring agencies to use formal cost–benefit analysis in submitting proposed regulations unless prohibited by law.

At the outset, the Reagan administrative presidency strategy affected agency risk assessments through the executive order and indirectly through its personnel and budgetary priorities. The Administration openly targeted a number of risk-related regulations for regulatory relief. Budget cuts seriously eroded the ability of social regulatory agencies to provide an adequate data base for risk assessments, particularly when the regulated industry was not obliged to provide the data. With reduced staff as the result of budget reductions and, consequently, without sufficient data, agencies were hampered in adequately assessing and managing health and environmental impacts and risks associated with products and technologies. During Reagan's first term, EPA's appropriations for its pesticide program were slashed by twenty million dollars and its staff complement by almost three hundred from fiscal years 1981 to 1983. At the same time, the load of pesticide registrations increased, with the result that some scientific reviewers routinely accepted without question industry's summary statements of its experimental results.[4] Moreover, some political loyalists appointed to environmental agencies affected risk management by their personnel and reorganization actions. Anne Burford, for example, shifted several EPA career officials out of the agency's risk management activities. The subsequent disclosure of closed-door meetings and discussions between EPA officials and industry representatives to discuss regulatory strategies, to resolve technical matters, and to draft documents to be filed by EPA officials in the *Federal Register* all served to weaken public trust in EPA's commitment, competence, and risk assessment procedures.[5]

EPA's use of "science forums" involving secret meetings of EPA officials with regulated industry representatives concerning possible effects of formaldehyde led to widespread criticism within the scientific community about the initial course of the Reagan Administration's cancer risk assessment policy. EPA's use of secret science forums and the Todhunter memorandum concerning impact estimates of formaldehyde were strongly criticized on the grounds that the agency had violated scientific procedures of peer review when EPA relied solely upon one source of information—the regulated industry. Furthermore, no transcripts were kept of the secret discussions.[6]

Whereas the Carter Administration's cancer risk assessment policies were based on a more risk-averse approach, the incoming Reagan Administration favored the position of some scientific critics who maintained that existing cancer policy principles rested on shaky scientific footing, thereby justifying the Administration's more risk-tolerant approach toward potential carcinogens. According to Mark Rushefsky, during Reagan's first term

> cancer policies stemming from EPA and OSTP (Office of Science and Technology Policy) were attempts to combine the scientific critiques and regulatory relief streams to produce more risk tolerant policies. That effort was stymied both by the scandals that affected EPA and the continued strong support for environmental protection in Congress and in the general public. Later cancer policies by EPA and the Office of Science and Technology were closer to the Carter Administration consensus, with OSTP adopting the principles approach to cancer-risk assessment and EPA adopting some of the ideas of the scientific critique.[7]

Another distinctive difference between the Carter and Reagan Administrations was OMB's increasing, if indirect, influence in risk assessment and risk management. OMB Director David Stockman urged the adoption of comparative risk analysis as part of the Administration's legislative package of regulatory reform. Unable to obtain congressional approval, he used his authority under E.O. 12291 to issue some minimal guidelines encouraging the use of risk analysis methods. Risk assessment techniques were required in regulatory impact statements when these techniques contributed to more informed regulatory decision making.[8] But beyond minimal guidelines issued in the early 1980s, OMB did not standardize any guidelines for the conduct of risk assessment analysis.[9]

Under the Paperwork Reduction Act, OMB was also able to influence the risk assessment process of agencies by canceling, revising, or delaying information collection requests by agencies, information that might eventually be used as a data base to gauge hazards and risks leading to a proposed regulation. Through its budgetary powers, OMB played a significant role in cutting budgets for scientific personnel and in research for environmental agencies, such as EPA and OSHA, during the first term of the Reagan Administration. It was also instrumental in allocating greater research funding on the impacts of radon to the Department of Energy, much to the dismay of the EPA in the president's second term. Through the use of E.O. 12291, critics maintained that OMB was able to veto, revise, and delay the issuance of regulations, displacing congressional intent and agency authority even though agencies are legally charged with the promulgation of regulations.

Risk assessment was defined by OMB as "a purely scientific process that measures the riskiness of various activities and combines it with other information, such as the cost and feasibility of reducing risks, to determine how to reduce risks more efficiently."[10] A more detailed analysis of risk assessment and risk management by the Administration's Council on Environmental Quality (CEQ) accepted the major functions and distinctions between the two but noted that the boundaries between them are not easy to draw. "Assessments of risk are inherently imprecise because knowledge is incomplete, and because the results of the process depend heavily on the procedures and assumptions used. The line separating 'science' from 'policy' is not a sharp one in that judgment must be used where data are absent."[11]

Although there was neither any provision nor specific reference about risk assessment in E.O. 12498 and 12291, the former order was used as a vehicle to express OMB's perspective and priorities on risk assessment. OMB traced its authority to issue pronouncements on risk assessment to one of the Administration's regulatory guidelines set by the President's Task Force on Regulatory Relief, which declared, "Regulations that seek to reduce health or safety risks should be based on scientific assessment procedures, and should address risks that are real rather than hypothetical or remote."[12] In turn, the claim of authority that the Administration cited for the task force itself was based on a broad interpretation of the

Constitution's Article II's executive power clause and the *Sierra* v. *Costle* decision.

OMB proceeded to connect the cost–benefit process mandated by E.O. 12291 to risk reduction benefits and the risk assessment process and stated, "In Executive Order 12291 President Reagan has required that 'regulatory objectives shall be chosen to maximize the net benefits to society.' This cannot be achieved without understanding both the costs and the risk reduction benefits of regulatory options."[13]

E.O. 12498 gave OMB another important level at which it could influence risk assessment before it was incorporated as part of a proposed regulation. Under E.O. 12498 it was possible for OMB to veto a proposed study by an agency in its regulatory agenda involving or leading to risk assessments that could eventually be required in a proposed regulation. Unless there was a leak by agency officials to the press or to congressional staff, the public was unaware of the cancellation of the study.

Under E.O. 12498, the regulatory program was envisioned by OMB as a counterpart to its powers in priority setting, explanation, and coordination of proposed agency funds in the federal budget. It established a form of regulatory clearance and coordination whereby agencies submitted their regulatory agenda for each year to OMB. The regulatory program was perceived not only as a vehicle to coordinate various regulatory agendas but also as a means of blocking regulatory initiatives deemed inconsistent with regulatory priorities of the Administration and its perception of agency discretion. However, the power to curb regulatory initiatives was limited, since many regulatory mandates are spelled out in statutes or can be required by riders and revised legislation.

OMB used its power granted under E.O. 12498 not only to coordinate the Administration's regulatory agenda in line with the Administration's priorities but also to advocate greater consistency in risk assessment and risk management. An OMB report stated: "More review by regulatory departments and by the Executive branch has already begun to improve consistency in risk assessment and risk management, and thereby improve societal welfare. E.O. 12291 provides a mechanism to help ensure consistency."[14] From its vantage point as a fiscal watchdog advisory agency and in view of President Reagan's goal of regulatory relief, OMB maintained that "the goal in managing risks is to provide the greatest net benefit to the general public. To do this regulators must have a way to compare the effectiveness of different approaches for reducing various risks to society. Without such a comparative, quantitative procedure, the government could spend society's resources on efforts that do not reduce risks effectively."[15]

A number of risk specialists outside of the government have also supported the use of quantitative risk assessment in order to reduce risks and to provide net benefits to society. Lave, for example, declared that quantitative risk assessment, despite its imperfections, can help inform political judgment and decision making relating to risk. He and others acknowledge the inevitable role of political accountability and judgment in risk-related decisions.

Despite its limitations, quantitative risk assessment has no logical alternative. With the exception of a policy of no risk, which is impossible to implement in a modern industrial society, risk assessment is the only systematic tool for analyzing various regulatory approaches to health and safety. All other frameworks involve some sort of intuitive balancing that is inappropriate where quantitative analysis is possible and where the stakes are high.[16]

OMB emphasized the need for coordination, consistency, and economic efficiency in the reduction of risks. It criticized the large differences in cost effectiveness for different regulations, declaring that greater risk reduction could have been provided at the same or lower total cost by regulating other, more cost-effective risks. While it acknowledged that there are more considerations in establishing regulatory policy than risk–cost tradeoffs and that many laws mandate weighing factors besides (or, in some instances, instead of) cost–risk reduction, thereby making it inappropriate to establish a single value-of-life estimate for all situations, it still urged agencies to evaluate cost effectiveness in proposed regulations.

An OMB report noted:

Critics have claimed that one cannot place "a value on life" and therefore we should not estimate the cost per life saved implied by proposed regulations. It is true that a specific individual's life cannot be assigned a dollar value since most people would be willing to spend almost any amount of money to avoid certain death and to continue a healthy life. But this is almost never the situation that government regulators face. The kinds of risks government usually regulates are small risks of death for a large number of individuals. Under these conditions, it is essential to have some uniform measure of cost and benefit so that the maximum number of lives can be saved with society's limited resources. If policy officials do not use estimates of cost per statistical life saved, they will not know if alternative options might save more lives.[17]

There has been no systematic broad-scaled study of the problems, differing perspectives, interactions, and conflicts between OMB officials and regulatory agency personnel in the field of risk assessment. The National Academy of Public Administration (NAPA) interviewed OMB and regulatory agency officials in its examination of presidential management of agency rule making, but most agency officials' comments were made without attribution. Unable to apply any definitive method in weighing the claims of those who believed that OMB had displaced agency authority in the rule-making process and those who claimed that it did not, the NAPA report concluded that "OMB arguments are more than advisory but still less than mandatory. The review process is more one of negotiation and accommodation than of agency initiatives being overruled by OMB demands."[18] Agency officials disagreed on whether OMB had abused its powers in the regulatory review process, but the NAPA survey did not identify or distinguish between those who thought that OMB overreached its powers and those who believed that it had not.

The NAPA report indicated that "there are, however, some clear and regular patterns of difference between the regulatory agencies and OMB, as exemplified by three areas of controversy that are central to the formulation of regulations: (1) the assessment of environmental and health risks; (2) the calculation of the costs and benefits of reducing those risks; and (3) comparisons of the cost-effectiveness of different regulations."[19] OMB and regulatory agency officials disagreed over the calculation of both costs and benefits, as well as the choice of discount rates in estimating the effects of regulations over time. Critics maintained that OMB generally uses a higher discount rate than is applied by the agencies, making it more difficult to support the imposition of new regulations. OMB's written guidance for the preparation of Regulatory Impact Analyses for proposed major regulatory agencies assumed that present lives saved are worth more than those protected in the future. Some agency officials, concerned about distributional impacts of regulations, have opposed discounting future benefits:

> They argue that one life saved in the future should be equated with one saved in the present. They reject analogies with financial investments and rates of return. Regulatory statutes, they maintain, do not give regulators the option of deferring regulatory burdens, so that regulated interests can invest the funds for alternative uses.[20]

Thus, critics within and outside regulatory agencies argued that important normative and ethical questions can be neglected if OMB's emphasis on short-term economic considerations prevails in regulatory policy making.

In connection with EPA's proposed asbestos regulations, OMB claimed that benefits should be discounted to indicate that those individuals exposed to carcinogenic agents suffered no loss until they actually contracted cancer over the estimated thirty- to forty-year latency period. This approach did not square with EPA's previous practice and, in fact, up until that time EPA's Office of Toxic Substances had never utilized discounting over the estimated latency period of a chronic hazard. The EPA programs that did use discounting typically discounted benefits from the time when exposure to a substance was avoided instead of from the moment of onset of the disease. EPA officials expressed some misgivings about OMB's discounting approach, maintaining that it would greatly reduce the projected benefit of EPA's proposed asbestos regulations. They also urged that the issue of discounting over the latency period of cancer-causing agents be fully debated in public forums, but OMB ignored the request.[21]

OMB AND CANCER RISK ASSESSMENTS

Differences between OMB's pronouncements and regulatory agency policies were evident in carcinogen risk assessments. According to the Office of Technology Assessment, OMB's pronouncements in this area "are contrary to the general consensus that has evolved in the regulatory agency policies."[22] OMB's perspective on risk assessment and its differences with some regulatory agencies reflected in part the fact that much of the cancer risk assessment process is controversial among scientists and is marked by uncertainty. One school of scientists believes that benign tumors in laboratory animals almost always indicate early stages of malignancy, while another group maintains that benign tumors should be discounted or weighted differently from malignant ones in estimating whether a substance is likely to cause cancer. OMB ascribed to the viewpoint of the latter scientific school and stated that the use of benign tumor data in risk assessment can lead to overestimates of real risk, since all tumors do not evolve malignantly.

Scientists have also disagreed about the significance of negative results in cancer studies in which animal exposure to carcinogens does not produce tumors or other health problems. One scientific group found that animal studies are not particularly sensitive means of cancer production, and, therefore, negative results are ignored when other clear positive results may be found. OMB maintained that the use of the most sensitive species studies can lead to biases in risk assessment, and it sided with a scientific approach called the weight-of-the-evidence approach. That method seeks a weighted average of all available scientifically valid information, including both negative and positive results in cancer risk assessment. The approach embodied in most agency risk assessment policies has been to use negative epidemiological studies only to gauge an upper boundary limit on estimated risks and not to employ such studies to question positive evidence. OMB was also concerned about the use of the upper confidence limit in agency extrapolation techniques, maintaining that such an approach presents a 95 percent chance of overstating true risks. However, its perspective in extrapolation techniques was criticized in an Office of Technology Assessment report on the grounds that, "in fact, OMB is misinterpreting the meaning of the upper bound estimates prepared by the regulatory agencies."[23]

In 1986 in OMB's regulatory review of EPA's long-awaited cancer risk assessment guidelines, Wendy Lee Gramm, head of OMB's Office of Information and Regulatory Affairs (OIRA), criticized EPA's guidelines in four key areas. The areas involved: (1) interspecies comparisons; (2) the counting of benign tumors; (3) the selection of extrapolation models; and (4) the choice of the most sensitive species. Gramm, for example, disagreed with a provision in EPA's proposed guidelines that stated, "Because it is possible that human sensitivity is as high as the most sensitive responding animal species, in the absence of evidence to the contrary, the biologically acceptable data set from long-term animal studies showing the greatest sensitivity should generally be given the greatest emphasis, again with due regard to biological and statistical considerations."[24] Gramm declared that an official should base his or her decision on all scientifically sound available studies, and that OIRA was concerned that those undertaking risk assessments might simply choose those animal studies indicating the greatest sensitivity without adequately considering comparative risk estimates based on other animal studies. She urged EPA to replace the sentence emphasizing most sensitive animal studies with the statement that "all data from scientifically valid long-term animal studies shall be used to assess the possible risk to humans with regard to biological and statistical considerations."[25]

OIRA's head also took issue with provisions in EPA's proposed guidelines dealing with cancer exposure, which stated, "When there is uncertainty in the scientific facts, it is Agency policy to err on the side of public safety. The Agency intends to be realistic, but will not arbitrarily select midranges of environmental distributions that may compromise human health," and "the Agency will err on the side of public health when evaluating uncertainties when data are limited or nonexistent." She charged that these passages were inconsistent with the body of EPA's guidelines, which emphasized unbiased exposure estimates, and that the "agency's policy to err, regardless of the direction of the error" was "the kind of ambiguous language that is sometimes cited as the excuse for not presenting the full range of information to decision-makers."[26] Gramm finally warned EPA that OIRA planned to review the agency's draft regulations carefully to assure their compliance with OMB's views if EPA did not change its generic guidelines.

OIRA's efforts to change provisions in EPA's cancer risk assessment guidelines, Gramm's speech on risk assessment to the American Industrial Health Council, and OMB's comments on formaldehyde triggered a vigorous response from Representative John Dingell, chairman of the Subcommittee on Oversight and Investigation, House Energy and Commerce Committee. Gramm had described OIRA criteria on risk assessment to the American Industrial Health Council and mentioned that OIRA staff projects were proceeding on comparative risk assessment and cost effectiveness, as well as statistical studies in risk assessment and the impact of conservative assumptions on risk assessment. She also mentioned that OIRA was considering the development of "more specific guidance for risk assessments."[27] Dingell charged that OIRA had ventured beyond its limited authority under the Paperwork Reduction Act and was abusing its powers and resources in attempts to direct federal cancer policy. He requested that Gramm provide the House Oversight Subcommittee with names of OMB officials and consultants who were involved in the review of EPA's five draft final regulations, the curricula vitae and expertise of such officials in sixteen specific scientific disciplines and in statistics, and copies of all written material, as well as a list of oral communications on this matter between OMB and organizations and individuals outside the government.

Dingell also requested that EPA Administrator Lee Thomas provide his subcommittee with extensive information, including all written communications between OMB and EPA on the draft guidelines, other pertinent documents, and the names of all individuals in and out of the federal government who participated in the internal peer review of the guidelines. Parenthetically, Dingell also requested that OMB provide his subcommittee with the names and educational and professional backgrounds of those individuals who had prepared the policy statement on risk assessment in OMB's *Regulatory Program of the United States*. He also called upon OMB to provide more detailed data to explain its charts and information on risk–cost transactions for selected regulatory agencies in the regulatory program.

Gramm indicated that only twelve OIRA staff members were involved in the review of EPA's guidelines. No consultants were brought in, but supplementary analysis of the guidelines was provided by staff of the

National Science Foundation and the Office of Science and Technology Policy (OSTP). OSTP officials reportedly claimed that the EPA guidelines were generally in compliance with OSTP policy on cancer risk assessment, but that EPA guidelines contained statements that were broader, including statements that were unclear, inconsistent, and differing with the OSTP document on chemical carcinogens.[28] In addition, an official of the National Science Foundation claimed that EPA's draft guidelines did not draw a clear enough distinction between risk assessment and risk management.

Pressure by Congressman Dingell forced OIRA to disallow any plans to implement cancer risk guidelines and to back off on its pressure to modify provisions in EPA's proposed cancer risk assessment guidelines. OMB reached an accommodation in negotiations with EPA, with EPA adding two introductory paragraphs to its cancer risk guidelines, but it did not change the specific language that OMB requested.

The Reagan Administration managed to avert the movement by some powerful congressional committee chairmen to defund OIRA. Congress, however, finally tightened its control over OIRA in the reauthorization of the Paperwork Reduction Act in 1986. It stipulated that OIRA would become a line-item budget account limited to $5.5 million a year over a three-year period and that the appointment of its head would be confirmed by the Senate. The outcome of the 1986 congressional elections further weakened the political clout of the Reagan White House in domestic policy because the Democratic Party recaptured the Senate. OMB continued to play a significant role, but OIRA's power was diminished, marked by Gramm's resignation. For the remainder of the Reagan Administration, OIRA operated with an acting director.

By the end of Reagan's second term, the influence of OMB in risk assessment had diminished, not only because the Administration's political power waned in the closing months but also because risk assessment had become a major management tool for EPA under Administrator Lee Thomas and his predecessor, William Ruckelshaus. OMB and the Reagan White House supported risk assessment as a means of curbing extensive regulation by requiring more proof to justify regulatory efforts. At the same time, however, EPA's greater reliance on risk assessment strengthened its dealings with OMB, since the focus of debate and analysis had shifted more in the direction of scientific and technical issues, areas of EPA's expertise, with less focus on economic considerations. According to Andrews:

> Risk assessment made risk rather than dollars the new focus for policy
> analysis and a criterion by which to compare progress and proposals

on terms relevant to EPA's mission and expertise. . . . Whatever its imperfections, therefore, risk assessment allowed EPA to wrap its decisions in the legitimacy and apparent objectivity of science, and in the language of health effects rather than merely economic benefits.[29]

Critics of OMB during the Reagan Administration charged that it ventured beyond its intellectual depth in the review of cancer risk assessment guidelines. A large part of OIRA's problem in reviewing EPA's cancer guidelines was that the issue was scientific rather than economic, and OIRA was understaffed in the scientific field. Critics claimed that OIRA lacked sufficient expertise in biology, epidemiology, and toxology so necessary in understanding cancer risk assessments. For example, an OMB official stated that OSHA's proposed formaldehyde rule was analyzed by three economists, whereas OSHA involved an epidemiologist, a toxologist, a biochemist, a biostatistician, and an industrial hygienist in its formaldehyde draft regulation.

Some criticized OMB's regulatory review operation for being too heavily staffed with economists. According to Lave,

The problem is that OMB has a lot of economists and economists have one song to sing. That song is about efficiency and cost effectiveness. The political process is not fundamentally about efficiency and cost effectiveness. That's why these decisions about what is an "adequate" level of protection ought to be made by Congress, writing laws with guidelines about what are permissible risks.[30]

Observers criticized OMB for delaying the adoption of health standards; for prescribing tests that science cannot meet; and for being unaccountable, ignorant, and arrogant in second-guessing agency cancer risk assessments. Defenders of OMB's role maintained that tough questions are needed to make sure that decision makers in regulatory agencies understand their overly conservative assumptions. Paul Portney, senior fellow at Resources for the Future, pointed out that OMB contributed to its problems by operating in secrecy, but that it posed vitally needed questions. He said, "Regulations cost the public a lot of money, and somebody has to ask, 'Is it worth it?' Therefore, 'There is nothing wrong with OMB second-guessing its regulatory agencies and occasionally questioning their science.' "[31] He maintained that OMB works for the president, and its role is justifiable in pressing an agency concerning a proposed standard. OMB may feel that the agency is too conservative regarding its risk assessment or it may disagree with the agency on the projected costs of a proposed rule. Although there were criticisms about OMB's preponderance of staff people with economic backgrounds and its orientation toward cost effectiveness and efficiency, there was no significant pressure by congressional oversight and appropriations committees to expand OMB's complement with staff members of varied scientific training in epidemiology and toxology.

The appropriate role of OMB and its relationship between agencies in cancer risk assessment cannot easily be defined, in part because the line between science and policy cannot easily be demarcated. In theory, OMB has a justifiable role raising questions concerning proposed standards of regulatory agencies and their procedures, and in serving as a presidential watchdog over regulatory costs; but in practice and in the manner of its operation, OIRA demonstrated that political controls on behalf of the president can overshadow scientific and professional judgments, jeopardizing the legitimacy of the regulatory enterprise.[32] Risk assessment and risk management operate in a pluralistic, sometimes confrontational, political arena. Portney believes that "we will tolerate a lot of inefficiency in order to get fair play. We are process oriented."[33] Negotiations between some of the actors, particularly OMB and agency officials, are an integral part of the politics of risk management. Conflict between the Budget Office and the agencies is also inescapable, particularly when Congress is controlled by one party and the presidency by another. But the complexity of the process and the range of uncertainty concerning the limits of scientific knowledge as well as the costs and benefits of risk management call for cooperation and patient negotiation.

There has to be some regulatory oversight group within the Executive Office of the President (EOP), whether it is located in the OMB, OSTP, or in another unit. But it should be an interdisciplinary group. Part of OIRA's problem in regulatory review and risk assessment is that it does not have enough scientists. Another problem, particularly during much of the Reagan Administration, was that agencies and the public were not apprised of private meetings and oral communications between OIRA officials and members of private groups. This perpetuated the view that OMB sided with business interests. Finally, after much criticism by Congress and by the legal community, OMB made available to agencies and to the public written material, pertinent meetings, and communications with individuals outside the federal government. During the Carter Administration, RARG always wrote down comments concerning a proposed regulation, sometimes forty to fifty pages in length, and the comments were submitted as part of the public docket on a proposed rule. In the Reagan Administration OIRA was also criticized for not undertaking a greater effort to meet with public interest and environmental groups and for not publicly supporting an agency when it was doing something right.[34]

The politics of risk management operate in a political arena peopled by many actors, sometimes in overlapping, untidy jurisdictions. Apart from Congress and its oversight committees and subcommittees and the Office of Technology Assessment, there are the federal courts; the EOP, including OMB, the Office of Science and Technology Policy, and interdepartmental committees; the bureaucracy, with its scientifically trained personnel and advisory science committees; regulated chemical and business interest groups, with their allied national organizations; and public interest law groups, with their issue networks of environmental and public health organizations. The political path of risk management is filled with many checkpoints and can be excruciatingly slow and inefficient to some observers in comparison with the political culture of science policy and risk management in other nations.

One school of thought believes that Congress should sketch out broad policy goals in legislation, leaving detailed regulations and risk assessment to the agencies. But the potentially redistributive impacts of some risk policies may make some Congressmen wary of approving policies that might be opposed by some of their constituents. Lack of information and scientific uncertainty related to risks also present problems for effective congressional oversight. One close observer noted that an analysis of risk legislation "suggests that Congress has largely avoided a role in determining acceptable risk."[35] Congress, for example, by adopting vague standards and avoiding answers to critical questions, has shifted problems to the courts, loading them with more litigation. This was no accident, according to Norman Vig, as "Congress evidently *intended* the courts to play an active part in refining agency policy" and thus, inescapably, courts have been involved in reviewing risk policy decisions.[36]

In some legislation Congress granted agencies a considerable measure of discretion in choosing regulatory strategies. But ambiguity in some laws permitted political loyalists in the Reagan Administration to put their imprint on policies reflecting Administration priorities, rather than the intentions of congressional architects reflected in the legislative history of such laws. Congress was unwilling to adopt legislation during President Reagan's first term that would have sanctioned OMB's role in cost–benefit analysis in regulating policy; the Senate approved passage of a bill in a bipartisan unanimous vote, but House opponents defeated the measure. The White House had previously issued E.O. 12291 adopting cost–benefit analysis and later expanded its power over the regulatory process with E.O. 12498, issuing pronouncements on risk assessment under broad interpretations of the Constitution's Article II on executive power. Congressional oversight committees monitored OMB's application of cost–benefit analysis and risk assessment, but they were unwilling to grant the president and presidentially designated agencies, such as OMB and OSTP, any additional power by statute to promote or coordinate the benefits of risk assessment and risk comparison techniques in key regulatory agencies. Witnesses from the environmental, public health, labor, and public interest law network opposed the proposed Risk Analysis and Demonstration Act of 1983 on the grounds that there are serious methodological problems with comparative risk assessment. They also maintained that the choice of any coordinating agency of risk demonstration studies should be in the hands of Congress, a more representative body, rather than with the president. Previous versions of the bill identified OMB or OSTP as possible coordinators of risk demonstration projects in federal regulatory agencies. Citing some of the abuses that had occurred in the regulatory process and political manipulation of scientific information in the first term of the Reagan Administration, opponents managed to kill the bill at the committee level.[37]

The Reagan administrative presidency strategy and its ideological objectives involved the institutional presidency, particularly OMB, deeper into regulatory management and risk management at the expense of political conflict with congressional oversight committees and their political allies. OMB's powers were abused but also short-term gains were made, from the Administration's perspective. It is not likely, however, that the powers assumed under President Reagan's E.O. 12291 and E.O. 12498 will be substantially curbed by President Bush or by the Congress. But the longer-term danger in the heightened politicization of OMB, part of a trend since the Nixon Administration, has been the loss of its credibility and a growing distrust of its motives and activities by Congress. This legacy presents problems in obtaining the necessary accommodation with Congress to establish by statute a centralized regulatory review process as an appropriate exercise of presidential power, as well as the requisite cooperation and coordination of Congress and the presidency in dealing with risk-related issues.

NOTES

1. Sheila Jasanoff, *Risk and Political Culture* (New York: Russell Sage Foundation, 1986), 56.

2. Edward Paul Fuchs, *Presidents, Management and Regulation* (Englewood Cliffs, N.J.: Prentice-Hall, 1988), 69–70.

3. Mark E. Rushefsky, *Making Cancer Policy* (Albany: State University of New York, 1988), 96.

4. Alfred A. Marcus, "Risk, Uncertainty, and Scientific Judgment," *Minerva* 26 (1988): 148.

5. Thomas O. McGarity, "Risk and Trust: The Role of Regulatory Agencies," *Environmental Law Reporter* 16 (August 1986): 10, 207; see also Michael E. Kraft and Norman L. Vig, "Environmental Policy in the Reagan Presidency," *Political Science Quarterly* 99 (1984): 438–39.

6. Mark E. Rushefsky, "The Misuse of Science in Governmental Decision-making," *Science, Technology, and Human Values* 9 (1984): 51.

7. Rushefsky, *Making Cancer Policy*, 149.

8. *Risk Analysis Research and Demonstration Act of 1982*, H.R. Rep. No. 97–625, 97th Cong., 2d sess., 10.

9. National Academy of Public Administration, *Presidential Management of Rulemaking in Regulatory Agencies* (Washington, D.C., 1987), 37.

10. Executive Office of the President, OMB, *Regulatory Program of the United States Government*, 1 April 1986–31 March 1987, 22.

11. Special Report, "Risk Assessment and Risk Management," 15th Annual Report, Council on Environmental Quality, 1984, 212. In its 14th Annual Report, CEQ stressed the need for consistency in the assessment of environmental and health risks and favored balancing costs and benefits as an explicit part of risk management.

12. President's Task Force on Regulatory Relief, *Regulatory Policy Guidelines, Reagan Administration Regulatory Achievements* (11 August 1983): 16.

13. *Regulatory Program of the United States Government*, 12.

14. Ibid., 16.

15. Ibid., 20.

16. Lester Lave, *Quantitative Risk Assessment in Regulation* (Washington, D.C.: Brookings Institution, 1982), 2.

17. *Regulatory Program of the United States Government*, 22. Placing a value on life was not new with the Reagan Administration. The Carter Administration had been more circumspect, but RARG economists had answered critics by stating that all regulatory decisions implicitly put a value on human life. Richard Kirshstein, "Can Government Place a Value on Saving a Human Life?" *National Journal* 11, no. 7 (7 February 1979): 252–55.

18. *Presidential Management of Rulemaking in Regulatory Agencies*, 26.

19. Ibid., 28–29.

20. Ibid.

21. House Subcommittee on Oversight and Investigations, *EPA's Asbestos Regulations: Report on a Case Study on OMB Interference in Agency Rulemaking*, Committee Print 99–V, 99th Cong., 1st sess., 78–80.

22. Office of Technology Assessment, Congress, *Identifying and Regulating Carcinogens*, November 1987, 172.

23. Ibid.

24. Letter of Wendy Lee Gramm, Head, Office of Information and Regulatory Affairs, to Lee M. Thomas, EPA Administrator, 12 August 1986, 5.

25. Ibid.

26. Ibid., 8–9.

27. Wendy Lee Gramm, "OMB Sensitivity to the Need for Good Science for Cost-effective Regulation," Paper delivered at American Industrial Health Conference, Washington, D.C., 22 May 1986, 6.

28. *Inside the Administration* 5, no. 3 (21 August 1986): 3.

29. Richard N. L. Andrews, "Risk Assessment: Regulation and Beyond," in *Environmental Policy in the 1990s*, ed. Norman J. Vig and Michael E. Kraft (Washington, D.C.: CQ Press, 1990), 176–77.

30. Judith Haveman, "Assessed Cancer Risk is Inflated, OMB Says," *The Washington Post*, 13 July 1986, A 8.

31. Ibid.

32. Kraft and Vig, "Environmental Policy in the Reagan Presidency," 438.

33. Interview with Paul Portney, Resources for the Future, 25 September 1988.

34. Ibid.

35. Susan G. Hadden, "Introduction: Risk Policy in American Institutions," in *Risk Analysis, Institutions and Public Policy*, ed. Susan G. Hadden (Port Washington, N.Y.: Associated Faculty Press, 1984), 10.

36. Norman J. Vig, "The Courts: Judicial Review and Risk Assessment," in *Risk Analysis*, 62.

37. *The Risk Assessment Research and Demonstration Act of 1983.* Hearings on H.R. 4192, House Subcommittee on Natural Resources, Agriculture Research and Environment, Committee on Science and Technology, 98th Cong., 2d sess., 5 June 1984, 98–99, 170–75.

5

The Reagan Administrative
Presidency Strategy and the Politics of
Enforcement in Environmental Policy

Law enforcement can be achieved by a mixture of compliance and deterrence strategies by regulatory agencies. The major goal in a compliance enforcement system is to obtain conformity with legal mandates to encourage compliance without the necessity to detect and persecute violators. A deterrence enforcement approach, on the other hand, aims to obtain law-abiding behavior by detecting infractions of the law, determining who has violated the law, and penalizing violators in order to deter future infractions. Each strategy has its advantages and limitations, which the regulatory agency may consider if it has some flexibility of choice. The agency enforcement process may also be influenced by other factors in the political arena, including the perspectives of oversight and appropriations committees in Congress, interest groups, particularly regulated groups, the White House and its key advisory agencies, as well as by the mandate and resources of the agency, and the potency of its allies.[1]

The politics of enforcement is complex and difficult to trace and measure, particularly since enforcement patterns and strategies may vary by agency and by program. Since enforcement standards are rarely stipulated by statute and by regulation, actual enforcement falls within the discretion of the executive branch and appropriate agencies. When they are written, enforcement strategies may be spelled out in internal agency memoranda and directives. Universal and full enforcement of all laws and regulations is administratively impossible, and effective enforcement is difficult to define; therefore, agencies use some discretion in selecting or omitting or narrowing the range of penalties and remedial steps to apply against violators. More flexible enforcement approaches, which permit a considerable degree of administrative discretion, may estimate enforcement performance by overall results instead of the overall number of times that regulations and statutes are cited. However, allowing considerable discretion by public officials may provide occasions for favorite treatment. The use of flexible enforcement strategies can also make regulatory agencies vulnerable to onslaughts from the media and political quarters in Congress for such treatment and for giving the appearance of unwarranted leniency.

The best defensive strategy, according to Bardach and Kagan, is to act as "rule-following policemen."

> Additional security is provided by maintaining statistics showing that the agency is conducting regular inspections, imposing high numbers of citations and fines, and mounting prosecutions, often with resulting pressures on inspectors to do what is necessary to keep those statistics at a high level. Thus, these enforcement tactics are likely to become and remain entrenched, not because of their useful offensive function of providing more deterrence, but because of their defensive function of showing that the agency has been acting in conformance with the law and has been as systematic and as tough as existing manpower and sanctions enable it to be.[2]

When the politically flexible strategies of enforcement of the Reagan Administration led to widespread charges of mismanagement and corruption in the enforcement of the Superfund law, leading to the resignation of five top officials in EPA, the new leadership under William Ruckelshaus attempted to restore the credibility of the agency by maintaining annual statistics indicating that the agency was increasing the number of regular inspections, citations, and court cases.

From the outset the Reagan administrative presidency strategy sought to shape the law enforcement process in environmental policy in pursuit of its goals of regulatory relief and a reduced federal regulatory presence. The Administration's massive budget cuts obtained through the reconciliation process in 1981, combined with administrative changes in regulatory oversight, significantly influenced environmental regulation and environmental enforcement activity. A congressional budget office analysis of EPA's budget found that the real percentage drop in the agency's spending between 1981 and the proposed 1984 budget was high, with a real dollar decline of 39 percent in enforcement, along with a 38 percent reduction in research and development, and a 46 percent drop in pollution abatement and control.[3]

George Eads and Michael Fix noted some recurring strategies in their analysis of agency enforcement strategies in the first term of the Reagan

Administration. They included (1) a general reduction in the dollar amount of civil penalties assessed, (2) adoption of new and more exclusive screening criteria for identifying potential violators, (3) an unwillingness to test new legal or economic theories that might expand the existing classes of violators, (4) reduced discretion for field personnel, (5) a reliance on state and local and trade and professional associations as substitute federal enforcers, and (6) the adoption of a less threatening, more flexible posture toward regulated industries and greater interpretation in pursuing violators of regulatory statutes whose actions established criminal liability.[4]

The Reagan administrative presidency strategy of appointing political loyalists to regulatory agencies, particularly in Reagan's first term, affected enforcement activity in environmental policy. EPA Administrator Anne Gorsuch (Anne Burford) accepted the drastic cuts in enforcement funds and within a year there were four reorganizations of the enforcement structure and organization on both national and regional levels of the agency. She justified her reorganization efforts as a means of obtaining a more unified legal staff, but it was charged that these reorganizations complicated projected budgets for enforcement activity and that they resulted in confusion and a large number of resignations.[5] However, despite the reorganizations and personnel changes at EPA in the Burford regime, Dan Wood found significant resistance to the Administration's goals of regulatory relief with EPA officials actually increasing their activities in compliance with the Clean Air Act, only to be curbed by the 1982 budget cuts approved by Congress.[6]

Environmental organizations, spearheaded by the Natural Resources Defense Council and the Sierra Club, led a campaign of citizen lawsuits to force the Burford regime to greater compliance with the Clean Water Act. About two-thirds of the more than two hundred lawsuits filed concerned significant noncompliance.[7] The extent of noncompliance was documented in a GAO study of 531 major waste-water discharges in six states. The study covering an eighteen-month period ending in March 1982 found that noncompliance was widespread, frequent, and significant, with almost a third of the dischargers in significant noncompliance over that time frame. The report stated that the then-current enforcement climate permitted noncompliance to persist for long periods and that thousands of discharge sources either had not been issued permits or held permits that had expired. The study also noted that data on sampling inspections had been reduced, as were efforts by EPA and the states to check self-monitoring by dischargers.[8]

The impact of reorganization, agency mismanagement, budget cuts, and the Administration's policy of regulatory relief resulted in a significant drop in EPA enforcement activity from 1980 to 1981. Civil actions suits by EPA sent to the Department of Justice and cases forwarded by regional to EPA central headquarters dropped precipitously from the Carter Administration to the first year of the Reagan Administration. This amounted to a 70 percent decline in civil actions forwarded to the Justice Department and an 80 percent reduction in cases sent up from regional offices to the central Washington office. EPA's legal staff was also significantly reduced from 513 to 397 from fiscal year (FY) 1980 to FY 1983.[9] Cases involving environmental programs, filed in court by the Department of Justice, dropped their lowest to fifty-one in FY 1982.[10] Widespread charges of mismanagement and lack of enforcement, the Administration's preference for negotiation and voluntary compliance, and the inadequacy of settlements negotiated by EPA, particularly in handling the Superfund program, served to undermine the Administration's initiatives on regulatory relief.

Ruckelshaus was recalled to the helm of EPA by President Reagan after the firing or resignation of almost all of the agency's top management personnel. He reorganized EPA's enforcement structure, creating a new Office of Enforcement and Compliance monitoring, and reestablished the General Counsel as a separate office. President Reagan personally assured the EPA administrator that he would support appropriate levels of staff and fiscal resources and, although EPA had a net increase of fifty lawyers by the end of FY 1984, there were still fifty-six fewer lawyers than were on board in the closing days of the Carter Administration. Although Ruckelshaus managed to reverse the hemorrhaging of EPA's enforcement staff, the agency had acquired additional enforcement and compliance responsibilities, particularly in the Superfund law of 1980. The Reagan Administration's budget for EPA enforcement responsibilities increased by 27 percent in FY 1985, but the lion's share (60 percent) was targeted for the Superfund program. Increasingly, over the remainder of the Reagan Administration, EPA managed to produce a greater number of administrative orders and criminal case referrals to the Department of Justice dealing with environmental laws and regulations. Although the number of criminal case referrals was small, there were convictions, and even imprisonment of company officials and corporate officers. Working under a White House political environment that still continued to favor regulatory relief, EPA established a high enforcement priority in dealing with significant noncompliers and violators of environmental laws and regulations.[11]

EPA's enforcement and compliance efforts, as well as those in other federal environmentally related programs, were affected by the Reagan Administration's New Federalism policies. Many of these policies had roots in previous administrations, including grant consolidation, regulatory relief, and efforts to reduce the size, costs, and pervasiveness of the federal government. The Reagan Administration's New Federalism was marked by efforts toward a broad-scale devolution of programmatic responsibilities to state governments, a reduced federal presence in regional and multistate institutions, and a deregulatory effort that included a reduction of federal regulations impacting on the private sector as well as on state and local governments.[12] Some Administration priorities were achieved during 1981–82, but further changes were dampened when Congress, particularly the House of Representatives, exercised its budgetary oversight and investigation roles in dealing with other New Federalism objectives. Local governments, left out in many other New Federalism objectives, marshaled their opposition, along with interest groups. In addition, negotiations between federal and state government officials broke down over additional proposed transfers, reorganizations, and funding of domestic programs.

Critics charged that the Reagan Administration's devolutionary goals were sacrificed when they conflicted with other Administration objectives, such as paring the federal budget, advancing national security interests, deregulating the private sector, and advancing other parts of the conservative social policy agenda. These conflicts occurred, for example, when the Reagan Administration overrode state government opposition, increasing exploration for offshore oil and expanding its commitment to nuclear power.[13]

In the first term of the Reagan Administration, four New Federalism strategies devolved power in an ad hoc manner to state governments in environmental, health, and safety programs. These strategies included accelerating formal delegation of program authority to the states, promulgating generic regulations, reducing federal oversight of state regulatory authority, and relaxing federal compliance standards.[14] Some of these administrative actions were evolutionary, in compliance with environmental statutes, and some were a continuation of efforts of prior administrations.

In the New Federalism, formal delegation to the states was hastened in the Resource Conservation and Recovery Act, the Surface Mining and Reclamation Act, and the Occupational Safety and Health Act. Under Anne Gorsuch, EPA accelerated the delegation of environmental programs to the states, far beyond previous administrations. Initially, many states were pleased with the agency's steps to reduce red tape and delay and to provide more state flexibility in setting water quality standards. However, many state government officials bridled at the Administration's goals of short-term reduction and long-term phase-out of EPA grants to state and local governments to implement major environmental programs. Congress rejected the

Administration's proposed 20 percent 1983 budget cut in EPA grants—grants that had already been reduced by 11.9 percent from 1981 to 1982, and ended with a small decrease of 2.5 percent in appropriations. Even though Congress had prevented significant cuts, many state environmental officials felt whipsawed by the Administration's devolution actions and its budget cutting of state environmental program grants. A survey of state budgetary officials in November 1984 revealed that most of the states that responded were not about to replace federal grant-in-aid reductions from EPA from FYs 1981 to 1984 with their own funds, and those providing any replacement were mostly in the hazardous waste management field.[15]

Another strategy was the issuance of generic regulations, including the expansion of EPA's emission trading rules and the issuance of general permits under Section 404 of the Clean Water Act by the Corps of Engineers. A more common, flexible New Federalism strategy involved reducing federal oversight of state regulation. This included all the options whereby federal authorities could accept or overrule state environmental decisions relating to compliance and enforcement activity, such as the review of state-drawn permits; the extent of prosecutional activity, fines, and settlements; and the reduction of staff resources. The removal of all federal compliance officials from states that signed agreements with OSHA was an example of reduced federal oversight. The relaxation, cancellation, or revision of federal program standards provided another option permitting state regulatory authorities more flexibility in administering new, more lenient rules. Eliminating reporting requirements by federal authorities can have a significant impact on monitoring, compliance, and enforcement in environmental policy—an area that has had long-standing problems in achieving continuous compliance with laws and regulations.[16]

THE REAGAN ADMINISTRATIVE PRESIDENCY AND THE POLITICS OF ENFORCEMENT OF THE SURFACE MINING CONTROL AND RECLAMATION ACT (SMCRA)

The incoming Reagan Administration in 1980 sought to curb the Office of Surface Mining Reclamation and Enforcement (OSM) and its implementation of the controversial Surface Mining Control and Reclamation Act (SMCRA) as one of its high-priority targets for regulatory relief. Walter Rosenbaum noted, "It is hard to find a good word for the design of OSM's statutory mandate, its administrative structure or its implementation of SMCRA even among scholars normally sympathetic to environmental legislation."[17] OSM'S tumultuous history and its problems in implementating SMCRA have been due to a number of factors, including some rigid provisions in the law, the initial zealous implementation and enforcement of the law by environmental officials in the Carter Administration, resistance by coal interests, and the impact and counterreaction to the Reagan administrative presidency strategy. The ensuing struggle over two terms of the Reagan presidency between the Administration and key committees of Congress, particularly in the House of Representatives, and between the Administration and environmental groups in the judicial arena over OSM's regulatory and enforcement policies demonstrated both the power and the vulnerability of Reagan's administrative presidency strategy. An examination of the politics of enforcement in this chapter indicates the various strategies of the White House and key congressional oversight committees and environmental organizations, and the political costs borne by the embattled agency.

The near-decade-long effort to adopt the surface mining law involved a protracted struggle in Congress, two vetoes by President Ford, and finally an unsuccessful attempt to have the Supreme Court declare the law unconstitutional. As originally conceived, SMCRA was supposed to regulate all surface mining, but key congressmen from Western mining states engineered a compromise with environmentalists so that the law dealt primarily with strip-mining of coal, with a provision for studying the possibility of regulatory surface mining in other mineral industries. SMCRA's adoption was achieved by a strange alignment of environmentalists, some Western legislators, the United Mine Workers (UMW), and some Eastern states. The UMW and deep-mining coal interests joined together in supporting federal regulation of strip-mining in order to narrow the competitive edge of strip-mined coal. The greatest degree of opposition before and after the law came from states in the Appalachian region; and the losers, disproportionately centered in that region, were unmistakably small firms, particularly those utilizing contour and auger mining methods.[18]

Reagan's victory in 1980 set the stage for major changes in OSM and reduced enforcement of the 1977 strip-mining law. The Heritage Foundation urged the incoming president "to make an example of OSM and its regulatory excesses, to review reclamation regulations, to slash the agency's budget and reduce its enforcement personnel, and to bring in senior staff and regional directors who would be more attuned to state government implementation of the law."[19]

The Reagan Administration ensured that appointments in the Department of the Interior and top officials in OSM shared Reagan's goals on regulatory relief and greater state implementation of the law. Secretary of the Interior James Watt had previously challenged provisions of SMCRA, as one of the principal lawyers of the Western Mountain Foundation law firm. James R. Harris, the newly appointed OSM director, had previously supported the State of Indiana's challenge to the constitutionality of the law when he was a state legislator. Steven Griles, appointed second-in-command at OSM, had also been a strong opponent of SMCRA provisions when he was a state official in Virginia.

The battle to declare the strip-mining law unconstitutional failed before Reagan assumed power, and the new Administration was forced to employ the tools of the administrative presidency rather than undertake a more arduous route of legislative revision. The Administration's strategy involved appointing loyalists and shifting opponents within the agency, reorganizing administrative positions, budget cutting and shifting budgetary objectives, eliminating or revising existing regulations, and formulating new rules. The administrative strategy route allowed Secretary Watt and OSM chairman Harris "direct management of the deregulatory process" and more flexibility and control in rewriting regulations, with the expectation that there would not be a protracted struggle and confrontation with Congress.[20]

Through personnel changes, resignations, reorganization, and budget cuts, the agency's staff was reduced from 1,001 in the last year of the Carter Administration to 628 employees. Secretary Watt swiftly established a task force to consider the reorganization of OSM. The power of regional officials and the agency's existing organizational arrangements had angered some governors and coal companies. Some governors had been annoyed that an unelected regional director of OSM could determine policy for the chief executive of a state. Coal companies complained that sometimes they had reached accommodations with OSM headquarters and later discovered that a regional director would ignore such agreements. Watt's task force presented the agency with two organizational options. The secretary chose the more drastic plan, which called for the abolition of the agency's five regional offices, replacing them with six field offices and fourteen liaison offices located mostly in the capitals of the major coal-producing states. In implementing Reagan Administration objectives, Watt sought to reduce the agency's presence in the field from forty-two to twenty-two offices and from five regional, thirteen district, and twenty-four field offices to fourteen state liaison offices, six field, and two technical centers.[21] The secretary claimed that the reorganization was justified because the agency was shifting its role providing greater emphasis upon assistance, advice, and review of state efforts, as states moved closer to primacy in implementing the law. Some governors and business leaders supported Watt's reorganization, but he was opposed by others on the grounds that the separation of inspectors from the lawyers and the permit staff from the lawyers contradicted principles of effective regulatory administration.[22] Environmental group officials were also concerned about the reorganization and the proposed goal of reducing federal inspectors and enforcement personnel by 70 percent. Secretary Watt maintained that the proposed reorganization was a means of implementing the shift from a direct enforcement role to an oversight and assistance approach and that, in fact, the Carter Administration had cut the inspector force from 222 in FY 1980 to 156 in FY 1981 and had proposed 97 inspectors for FY 1982.[23]

A House appropriations subcommittee voted to prevent the Department of the Interior (DOI) from spending funds to implement the proposed reorganization of OSM. Watt countered by having the reorganization in place before the new fiscal year began. The full House Appropriations Committee voted to keep the spending prohibition in the appropriations bill for the Department of the Interior, but the Republican-controlled Senate Appropriations Committee dropped the spending ban, as did House-Senate conferees in the final appropriations bill. Secretary Watt and the administrative presidency strategy were successful in OSM reorganization due in large part to the fact that the presidency and the Senate were controlled by the same political party.

The reorganization struggle was an opening salvo in the developing conflict between the House and the Administration over implementation of SMCRA. One commentator noted:

> While it is possible that the secretary's reorganization was designed to cut costs and facilitate primacy, it seemed obvious that it would create some confusion, induce experienced personnel to leave OSM, impede coordination between technical and enforcement staff and impede liaison between OSM and other DOI bureaus. These impacts could not fail to weaken surface mining regulations in the short term.[24]

Secretary Watt and OSM's new management team also complied with President Reagan's E.O. 12291 mandating federal agencies to examine, review, and, if necessary, cancel all burdensome regulations. Watt and OSM head Harris solicited complaints from coal companies and trade associations concerning burdensome regulations. OSM staff eventually recommended that 89 rule sections be eliminated, 12 new sections be added, and 329 sections be revised, and that 112 provisions be fused with other sections.[25] The agency claimed that 91 percent of all of its regulations were rewritten in 1982. Some regulations, issued but not implemented by the Carter Administration, were remanded back to the agency by OMB and were later withdrawn by OSM. OSM also proposed thirty-five rules during 1982 dealing with abandoned mine lands, state programs, and the two-acre exemption. Ten rules were finalized in that busy year dealing with inspections and enforcement, abandoned mine lands, and the two-acre exemption.[26]

Under Secretary Watt's direction, OSM accelerated its approval of primacy for almost all coal-producing states. According to the surface mining statute, individual states were expected, after a transition period of federal direction, to have the principal responsibility for implementation and enforcement, with OSM providing continuous oversight to ensure that minimum national standards were met. The agency was obligated under the law to implement the federal regulatory provisions in any state which did not meet federal approval of its program, and if a state program was not deemed to be functioning properly after it obtained primacy, OSM was required to assume all or part of a state's program. In a number of ways, the strip-mining law had been adversely affected by vigilant federal inspectors in the initial years of the program, creating a backlash even among those states that were adamantly opposed to the law's detailed provisions. However, Secretary Watt's reorganization of the agency, the enforcement policies he helped to establish, and his confrontational reaction to congressional oversight not only created a powerful backlash in the House of Representatives but also contributed to a serious backlog of cases, leading to lawsuits requiring the agency to fulfill its enforcement obligations under the law.

OSM was required by court order in 1982 to assess and collect penalties against coal mine companies for failure to abate cessation orders and to remain up-to-date regarding timely assessment of such penalties. In complying with the order, the agency brought to light 1,100 previously unassessed orders, with an assessment charge of $59 million. OSM had vigorously fought the suit and pursued appeals on the court order. In the face of a possible contempt motion before District Court Judge Barrington Parker, DOI negotiated a modification of the initial court order in 1985.[27] The essential part of that negotiated settlement was the agency's agreement to set up and maintain a computer system to match surface-mining permit applicants and permittees with operators having civil penalties assessed against them as well as operators not in compliance with cessation orders. Because of the difficulties involved in collecting debts, the modified court order permitted the agency to base its collection efforts and options in part on estimates of the net worth of a coal mine company and its chief executive officers. The mandated computer tracking system was deemed a major achievement in redirecting the agency's enforcement role, but it was not expected to be operational until the end of the Reagan presidency. The court extended the compliance deadline to October 1987.[28] But even when the computerized "applicant violator system" went into operation in October 1987, with federal violations recorded in the computer system, it was not expected that state violation data would be in the computer system until 1988. In a previous suit decided in 1980, OSM agreed to set up and implement procedures to ascertain whether or not civil penalties for violators should be charged against individuals connected with corporations that violated the act. When it was demonstrated that the settlement agreement had not been implemented, the court ordered the agency to make written resolutions by March 1984 concerning whether or not individual penalties should be required.[29]

Environmental groups, as well as a House oversight congressional committee and the GAO, documented the abuses of the "two-acre exemption," a provision in the strip-mining law that exempted mines of two acres or less from many of the statute's environmental restrictions. Although a detailed settlement was reached between the agency and environmental groups involving a compilation of an accurate inventory of mines smaller than two acres in Virginia and Kentucky and the gathering of information on enforcement actions, inspections, and reclamation fees in those states, a year later environmental groups sought to reopen the case on the grounds that the agency had been lax in enforcing the agreement.

Regulatory reforms instituted by OSM and Interior Department officials brought about court cases that resulted in hundreds of overturned regulations. L. Thomas Galloway, an environmental lawyer involved in some key court cases, claimed that "we fought them to a standstill, losing three out of 105 challenges of first-level importance" and prevailing in seventy contested in the courts.[30] The three losses included a rule permitting the secretary of the interior to delegate environmental responsibilities relating to federal public lands to state officials and the water replacement and incremental bonding issues.

Secretary Watt's confrontational approach and controversial policies triggered lawsuits challenging OSM regulatory revisions and strengthened the alliance between environmental organization officials and House oversight committee leaders. Congressional architects of SMCRA, such as Congressman Morris Udall, who felt that their handiwork was being undermined, provided greater scrutiny of OSM operations. But even though there were pressures and some incentives for serious congressional oversight of OSM programs and enforcement of SMCRA provisions, "oversight does not come naturally or easily to Congress"; a continuous, systematic, and well-conceived evaluation of program performance or impact occurs with difficulty, and infrequently.[31] Agencies have their resources and allies (in this case, the White House) and can thwart and frustrate oversight committees by delaying tactics and other means. Sustained, comprehensive oversight activity is difficult due to the magnitude of the task, which can include scrutiny of personnel policies, budgets, organizational structure, decision-making processes, substantive policy matters, and patterns of enforcement of a particular agency.

House committees lost the first round to Secretary Watt and the Administration in the reorganization of OSM. The Interior Department continued to oppose efforts to increase the agency's enforcement program in budget hearings after Watt's resignation. Later, when the House Committee on Appropriations added funds for personnel to assist the agency in its inspection and enforcement program and to implement a court settlement, it was dismayed to learn that the agency had filled new positions in Congressional Liaison, Public Affairs, and External Affairs offices rather than in the enforcement and inspection operations. The next year the House Appropriations Committee rebuked the Interior Department, and Senator Howard Metzenbaum threatened to stall the Senate's confirmation of OSM Acting Director Jed Christiansen as head of the agency. When Christiansen assured the Appropriations Committee that added funds would permit the agency to step up its fines and collections, the senator dropped his threat of opposition to the nomination. Having been burned once before, the Appropriations Committee added funds for thirty-seven inspectors and troubleshooters, with the stipulation that the committee be notified on a bimonthly basis of hiring and assignment for these positions.

A serious complaint lodged against the Department of the Interior and OSM was their failure to collect millions of dollars in outstanding civil penalties under SMCRA, despite the issuance of federal court orders mandating the implementation of the act and congressional appropriations specifically targeted for the assessment and collection of civil penalties. Congressional subcommittee hearings in 1984 indicated that $6.8 million out of an estimated $150 million in civil penalties had been collected, some reaching back to the Carter Administration. Steven Griles, former OSM deputy director, claimed that the Reagan Administration inherited a disorganized enforcement records system from the Carter Administration in both regional offices and at OSM Washington headquarters. He claimed that there was no policy for the assessment and collection of "megabucks" enforcement cases and that violations in these cases issued between 1977 and 1980 totaled almost one-third of the agency's outstanding debt in 1985.[32] By 1986 an estimated 80 percent of the more than $150 million in unpaid civil penalties assessed since 1978 was deemed uncollectible as the result of the death or disappearance of business officials and business closings and bankruptcies.[33] Critics of OSM and the Reagan Administration claimed that the Administration's budget cuts and deemphasis on enforcement permitted too many assessed penalties to become stale and difficult if not impossible to collect. The first of three detailed House reports on OSM's performance over a four-year period concluded that Interior Department officials had misled Congress and the public and that the system had "virtually collapsed" and that "much of the action undertaken by the Department has been in response to Federal court orders resulting from suits brought by citizen groups. Even under court supervision, however, the Department's programs have had only marginal success."[34]

The House Committee on Government Operations drew up a list of detailed recommendations and requested William Clark, the new secretary of the interior, to provide a progress report within ninety days. Under Clark's direction, a management review of OSM operations was undertaken by a joint team of Interior Department officials and members of the House Interior and Insular Affairs Committee. Clark also requested the Internal Revenue Service (IRS) to analyze OSM operations and to provide recommendations for improving the agency's assessment and collection procedures. The IRS portrayed the OSM collections division as a "paper shuffler" operation and the Interior Department's response to its difficulties as inconsistent. Although Secretary Clark was more cooperative than his predecessor and there were some improvements in OSM operations, in fact the size of the debt in civil penalties increased while the collection rate had declined.[35] Although some initial steps were taken by OSM to comply with the 1982 Parker court order mandating the use of alternative enforcement actions (such as injunctions, assessment of individual civil penalties, and criminal penalties for failure to abate cessation orders), the House Committee on Government Operations claimed that DOI had not pursued such alternative enforcement remedies through to full implementation. The committee was skeptical about OSM's regulatory commitment but, because of the frequent changes in OSM leadership and changes in the secretaryship of DOI, it gave the agency another nine months to show improvement, warning that if significant improvement was not indicated within that time, the committee would recommend that Congress consider transferring OSM from DOI to another regulatory agency.

The House Committee on Government Operations issued another report two years later, charging that ten years after the strip-mining law was adopted there was still no accurate count of the sites that had been mined, abandoned, or left unreclaimed. Without a site inventory by OSM and the states, efforts to measure reclamation progress were hobbled by only rough estimates of the magnitude of the problem. The absolute dollar amount of civil penalties collected had grown since the previous congressional investigation. A significant problem in the collection of civil penalties reflected the problems of collecting old debts of some firms that had gone out of business, but even the amount assessed for 1986 citations remained at less than 1 percent.

Congress intended that a staff complement of eighty-one full-time employees be provided for surface-mining activities within the solicitor's office of DOI. Congress, however, provided a lump-sum appropriation rather than targeted funds for each functional category, leaving the solicitor legally free to distribute funds at his discretion. The net result was that sixty rather than eighty-one employees dealt with strip-mining issues, and the solicitor's office spent $1,139,928 less than had been budgeted for surface-mining responsibilities for that year. Surface-mining unexpended funds were diverted to conservation and wildlife, energy and resources, and Indian affairs activities within the Department of the Interior.[36]

Another problem examined by the House Committee on Government Operations was OSM's conference officers program. That program's objective was the settlement of cases by informal proceedings between coal mine operators and agency officials, thereby avoiding extended adjudicatory proceedings, and encouraging a speedier abatement of violations, and providing incentives for firms to pay penalties. The House committee requested a review of this program to determine whether such conferences had been held in accordance with Interior Department procedures. It found that in almost half of the statistical sample of case files examined, the reductions of penalties were inconsistent with the department's assessment manual or policy directives. In the course of this review, it also discovered that a number of conference case files had been altered. An inspector general's investigation and report sought by the House committee later confirmed that there had been tampering with some conference records.[37]

Under provisions of the strip-mining law, states were given primary responsibility for developing, issuing, and enforcing regulations, but this key provision raised potential conflict with other SMCRA provisions requiring uniform national standards and federal oversight of state actions. Secretary Watt succeeded in changing the interpretation of the "state window" provision of the law by adopting a regulation that expanded the flexibility of state regulations in comparison with OSM regulations, and his reorganization reduced the number of federal inspectors. Environmentalists were concerned that the lower number of federal inspectors would be inadequate to review state compliance with the law and that some states might revert or be encouraged to provide lax regulation and enforcement. A National Wildlife Federation report pointed out that in over two thousand of the four thousand instances in which coal companies received orders to stop illegal mining operations from 1979 to 1983, coal operators ignored these orders.[38] The report also noted that OSM knew about a significant number of violators of the law and had not stopped them in almost every major coal-producing state.

Deemphasis upon federal enforcement led to resentment by some firms that had complied with the law and OSM's regulations; some companies had indeed benefited by noncompliance. Eventually, as the result of complaints by coal firms and environmentalists, OSM was forced to take over enforcement and inspection operations in Oklahoma and Tennessee until those states demonstrated significant improvement to OSM head-quarters. The agency also warned West Virginia in 1985 that, in spite of a reorganization of its program, the state's regulatory operation would be terminated unless some additional recommendations were implemented. A GAO report revealed significant violations and lax enforcement of the two-acre exemption provision in the states of Virginia and Kentucky—this despite OSM's adoption in 1981 of a regulation to curb abuses of that exemption. Another GAO study of inspection activity in four coal-purchasing states found that state officials had undertaken most of the required inspections, but that they did not report 78 of 129 total violations that federal inspectors and GAO officials noted during their visits to eighty-two sites.[39] Through congressional oversight and litigation, the Reagan Administration's deregulatory effort and New Federalism approach was placed in the uncomfortable position of assuming and threatening to take over state enforcement and inspection programs in order to restore credibility and legitimacy to the overall program.

At the same time, OSM and the Reagan Administration had repeatedly frustrated the House Committee on Government Operations. In 1985 the committee concluded that "close congressional oversight and supervision by the Federal Courts had failed to effect fundamental improvements in OSM's surface mining program" and that the Interior Department's inactivity had rewarded unscrupulous coal operators.[40] Two years later the committee expanded its criticism and diagnosis of the problem at the surface mining agency:

The Committee is unable to determine the reasons: whether it is because of a fundamental lack of regulatory commitment on the part of key policy-makers; the lack of effective leadership; sheer incom-

petence; or its lack of will. . . . Repeatedly, problems which lie at the
very core of successful enforcement of the law have been identified
and repeatedly, constructive recommendations coming from both
within and without the agency have been ignored.[41]

There were, in addition, ideological factors relating to the agency's
regulatory and enforcement role. Although the strident confrontational
approach of Secretary Watt had disappeared, the Administration's
ideological thrust was still maintained, but was more muted and less
powerful at higher levels of the Interior Department, particularly by
Steven Griles, the assistant director for Land and Minerals Management, who supervised OSM activities.

The House Committee on Government Operations in 1985
threatened OSM with the stick of recommending the transfer of OSM
programs to another department if the agency failed to make significant
improvements. Two years later the committee's fundamental criticisms
remained approximately the same, but it tabled its threat of a transfer,
not wishing to grant added legitimacy to the agency's past failure and
provide it with another excuse to fail to undertake future improvements. When reminded by the OSM director that a transfer from DOI
would be quite disruptive, the committee opted for a GAO study of the
possibility of transferring OSM to another department or creating an
independent agency.[42]

Environmental groups won significant victories in defeating some
regulations, remanding many others, and forcing the agency to adopt new
regulations. But many of the regulations remanded back to OSM and the
Interior Department resurfaced as hard-line as ever from an environmentalist perspective. It took considerable time before court orders were
implemented by embattled OSM officials. For example, it took almost four
years before OSM was able to implement an automatic violator system, a
computer system matching surface-mining permit applicants with
operators who had outstanding penalty violations. This system—the result
of a negotiated modification of a federal court order—required a com-
puterized matching system as a means of denying additional permits to
known coal company violators until their existing infractions were corrected.

Environmental groups claimed some victories in promoting greater
enforcement as the result of litigation and settlement. But although settlements were one of the strategic building blocks to achieve more effective
enforcement, three major problems remained in implementing a court
settlement with OSM, according to L. Thomas Galloway, one of the

principal environmental lawyers involved with implementation of the strip-mining law. The first major problem was that the achievement of a settlement did not bridge the wide philosophic gap between environmental organizations and the Reagan Administration. The agency and DOI were charged with delaying tactics and attempts to wear out the opposition as the result of political and ideological differences. At times the White House was involved, according to Galloway, but a more constant presence and ideological thrust were maintained by higher-level DOI officials, particularly by Assistant Secretary Steven Griles. A second problem involved in implementing court settlements was the charge of incompetence within the ranks and top level of OSM. The Administration's personnel policies had a profound impact on the agency, resulting in an almost 50 percent turnover. In all, there were six directors and acting directors over the course of the Reagan presidency, three of whom were "plainly incompetent," according to Galloway. The turnover and short tenure of OSM's leadership contributed to the instability of the agency, heightening its inability to meet the directives of the House Committee on Government Operations and federal court orders. Within a period of less than a year from March 1984 to April 1985, there were three agency directors as well as two secretaries of the interior. The charge of incompetence threatened to undermine the credibility of both the agency and the Reagan Administration and its ability to accomplish some of its objectives. Environmental organizations actually benefited by the incompetence at OSM in their battles to win court cases and press for settlements. However, the same charge of incompetence may have proved an obstacle when it came to implementing the same settlements and court orders.[43]

A third problem in implementing court settlements and in enforcing the strip-mining law was state political influence in implementation and enforcement. This was particularly a problem in the eastern Appalachian states of West Virginia, Virginia, and Tennessee. Critics of the Reagan Administration, such as Galloway, maintained that some Interior officials and others in the Administration may have believed in states rights in the New Federalism, permitting states to assume control with relaxed federal oversight, but as a practical matter this encouraged too much state government leeway.[44] The Kentucky legislature, for example, adopted a law shifting the review of strip-mining cases from central state courts to local courts, where critics maintained local concerns and interests would be more likely to prevail. Moreover, Richard Harris, a specialist in coal legislation, noted that "as the states took over the program under the state primacy provision, regulation tended to fall to a lowest common denominator," and "state primacy encouraged competitive reduction of regulatory burdens among the states, a Gresham's Law of Regulation indeed!"[45]

The revision of 90 percent of the surface-mining regulations at the outset of the Reagan Administration led to a massive lawsuit in which Judge Thomas Flannery in four decisions remanded almost every major regulatory change back to the agency.[46] OSM prevailed in its emphasis on performance standards and in the state window rule permitting more flexibility in the state strip-mining regulations and in the rule permitting the secretary of the interior to delegate his environmental responsibilities to states on federal lands. However, as the result of lawsuits instituted by environmental organizations, OSM was required to broaden protection of wild and scenic river study areas along guidelines established under the Wild and Scenic Rivers Act to broaden historic preservation sites during mine-permitting activity, and to provide fish and wildlife additional protection from surface mining. Strip-mining was disallowed where habitats of endangered species might be jeopardized.

The problem for environmental organizations was that most of their challenges to OSM regulations were remanded to the agency by the federal court, with each regulation resubmitted "as hardboiled as ever" and at least as hard-line as those issued by the Watt regime.[47] Environmental organizations won out on the issue of standing to sue and expended hundreds of thousands of dollars on litigation. They won some victories, bought time, "stopped the hemorrhaging," and managed to slow down the regulatory reform effort.[48] But winning court suits and reaching court settlements was only half the battle; environmental organizations, as well as the Congress, faced major problems with the delays, resistance, and ineptitude of OSM in implementing federal court orders and settlements.

This was not the case with EPA. Initially, EPA officials resisted the Administration and managed to continue their efforts to enforce Clean Air Act provisions, until budget cuts undermined their efforts. Later, EPA adopted a defensive enforcement strategy as "rule-following policeman," raising the level of fines, inspections, and prosecutions after the Burford regime, with the result that its political legitimacy and support were raised. By contrast, OSM as a less powerful agency buckled under the Reagan Administration's pressures. Nowhere was the battle more polarized and sustained than that between environmentalists and their allies and offices in DOI over implementation and enforcement of the surface mining act. This was due to a number of factors, including some provisions of the law itself, the reaction against zealous enforcement of the law's deadlines and regulations written by environmental officials in the Carter Administration, the counterreaction and aggressive efforts of Secretary of the Interior

Watt to change OSM regulations and the structure of the agency. Other polarizing factors included congressional oversight activity, the extensive litigation and difficulties in complying with court settlements, the Reagan administrative presidency tactics and deregulation strategy, and the Administration's unwillingness to provide the agency with additional resources to fulfill its statutory mission and the requirements of court orders. Apart from the environmental implications of this polarization and political impasse, its net effect was a serious loss of the morale, competency, and legitimacy of the agency and its functional responsibilities.

NOTES

1. Albert Reiss, Jr., "Selecting Strategies of Social Control over Organizational Life," in *Enforcing Regulation*, ed. Keith Hawkins and John M. Thomas (Boston, Mass.: Nijhoff, 1983), 23 25.

2. Eugene Bardach and Robert A. Kagan, *Going by the Book: The Problems of Regulating Reasonableness* (Philadelphia, Penn.: Temple University Press, 1982), 207–8.

3. U.S. Congressional Budget Office, *The Environmental Protection Agency: Overview of the Proposed 1984 Budget*, 1984, 3.

4. George C. Eads and Michael Fix, *Relief or Reform: Reagan's Regulatory Dilemma* (Washington, D.C.: Urban Institute Press, 1984), 194.

5. Testimony of Senator Patrick J. Leahy, *EPA Oversight: One-Year Review*, Joint Hearings, House of Representatives, 97th Cong., 2d sess., 21 July 1982, 39.

6. B. Dan Wood, "Principals, Bureaucrats, and Responsiveness in Clean Air Enforcements," *American Political Science Review* 82 (March 1988): 218–19.

7. Clifford Russell, Winston Harrington, and William J. Vaughan, *Enforcing Pollution Control Laws* (Washington, D.C.: Resources for the Future, 1986), 219.

8. GAO, *Waste Water Dischargers Are Not Complying with EPA Pollution Control Permits*, RCED–84–53, 2 December 1983.

9. *EPA's Office of Research and Development and Related Issues*. Hearing, Committee on Science and Technology, House of Representatives, 98th Cong., 2d sess., 14 March 1984, 106.

10. Office of Public Affairs, EPA, *Environmental News*, 16 December 1986, 3.

11. Summary of Enforcement Accomplishments, Fiscal Year 1986; EPA Office of Enforcement and Compliance Monitoring, April 1987; Summary of Enforcement Accomplishments, Fiscal Year 1985; EPA Office of Enforcement and Compliance Monitoring, Washington, D.C., April 1986.

12. David B. Walker, "The Condition and Course of the System," in *Administering the New Federalism*, ed. Lewis G. Bender and James A. Stever (Boulder, Colo.: Westview Press, 1986), 333–34.

13. Timothy J. Conlan, "Ambivalent Federalism: Intergovernmental Policy in the Reagan Administration," in *Administering the New Federalism*, 16.

14. Michael Fix, "Transferring Regulatory Authority to the States," in *The Reagan Regulatory Strategy: An Assessment*, ed. George C. Eads and Michael Fix (Washington, D.C.: Urban Institute Press, 1984), 158–59.

15. James P. Lester, "New Federalism and Environmental Policy," *Publius* 16 (1986): 177.

16. Fix, "Transferring Regulatory Authority," 168.

17. Walter A. Rosenbaum, "The Bureaucracy and Environmental Policy," in *Environmental Politics and Policy*, ed. James P. Lester (Durham, N.C.: Duke University Press, 1989), 225.

18. Richard A. Harris, *Coal Firms under the New Social Regulation* (Durham, N.C.: Duke University Press, 1985), 51–54.

19. Charles L. Heatherly, ed., *Mandate for Leadership* (Washington, D.C.: Heritage Foundation, 1981), 344–47.

20. Harris, *Coal Firms*, 158.

21. Office of the Secretary of the Interior, news release, 21 May 1981, n.p.

22. Robert Yuhnke, former Solicitor, Office of Surface Mining in Denver, Colorado. Hearing, Subcommittee on Civil Service, 97th Cong., 1st sess., 5 June 1981, 106–7.

23. *Oversight and Reorganization of the Office of Surface Mining.* Hearing, Subcommittee on Energy and the Environment, 97th Cong., 1st sess., 16 July 1981, 12.

24. Harris, *Coal Firms*, 161.

25. U.S. Office of Surface Mining, *Annual Report*, Fiscal Year 1980 (Washington, D.C.: 1981).

26. U.S. Office of Surface Mining, *Annual Report*, Fiscal Year 1982 (Washington, D.C.: 1983), 1, 7.

27. *Save Our Cumberland Mountains, Inc.* v. *James G. Watt et al.* 650 F. Supp. 979 (1982); *Save Our Cumberland Mountains, Inc. et al.* v. *William P. Clark et al.* 725 F. 2d 1422 (1984).

28. *Save Our Cumberland Mountains, Inc. et al.* v. *Donald P. Hodel et al.* 622 F. Supp. 1160 (1986).

29. *Council of Southern Mountains, Inc. et al.* v. *Cecil B. Andrus*, Civil No. 79–1521 (D.D.C. Cir. 1980); *Council of Southern Mountains, Inc. et al.* v. *William P. Clark*, Civil No. 79–1521 (D.D.C. 1984).

30. Interview with L. Thomas Galloway, 10 February 1988.

31. Randall B. Ripley and Grace A. Franklin, *Congress, the Bureaucracy and Public Policy* (Homewood, Ill.: Dorsey Press, 1980), 222–23.

32. Jed Dean Christensen, Nomination to be Director, OSM, Senate hearing 99–507, 99th Cong., 2d sess., 1986, 73.

33. Nominations of Ralph Tarr to be Solicitor, Interior Department, and J. Steven Griles to be Assistant Director, Land and Minerals Management, Interior Department, Senate hearing 99–440, 99th Cong., 1st sess., 1986, 107.

34. H.R. Rep. No. 98–1146, 98th Cong., 2d sess., 1984, 43–44.

35. H. R. Rep. No. 99–206, 99th Cong., lst sess., 1985, 7.

36. U.S. General Accounting Office, "Financial Management: Information on Expenditures by Interior's Office of the Solicitor" (ATMD–87–16FS), 12 November 1986, 3.

37. Office of Inspector General, U.S. Department of the Interior, *Reports of Investigation*, File No. VI–22, February 1987.

38. *Failed Oversight. A Report on the Failure of the Office of Surface Mining to Enforce the Federal Surface Mining and Reclamation Act* (Washington, D.C.: National Wildlife Federation, 1985).

39. U.S. General Accounting Office, "Surface Mining: Interior Department and States Could Improve Inspections" (RCED 87–40), 29 December 1986.

40. H. R. Rep. No. 99–206, 99th Cong., 1st sess., 23.

41. H. R. Rep 100–183, l01st Cong., 1st sess., 1987, 15.

42. Ibid., 4.

43. Interview with L. Thomas Galloway, 10 February 1988.

44. Ibid.

45. Harris, *Coal Firms*, 172–73.

46. *In Re: Permanent Surface Mining Regulation. Litigation* (consolidation), 620 F. Supp. 1519 (D.C.D.C.)(1985).

47. Ibid., 1520–21, 1583.

48. Interview with Norman Dean, 29 January 1988.

6

The Bush Presidency and Environmental Policy

President Bush inherited an enormous deficit problem, a savings and loan bailout and a nuclear weapons plant cleanup estimated to cost hundreds of billions of dollars, other neglected environmental problems, and a polarization between Congress and the White House. Although Bush claimed he was a conservationist and an environmentalist presidential candidate in 1988, environmentalists viewed his commitment and credentials with some suspicion since he had served as President Reagan's loyal lieutenant and chairman of the President's Task Force on Regulatory Relief. This chapter first examines the checks applied by Congress and the federal judiciary on the Reagan administrative presidency strategy in environmental policy and the legacy of that strategy. That discussion serves as an introduction to a more detailed examination of the Bush Administration's use of the tools of the administrative presidency in environmental policy. The administrative approach to regulatory policy is analyzed, along with some key environmental and energy issues in light of Bush's commitment to be an environmentalist president.

THE AMERICAN POLITICAL SYSTEM'S CHECKS AND BALANCES ON THE REAGAN ADMINISTRATIVE PRESIDENCY STRATEGY IN ENVIRONMENTAL POLICY

The Reagan Administration was unprecedented in its integrated approach and assault in reducing social regulations, particularly in the president's first term. It also demonstrated some of the practical difficulties for opponents of an administration to require it to enforce so many laws with which it disagreed. But despite the difficulties associated with congressional oversight, that assault also produced a strong congressional counterreaction and an exceptional, atypical degree of coordination between environmental organizations, public health associations, unions, and consumer groups and their respective allies in Congress.

Congressional oversight was thwarted in getting the Administration and some agencies to comply with congressional intent, but oversight played a significant role in documenting mismanagement, corruption, omissions, and inequities in regulatory policy, thereby damaging the credibility of the Administration. Oversight committees did their work, but it took a considerable amount of effort and time to alert the entire Congress and to coordinate responses to the more organized, ideologically motivated Administration.

In 1986 the 99th Congress finally broke the legislative logjam and adopted strengthened reauthorizations of environmental laws including the Clean Water Act, over Reagan's veto, the Toxic Substances Control Act, the Safe Drinking Water Act, and the Superfund Amendments and Reauthorization Act (SARA) as well as new laws, including the Water Resources Development Act and the Emergency Wetlands Act. In its reauthorizations, Congress restricted the discretion of agency officials with detailed statutory directives. However, Congress's role as a more detailed supervisor of regulation raised concerns about the increasing tendency of members of Congress to rely on their professional staff in interpreting complex technical provisions in environmental and other social legislation. Concerned observers believed that regulatory agency officials could be denied the flexibility and resourcefulness necessary to balance the economic, environmental, and technical factors that Congress so often expects in the implementation of laws. While it appeared that Congress was the victor in the reauthorization of environmental legislation, the price included the likelihood of a higher workload for congressional staff with more agency conferences and congressional hearings, adding to an overloaded congressional agenda.[1]

The federal judiciary served as another important institutional check on the Reagan administrative presidency. The Reagan Administration's expanded interpretation of executive privilege involving EPA administrator Anne Gorsuch received a federal district court rebuff. In addition, the Administration's interpretation of presidential deferral powers under the Congressional Budget Act of 1974 resulted in another confrontation with Congress and was eventually rejected by a federal court. A federal court of appeals panel, including Judge Robert Bork, ruled that the president had no legal power to make de facto policy deferrals of appropriated funds.

Federal courts also placed constraints on the Reagan Administration in their rulings against arbitrary agency deregulatory actions and agency disregard of statutory requirements. In *Motor Vehicle Manufacturers Association* v. *State Farm Mutual Automobile Insurance*, the Supreme Court ruled that an agency regulation cannot be revoked without providing a "reasoned analysis" and a "satisfactory explanation" for the agency's decision. The Court ruled that it was acceptable for the National Highway Traffic Safety Administration to weigh the costs and benefits of the rule in question, but that the agency failed to consider that safety was the principal concern in the Motor Vehicle Safety Act.[2] The Supreme Court in *American Textile Manufacturer's Institute* v. *Donovan* also rebuffed the Administration and upheld OSHA's cotton dust regulation on the grounds that the agency was required by law to protect workers to the greatest extent feasible without being required to provide a strict balancing of costs and benefits.[3] Courts also ruled that agency decisions had to be substantiated by the record of pertinent evidence. A court of appeals ruled that an OSHA decision to delete short-term, permissible worker exposure limits to ethylene oxide in a final rule was not substantiated by the record, and the rule was remanded to the agency. The Public Citizen Health Research Group maintained that OMB, in engineering the deletion, had no authority to force OSHA to change scientifically based health standards.[4] While the courts were reluctant to judge the legality and constitutionality of the regulatory review system established by President Reagan's E.O. 12291, a district court ruled in *Environmental Defense Fund* v. *Thomas* that OMB had no authority to hold up rules beyond their statutorily imposed deadlines.[5]

Although the courts constrained regulatory agencies and OMB when they ignored specific responsibilities and procedural requirements stipulated by law, the Supreme Court in *Chevron U.S.A.* v. *Natural Resources Defense Council* envisioned an active and appropriate role for the presidency in dealing with administrative agencies:

> While agencies are not directly accountable to the people, the Chief Executive is, and it is entirely appropriate for this political branch of government to make such policy choices—resolving the competing interests which Congress itself inadvertently did not resolve or intentionally left to be resolved by the agency charged with the administration of the statute in light of everyday realities.[6]

The Supreme Court in the *Chevron* case and in *Heckler* v. *Chaney* also circumscribed the scope of judicial review in regulatory issues to those that Congress clearly indicated should be reviewed. The Court declared agencies are granted considerable discretion in the interpretation of statutes as long as they use a standard of reasonableness within their expertise in their interpretations.[7] Although these and other decisions of the Supreme Court related to the political control of rule making, still the Court's "efforts to deal with rulemaking have not produced a clear delineation of presidential and congressional supervisory power," according to a report of the National Academy of Public Administration.[8]

The Reagan Administration was forced to change some of its tactics, if not some of its major goals, over two terms as the result of checks and balances in the American political system. Although Congress supported the Omnibus Reconciliation Act of 1981 and tax cuts that had a profound impact on environmental and natural resources programs, it did not approve major revisions that weakened existing environmental legislation. Negotiations to revise the Clean Air Act, which the Administration supported, were killed in the House. Moreover, presidential statutory authority in regulatory review, advocated by a number of legal and public administration authorities, was set back when the House rejected a proposed bill toward that end, which was supported by the Reagan Administration.

The politicization of the institutional presidency, developed in prior administrations, became more broadly rooted in the Reagan years, not only in OMB, but also in the Council on Environmental Quality, the Office of Science Advisor, and, for a time, the science advisory system of federal agencies. This politicization may have been deemed necessary for the White House's need for responsive competence, but it provoked a strong counteraction by congressional oversight committees and closer analysis of administration proposals and activities by a variety of congressional institutions, including the General Accounting Office and the Congressional Budget Office.

From an environmental perspective, the Reagan Administration's legislative and administrative presidency strategies were instrumental in the loss of key technical, scientific, and seasoned administrative personnel in environmental agencies, the reduction of monitoring activity and scientific research, the withdrawal of the United States from participation in international organizations relating to environmental issues, the reduction of enforcement actions, particularly in the first two years, a downgrading of energy conservation programs and alternate energy options, an ineffectual implementation of the Superfund program, and blockage of acid rain legislation. The Administration became less resistant to funding environmental programs, and it exercised political damage control by allowing a wider berth for new leadership at EPA. Congress managed to raise appropriations, but it took some time before appropriations were above pre-1980 levels for some environmental activities. However, the deficit problem and the Gramm–Rudman law in Reagan's second term dampened support for increased appropriations for social and environmental problems.

In Reagan's second term the Administration attempted to tighten controls over line agencies and their heads with the adoption of E.O. 12498, mandating an annual regulatory agenda to be submitted to OMB. That order, considered the capstone of the Administration's control of regulatory policy, required that all proposals for study or regulatory action be squared with the priorities of the Administration, unless they were required otherwise by statute or court order. The remainder of the Reagan presidency witnessed a battle between the Administration and opposing forces in Congress, with the latter prevailing in their efforts to attain greater public disclosure of drafts of agency submissions of proposed regulatory action, correspondence between agency heads and OIRA, and drafts of proposed and final rules submitted for review. However, the legality and basic framework of the centralized review system of proposed agency regulations and annual regulatory agenda remained unscathed. With the reauthorization of the Paperwork Reduction Act and OIRA, Congress tacitly accepted the framework established by the president's E.O. 12291.

The Reagan administrative presidency strategy clearly demonstrated an aggressive approach in dealing with policy areas that it opposed and a willingness to risk retaliation by Congress and other interests that favored the regulatory state. Reagan's style of leadership was atypical in the fervor of his ideology and commitments, and he was more willing than most presidents to risk a confrontational approach with Congress and an openly critical outlook vis-a-vis the federal bureaucracy that he headed. However, "Reagan left Bush a bureaucracy that was at least somewhat more Republican and noticeably more conservative than had formerly been the case in recent history."[9] Civil servants surveyed during Reagan's second term acknowledged that they had realized a significant loss of influence in the policy process. But the political benefits of running against Washington dissipated and were evidenced in the overall decline in power of the conservative movement in the congressional elections of 1990. The initial successes of Reagan's tacticians depended on the surprise, secrecy, and flexibility that administrative powers can provide and on Republican Party control of the Senate. That control lasted six years and, although the White House could not always count on the support of some Senate Republican moderates on social and environmental policy issues, party control of the Senate protected OMB from stronger opposition in the House, particularly in the president's first term. By Reagan's second term,

Senate Republicans were involved in more rigorous congressional oversight and in bipartisan negotiations to require OMB to provide greater public disclosure provisions in regulatory policy. Congress and the courts checked the excesses of the Reagan administrative presidency strategy but did not dissolve the high level of distrust between Congress and the White House over regulatory policy.

THE BUSH PRESIDENCY AND ENVIRONMENTAL POLICY

The administrative presidency of George Bush differed from his predecessor's approach in appointments strategy, in budgetary policy, in its deemphasis on administrative reorganization and lesser use of executive orders, and in the deescalation of presidential rhetoric about the size and scope of the federal government.

From the beginning, President Bush indicated the federal bureaucracy was more of an ally than an adversary and stated he would favor a pay raise for personnel in the Senior Executive Service. He praised the federal bureaucracy and some of its unsung heroes, stating that in "his conservative vision," there was "no strain or tension between those values and the value of professional civil service."[10] As president-elect he met with congressional chieftains of both parties and with officials of thirty environmental organizations who submitted an exhaustive list of seven hundred proposals for consideration by his Administration.

The new Administration's personnel policy on appointments of top- and middle-management political executives placed emphasis on team play, competence, loyalty to the president, and ethical probity. Compared with the Reagan Administration's initial appointments, which emphasized ideological credentials in selecting top- and mid-level political executives, the Bush White House permitted more discretion by agency and cabinet heads in the selection of top subordinates and dispensed with ideological litmus tests. President Bush also let it be known that a high standard of ethical behavior would be expected of all officials in the federal government and dexterously attempted to dissociate his Administration from the ethical improprieties of the Reagan era without offending the former president and his supporters.[11]

Compared to President Carter, who invested a great deal of political capital on administrative reorganization and reform, and to President Reagan, who sought to roll back the federal bureaucracy by favoring the abolition of some cabinet-level departments, starving other agencies he could not abolish, and seeking to "privatize" many federal government functions, President Bush has been less committed to using administrative reorganization and privatization as major tools in his administrative presidency. In the environmental policy field, however, he did support raising the Environmental Protection Agency to cabinet-rank status and revived and reorganized the President's Council on Environmental Quality.

In comparison with Presidents Nixon and Carter, who issued a number of executive orders promoting environmental policy, and President Reagan, whose executive orders profoundly constrained environmental policy, President Bush issued relatively few, mostly unimportant orders but kept Reagan's key executive orders on regulatory policy. The Bush Administration sought to preserve and refine the power of presidential and OMB oversight of agency regulatory policies and their annual agendas under Reagan's executive orders, and to expand OMB's oversight of agency risk assessments. He also supported a bill that sought to transform Reagan's "takings" executive order into a statute.

As legislative leader, Bush undertook a selected and limited domestic policy agenda. In his first term he used his veto more often than his predecessor and achieved an unbroken successful veto record over the first three-and-a-half years. There were no vetoes of environmental, energy, or natural resources legislation, but the Administration issued an ample number of veto threats of major bills in those policy areas. Along with his veto strategy, the president adopted the practice of rejecting some specific provisions in bills that he signed, indicating that he would ignore congressional directions that he maintained intruded on his constitutional powers. Bush's claim of selective authority to reject provisions of bills was applied not only to national security and foreign policy questions but also to domestic policy and environmental and national resources legislation. In those latter categories, he construed a number of provisions of laws as advisory rather than mandatory in order to avoid a constitutional clash between the two branches.

Bush's reputation as a moderate, pragmatic, consensus-type leader in domestic policy was also reflected in his appointments to environmental, energy, and natural resources agencies. He appeared to balance his commitment to be an environmentalist president in the appointments of William Reilly as EPA administrator and Michael Deland as chairman of the Council on Environmental Quality (CEQ) with his desire to satisfy development interests and more conservative allies in some of his appointments in the natural resources field, particularly in the Departments of the Interior and Energy.[12] Environmental groups were leery of the appointment of Secretary of the Interior Manual Lujan and of his commitment to environmental and conservation issues. According to the League of Conservation Voters, he had one of the lowest congressional rating scores on natural resources issues. He was seen as a supporter of Western development interests and, after several years, as a flexible, conservative, sometimes bumbling secretary, basically not interested in changing direction in the Interior Department.

The Senate confirmed Lujan's appointment and almost all of Bush's appointees in the Interior and other domestic cabinet-rank departments without serious or united opposition by environmental organizations. Two notable exceptions were the withdrawn nominations of James E. Cason as head of the U.S. Forest Service and Victor Stello, Jr., as assistant secretary of energy in charge of defense programs. Some conservation and wildlife organization officials were disappointed with the president's appointments. One official stated that Bush could not claim the title of an environmentalist president on the basis of some of his appointments in energy and natural resources departments. Another official claimed that some appointments appeared to be based more on political considerations than on training and experience.[13]

Undoubtedly, one of the most powerful "sleeper" appointments to influence environmental and energy policies was the choice of Governor John Sununu as the president's chief of staff. Until his forced resignation in 1991, Sununu was a more important influence and key player in some critical energy and environmental policy issues than previous presidential chiefs of staff. Thus, at the outset of the Bush Administration, environmental, natural resources, and energy officials faced not only the scrutiny of OMB Director Richard Darman, who voiced misgivings about Bush's commitment to be an environmentalist president, but also the possible opposition of the Council of Economic Advisers and Chief of Staff Sununu.

Although President Bush promised a new direction in environmental policy, he inherited a legacy of fiscal problems from the Reagan presidency. Both the White House and Congress had contributed to the high level of deficits which had amounted to $271 billion at the beginning of the Reagan Administration and ended at over $3 trillion. Together they had also neglected to monitor the banking community and nuclear weapons programs, resulting in a savings and loan crisis and bailout and nuclear weapons cleanup and public safety costs of hundreds of billions of dollars. President Bush promised a new direction in environmental leadership, but initially his Administration in its revision of the Reagan Administration FY 1990 budget provided little new funding for environmental, energy, and natural resources programs. The president's FY 1990 budget amendments proposed an additional $360 million to clean up and modernize the nation's nuclear weapons plants and raised the request for the clean coal funding program to honor the U.S. commitment to Canada. At the same time, however, the Administration submitted a series of tax incentives for oil and natural gas exploration and development, estimated to cost almost $500 million a year in lost revenues.[14]

Given the fiscal legacy of the 1980s and the president's pledge of no new taxes, the Bush Administration's budget for environmental and natural resources programs for FY 1991 was a modest 3.8 percent increase over the prior year. EPA's budget request increase was about 1.7 percent without the proposed $300 million spending cut for sewer construction grants. The Administration's request was 13.8 percent higher than FY 1990, with significant boosts in funding of EPA operations, its enforcement activities, and for the Superfund. However, even with the president's request for an increase of 11.8 percent in EPA's operating programs for FY 1991, and later with an increase of 7 percent in the FY 1992 budget, the raises put the agency's operating budget at only a slightly higher level in real terms than it was in FY 1979, according to the League of Conservation Voters.[15] Moreover, the agency's responsibilities and workload had more than doubled since then with the addition of new and expanded programs.

Constrained by spending caps on domestic policy under the Omnibus Budget Reconciliation Act of 1990 that the White House negotiated with congressional leaders, Bush proposed modest changes in environmental and natural resources programs for FY 1992, sometimes balancing boosts with reductions, and providing more focused interagency efforts in dealing with problems.

The president's FY 1992 budget request for EPA called for over a half billion dollars to carry out the requirements and deadlines of the Clean Air Amendments of 1990. More than 70 percent of the projected increase in EPA's operations budget was targeted for air-quality programs. Other environmental programs—in particular, toxic substances, water quality, and drinking water—proposed relatively slight increases or may have lost ground when inflation was considered. These increases were paired with a 9.5 percent proposed cut in federal money to state revolving loan funds for the construction of municipal waste treatment facilities in accord with the Clean Water Act of 1987.

In the natural resources area, the Bush Administration's budget requests for FY 1991 and FY 1992 centered on its America the Beautiful program, wetlands protection, and soil conservation. The centerpiece of the Department of the Interior's budget request was its America the Beautiful (ATB) initiative, a $630 million program in FY 1991 and $925 million in FY

1992, which selectively summarized the agency's natural resources activity in land purchases, reforestation, protection of natural resources, and recreational opportunities, with a small ATB protection program added in FY 1992. Allied with the ATB initiative was the Agriculture Department's FY 1991 request for $110 million for a tree-planting cost-sharing program with private land-owners (excluding timber companies) to encourage improved forest management and reforestation. An additional $45 million was earmarked for planting thirty million trees in cities, towns, and communities, which was aimed to improve the quality of life in urban and rural areas, to reduce energy demand for heating and cooling of buildings, and "to address concerns about the build-up of atmospheric carbon dioxide." The Soil Conservation Service also funded a tree-planting forestry incentive program. Funds for wetlands protection and management were sought as part of the ATB initiative and in other agency programs to fulfill the president's pledge of "no net loss of wetlands."[16] Wetland protection budget requests were raised from $400 million in FY 1991 to around $710 million in FY 1992.

The Interior Department's 1992 budget request assumed that the first tract in Alaska's Arctic National Wildlife Refuge (ANWR) could be leased in 1992 and that an estimated $1.9 billion could be realized from the leasing operation. Environmentalists and energy conservation specialists were critical of Administration budget proposals and its National Energy Plan strategy to seek oil in the Alaska refuge, the former group concerned about the impact of oil exploration and development on wildlife and the ecosystem, and the latter doubtful about the very limited reserves of oil. They recommended that the long-term, more benign approach should be on encouraging energy conservation and energy efficiency. More than one hundred groups requested the president to call for a National Academy of Sciences' study of the consequences of oil drilling in the refuge area, but the Bush Administration refused.

The League of Conservation Voters looked favorably on the president's substantial increase in the budget requests for CEQ, the Superfund, and some conservation programs. It noted, however, that some budget requests, in fact, constituted a real decline after inflation and that most of the ATB programs were already in existence and there were only marginal or slight budget increases.[17]

In its midterm evaluation of President Bush's performance, the league stated:

President Bush's record on environmental budget items has been mixed. He has provided increases for some important programs and has ignored a cut-back on others. The Bush Administration's environmental budget proposals have been better than Reagan's, but most of the increases have been marginal. Total incremental spending comprises one cent of each federal dollar expended, much less than a decade ago, despite the fact that the federal government's environmental responsibilities have roughly doubled in the last decade.

The Bush Administration has played a shell game with environmental budget initiatives, trying to buy the "Environmental President" image on the cheap. The President's FY 91 and FY 92 budgets feature environmental spending initiatives, portrayed as new spending, but there are frequently existing programs repackaged or new ones paid for with cuts in other environmental programs.[18]

The largest portion of the Bush Administration's requests for the Department of Energy (DOE) related to atomic energy defense activities dealing with the cleanup and environmental safety activities of the nation's atomic utility facilities. Funds were also sought for nuclear space and defense reactors, including a reactor that could be used in the Strategic Defense Initiative. There were, however, some modest changes and, compared to the Reagan Administration, more funds were sought for solar-related and alternative energy options. Given the rising concerns about acid rain, global warming, and the health impacts of air pollution, and the Bush Administration's large requests for hard-path magnetic fusion, nuclear energy research, and the projected $8 billion supercollider project, the president's requests for solar-related options, including the request of $13 million for an expanded solar research institute, were deemed minuscule or, at best, inadequate by soft-path and energy conservation advocates. The Bush White House was more aggressive in its budget requests and political support for reviving the moribund nuclear power industry and was reported to have wanted to triple the country's nuclear capacity by 2030. Toward that end, one million dollars was spent on demonstration projects cosponsored by DOE and industry to develop designs for a new generation of reactors.[19]

The regulatory wings of OMB were clipped somewhat by Congress in 1986, but it continued to wield significant and controversial power in information collection and regulatory review in the Bush Administration. Although the percentage of agency rules deemed consistent with change by OMB in 1989 was slightly less, at 19.4 percent, than that of Reagan's last year, the number of rules withdrawn by an agency, returned for reconsideration, or suspended by OMB was slightly higher in the first year of the Bush Administration. In addition, of eight federal agencies, constituting almost three-fourths of all agency rules reviewed by OMB, EPA had the largest percentage of agency rules deemed consistent with change (at 29.3 percent) and the largest number of rules returned by OMB for reconsideration.[20] It also tied with HUD for the total number of agency rules withdrawn by an agency, returned for reconsideration, or suspended by OMB. The average review time by OMB for major EPA regulations in 1989 was 104 days, higher on average than any of the years of the Reagan presidency.[21] However, this increase was due, in part, to the result of reauthorized environmental legislation in Reagan's second term, and the backlog of some rules submitted in Reagan's last year, as well as increased time in the review process as the result of revisions in the PRA in 1986.

The General Accounting Office documented the limitations and flaws in OMB's information collection processes during the Reagan Administration. For some time federal courts overruled OMB's efforts to change or delay health and safety rules issued by OSHA. The Bush Administration and OMB received another powerful setback in regulatory policy in the Supreme Court's ruling in *Dole, Secretary of Labor et al.* v. *United Steelworkers of America et al.*[22] The Court decided seven-to-two that OMB had no authority to block OSHA's revised rule that required businesses to make available to their employees and to the public critical health and safety information. Justice William Brennan, writing the Court's majority opinion, concluded:

> There is no indication in the Paperwork Reduction Act that OMB is authorized to determine the usefulness of agency-adopted warning requirements to those being warned. To the contrary, Congress focused exclusively on the utility of the information to the agency. And the only criteria specified are whether the agency can process the information quickly and use it in pursuit of the substantive mandate.[23]

The Supreme Court's decision indicated that OMB was not authorized to review disclosure rules issued by federal agencies requiring businesses to inform third parties, either consumers about their products or employees about harmful manufacturing processes. The *Dole* decision took away a powerful lever that OMB previously applied to rules submitted by some key regulatory agencies, including OSHA, EPA, the Food and Drug Administration, and the Federal Trade Commission. The Court's decision was a setback for OMB, but some commentators noted that it still had a significant range of power to affect regulations issued by agencies in the health, safety, and environmental fields, including power over agency budgets and power to review agency information collection requests and proposed regulations.[24]

The Supreme Court's *Dole* decision was issued in the midst of congressional hearings that were considering additional statutory limits on OIRA's powers and other changes in the reauthorization of the PRA. OIRA was still operating without a full-time director and its staff had been reduced from a high of eighty in 1984 to a low of fifty-seven (not including vacancies) in mid-1989.[25] Some changes sought by congressional critics in the reauthorization of the PRA and OIRA included: (1) requirements that OIRA log and make available oral and written communications concerning regulations that it received; (2) provisions requiring OIRA to consider public comments in the decision-making process, thereby increasing public participation; (3) provisions stipulating that OMB place in the public record more detailed written explanations for its disapproval of proposed rules submitted by an agency; and (4) tighter observance of mandatory deadlines requiring OIRA to conclude its review, with an extension under certain circumstances. Congressional critics argued that, despite constraints imposed in 1986, OIRA continued to impose its ideological agenda in the Bush Administration, circumventing the intent of Congress in its emphasis on regulatory review and "micromanagement" of agencies, with the result that it provided insufficient attention to statistical policy. During the Bush Administration there were also complaints that OMB was dictating to agencies on highly technical questions of risk assessment. For example, OMB was criticized for interfering with OSHA's efforts to issue a standard dealing with workers' exposure to cadmium by displacing OSHA's risk assessment estimates with its own.[26]

The Bush Administration seemed amenable to some of the proposed legislative changes in the PRA and in the operation of OIRA, but it maintained that some of the proposed statutory disclosure and review provisions would place too many restraints on the Executive Office of the President. The Justice Department stated that the proposed disclosure and review provisions in the Senate bill struck at the core of presidential constitutional authority over rule making by opening up deliberative materials to public scrutiny in the regulatory review process.[27] Protracted negotiations between OMB officials and congressional oversight committees failed to reauthorize OIRA and the PRA. Three years after Bush's election, OIRA was still operating without a full-time director and with a much lower staff complement than it had in the Reagan years. OIRA's funding under the 1986 reauthorization ran out, and it was forced to obtain its funds from OMB's general appropriation in 1991.

However, OMB and its regulatory division continued to exercise significant power in reviewing proposed agency regulations and annual agency regulatory agendas under former President Reagan's E.O. 12291 and E.O. 12498. OMB continued to advance its perspectives on risk assessment and risk management in a more sophisticated form, noting its criticisms of conservative risk assessment procedures, as well as differences it had on risk-related matters with EPA and OSHA. President Bush also requested the President's Council on Competitiveness, chaired by Vice President Dan Quayle, to work with OIRA to continue the regulatory review oversight work of the former President's Task Force on Regulatory Relief, which Bush had chaired as vice president in the Reagan Administration. By 1991, environmentalists were critical of the council's efforts to weaken EPA's proposed regulations for the Clean Air Act of 1990 and for its role in pressuring EPA to accept a 70 percent reduction, rather than a 90 percent reduction, in sulfur dioxide emissions from the Navajo Generating Station, affecting Grand Canyon visibility.[28]

In 1990, after protracted negotiations with Congress, President Bush signed the Clean Air Amendments of 1990, the Omnibus Budget Reconciliation Act of 1990, and the Oil Spill Liability Act. The president could claim credit for fulfilling his campaign pledge with the adoption of the Clean Air Act Amendments, one of the most complex laws in a decade, which (1) tightened auto emission standards and pollution control requirements for cities that have not fulfilled federal air quality standards; (2) mandated a 40 percent reduction in sulfur dioxide to promote acid rain control, and required control technology for major toxic air installations; and (3) prescribed cleaner gasoline and the introduction of clean fuel vehicles in the country's most polluted areas. The law also included an elaborate and detailed command and control system of permits, standards, deadlines, and stronger civil and criminal penalties. President Bush was credited with supporting economic incentives in the law, including a system of marketable pollution allowances for sulfur dioxide emissions, banking emissions credits for utilities, emission tradings for chemical companies, and some incentives for conservation and renewable energy power plants.

In the same year Bush finally reversed his campaign pledge on no new taxes and addressed the deficit problem. After protracted delay, maneuvering, and conflict with Congress, the president signed the Budget Reconciliation Act of 1990. Under the act, deficit reduction targets were established, along with caps on discretionary spending in domestic, defense, and international programs from 1991 to 1993. Overall spending caps were set for 1994 and 1995. This arrangement forced all domestic policy programs from 1991 to 1993 to compete for the discretionary dollars targeted for domestic policy and prohibited any tapping of funds allotted to defense or international programs. Thus, environmental and natural resources agencies had to compete with one another and with other social programs for the limited discretionary funds. Moreover, the law granted OMB a great deal of potential fiscal power at the expense of the Congressional Budget Office and the Joint Committee on Taxation to exercise continuing authority (rather than at the end of the year) to keep tally on the costs of all tax and spending bills as they went through Congress. However, OMB's new power may have been short-lived. The House of Representatives adopted a new rule—voting on party lines—that gave the critical authority to make cost estimates for tax legislation or House entitlement programs to the Congressional Budget Office or to the Joint Committee on Taxation. The new rule did not bind the Senate but affected the consideration of House–Senate conference reports in the House. Republicans charged that the rule violated a key provision in the Reconciliation Act, and President Bush declared that he would veto any bill in which cost estimates were mandated by the new House rule.[29]

In the environmentally related energy policy area, the Reconciliation Act increased taxes on motor fuels and gas-guzzler automobiles, boosted aviation excises, increased fees on licenses for nuclear power plants, and adopted a variety of user fees for Coast Guard services, railroads, and entities serviced and regulated by EPA. The Reconciliation Act also included an Administration initiative favored by EPA Administrator Reilly, called the Pollution Prevention Act of 1990. This act set up a modest sixteen-million-dollar pilot program for 1991–93 with technical assistance and matching grants to states to create and encourage pollution source reduction programs.

President Bush also supported raising EPA to cabinet-group status after legislation was proposed in Congress, but the White House threatened to veto the bill unless key provisions were changed. The Administration was particularly concerned with the creation of an independent environmental statistics bureau within EPA, which Bush officials maintained would undermine the president's supervisory powers as chief executive, including his power of appointment or removal of key officials.

The Bush Administration's efforts to balance economic considerations with environmental goals was no more controversial than in the natural resources area, particularly in the Administration's logging policies in ancient forests in the Pacific Northwest and in its wetlands policy. Environmentalists criticized the Administration for permitting logging levels in ancient forests to go beyond scientists' recommendations and for supporting a failed Senate amendment that would have exempted timber-cutting operations from the Endangered

Species Act for ten years. The amendment favored logging interests over environmentalists, who sought to force the Administration to protect the northern spotted owl under the Endangered Species Act. Responding to a federal court order, the Fish and Wildlife Service identified the spotted owl as a threatened species, but the White House delayed implementation of a conservation strategy advocated by government scientists and permitted logging the owl's ancient forest habitat at the level of seventy thousand acres a year. Environmental groups sued the Administration, and eventually the Fish and Wildlife Service submitted a plan to set aside 11.6 million acres of lands in Oregon, Washington, and California considered essential to the owl's survival. However, Fish and Wildlife Service Director John Turner indicated that some logging would be permitted in parts of the identified lands.[30] In order to protect American jobs and provide less pressure to log on federal lands, President Bush signed a law granting states the power to restrict exports of unprocessed logs from state lands and to establish a permanent federal ban on raw log exports from federal lands. However, as the recession deepened from 1991 to 1992, timber industry interests and labor groups, as well as conservationists and the White House, still faced the problem of reaching accommodation on protecting the spotted owl and guaranteeing a level of lumber supply and jobs in the area. Negotiations proceeded with a presidential election, congressional elections, and the reauthorization of the Endangered Species Act looming ahead in 1992. Finally, Secretary of the Interior Lujan proposed an amendment to the Endangered Species Act allowing cutting on two million acres of the owl's habitat and a cabinet-level committee voted to waive requirements of the act on another 1700 acres.

In the 1988 presidential campaign, George Bush pledged to be an environmental president and declared "all existing wetlands, no matter how small, should be preserved."[31] By 1989 scientists and officials from EPA, the Corps of Engineers, the Soil Conservation Service, and the Fish and Wildlife Service reached agreement on the criteria for defining wetlands and issued a manual on wetlands protection. The 1989 standards were initiated on a trial basis, and it was believed that they still required some revisions and fine-tuning. The wetlands regulations were also issued with limited opportunity for public comment, which raised the ire and organized opposition of oil, farming, real estate, and other development interests.[32] Environmental groups were not prepared for the uproar and level of opposition. A National Wetlands Coalition of oil, gas, and utility interests was formed to overturn the criteria for defining a wetland. Farm and real estate organizations and labor groups from the construction and timber industries joined forces with the coalition to pressure the White House and Congress to change the wetlands definition. In Congress 160

House members and 70 Senators cosponsored legislation, supported by the coalition, to recast wetlands policy. The President's Domestic Policy Council created a task force that supported limits on the wetlands program, along with OMB and the President's Council on Competitiveness. EPA Administrator Reilly attempted to prevent a sharp cutback in the 1989 wetlands criteria, but he acceded to the White House wetlands redefinition and CEQ Chairman Michael Deland was charged with defending it. A White House spokesman, acknowledging that fewer wetland areas would be protected, stated, "The President's pledge will be preserved," and "The new definition would preserve land that really is wetland."[33] Two experts from EPA who served on the technical review panel that drew up the 1989 wetlands manual resigned from the panel in reaction to White House pressure to change the wetlands definition.[34] Environmental organizations, including the National Audubon Society and National Wildlife Federation and some wetlands experts, claimed that the proposed redefinition had little scientific justification and threatened fragile ecological resources. Critics charged that the changes were politically inspired with little effort to justify them on scientific grounds. Under the proposed redefinition, one expert claimed that parts of the Florida Everglades would no longer be identified as wetlands. Dr. Joseph S. Larson, an expert on wetlands, declared: "The wetlands at risk are the very wetlands that give us clean drinking water, prevent our basements from flooding, and provide habitat for wild life, including a third of the nation's threatened and endangered species."[35]

The Bush Administration's long-awaited National Energy Strategy (NES) was unveiled in 1991. The objectives that Bush enunciated in 1989 were to strike a balance between assuring "reasonable" energy prices, maintaining a vigorous economy, upholding the Administration's commitment to a safer, healthier environment, and reducing the dependence of the country and its allies on unreliable energy suppliers. A prime objective was to provide maximum use of market-based mechanisms, for example, in determining energy prices, along with economic incentives to realize environmental goals at lowest cost. However, the Bush Administration's reliance on market incentives did not include a call for energy taxes. The president's energy strategy rejected energy taxes, import fees, and a carbon tax on fossil fuel emissions. Some market economists, however, perceive taxes as excellent means of encouraging energy conservation:

> If energy, oil, or imported oil is underpriced because the market price fails to reflect the environmental or security risks caused by its use,

we should raise its price to induce all consumers to conserve it, not just those few who buy a new car. . . . If we are trying to discourage oil consumption, the tax should be only on oil and its byproducts. If global warming is the concern, a tax on carbon is more appropriate.[36]

The Administration was more amenable to adopting investment tax credits, expediting deregulation of natural gas programs, and promoting advanced technology in energy policy. Bush's energy strategy also focused heavily on energy supply options, including controversial initiatives to promote oil and gas leasing on the coastal plain of the Arctic National Wildlife Refuge area and accelerated development of five Alaska North Slope oil fields. It also recommended the eventual lifting of congressional moratoria on exploration and development of some offshore continental shelf areas.[37]

Proposals to promote greater automobile fuel efficiency by increasing corporate average fuel economy (CAFE) standards, from the legally required 27.5 miles a gallon to 40 miles a gallon, were once again rejected by the Bush Administration in its energy plan. In order to protect a beleaguered auto industry, the energy plan recommended advanced and improved technology, sometimes through joint business and government cost-sharing research and development on alternative fuels, high performance electric vehicles, advanced diesel engines, and automotive gas turbines. These recommendations were in addition to 1990 Clean Air Act provisions considered an integral part of the president's energy strategy. The NES also encouraged alternative fuels, such as ethanol, methanol, and natural gas for automobiles, improved inspection and maintenance of vehicles, and stringent emission requirements for new vehicles.

Under both domestic and international pressure, the Bush Administration submitted substantial budget requests, as well as recommendations in its NES plan to deal with the global warming problem. The president filed more than $2 billion in budget requests over his first two years for a Global Climate Change Research Program. There were criticisms, however, at home and abroad that the Bush Administration lagged in addressing the carbon dioxide buildup with more concrete, corrective steps. The Administration argued that there was an insufficient scientific basis for understanding all of the interconnecting factors involved in climatic change and global warming.

The NES report stated the United States had committed itself to phasing out chlorofluorocarbons (CFCs) and related gases under the updated Montreal Protocol. It also cited adoption of the Clean Air Act Amendments of 1990 as a major step in hastening the reduction of greenhouse gases, carbon dioxide and methane, and indirect greenhouse gases, nitrogen oxide and carbon monoxide. Large-scale tree-planting programs calculated to capture CO_2 were also under way under the direction of the Departments of Agriculture and Interior. A variety of NES actions to promote both energy efficiency and improved and new energy technologies were calculated to keep the country's contribution to global warming at or even below its 1990 amount into the foreseeable future. These measures included energy efficiency in buildings and transport, accelerated development and improvement in nuclear power production of electricity, expanded use of natural gas and clean coal technology, and renewable energy alternatives including hydropower, biomass, and solar and wind technology.[38]

A National Academy of Sciences (NAS) report, released in 1991, urged the United States to act immediately to reduce the dangers of global warming and recommended a variety of steps without calling for quotas or target dates. The recommendations included raising CAFE standards for automobiles from 27.5 to 32.5 miles a gallon; producing a new generation of more efficient, safe nuclear-power facilities; adopting national energy-efficient building codes; sharply increasing research and development budgets for energy efficiency and energy conservation; providing more federal support for mass transit; and participating fully in international programs aimed to slow world population growth. The Bush Administration welcomed the report, but it did not support NAS's recommendations on CAFE standards, adoption of national building codes, major investments in research and development on renewable energy, and full U.S. participation in international population programs. D. Allen Bromley, the White House science adviser, declared steps had already been taken that would result in emission reductions on the level of those advocated in the NAS report. However, environmentalists maintained that initiatives already undertaken by the Bush Administration would only permit a stabilization in the short term but not an absolute reduction of greenhouse gases in the longer haul.[39] Later in 1992, President Bush was widely criticized for his role in killing targets and timetables for reducing greenhouse gases, thereby weakening the international convention to stabilize the global climate. The Bush Administration was also faulted for weakening the international treaty to protect world resources of biological diversity.

The president's energy strategy was strongly criticized in Congress and by officials in the environmental and natural resources community. The Critical Mass Energy Project of the Public Citizen group found Bush's strategy wanting and it offered a sustainable Energy Future Plan, supported by a coalition of more than 170 national and community-based environmental, consumer, religious, business, and student organizations. The coalition made energy efficiency and energy conservation the cornerstone of its energy plan, along with rapid expansion of renewable energy technologies, phasing out of nuclear power, and reduction in the use of coal and oil, with natural gas serving as the interim bridge fuel until the transition to renewable energy technologies and a more energy-efficient economy could be realized.[40]

Environmental and natural resources organizations, on the whole, have been disappointed with President Bush's brand of leadership, particularly in light of his campaign pledge to be an environmentalist president, and the pro-environmental rhetoric of the president and his appointees in the initial months of his presidency. The Wilderness Society, for example, declared that President Bush and his Administration had undertaken only a few environmentally sound positions, and only in the Clean Air Act had he provided effective leadership. By contrast, the society claimed that the Administration had taken anti-environmental stands or attempted to water down pro-environmental positions of federal agencies on global warming, oil drilling, and ancient forest protection. On balance, it declared the Administration's positions leaned toward development interests at the expense of public lands issues and natural resources protection.[41] The League of Conservation Voters also praised the president for his leadership in adopting the Clean Air Act Amendments of 1990 and for his appointments to EPA and to the Council on Environmental Quality and other agencies, but at midterm the progress of the first year faded to neglect and indifference. The league gave Bush's overall environmental record a "D" grade.[42]

President Bush's decision making on environmental problems has attempted to balance and placate opposing interests, meeting the impact of difficult political choices by straddling issues and buying time when possible.[43] On the one hand, he canceled leases for offshore drilling in Florida and California coastal areas to appease environmental concerns, but he raised hopes for oil and gas interests with the Administration's NES strategy, which opposed permanent moratoria for oil and gas exploration in critical offshore coastal areas. He signed two wilderness bills and supported the adoption of two others, but the Bush Administration's actions in dealing with the preservation of the northern spotted owl were criticized for setting a precedent for undermining the Endangered Species Act.

Environmentalists and natural resources organizations' officials view the president's consensus style of decision making and stated goals to balance economic growth, energy policy, and environmental protection as having some damaging consequences. However, President Bush and his advisers, aware of the relatively high and sustained public support for environmental protection registered in public opinion polls, know that presidents are judged at reelection time mainly on the state of the economy and the public's perception of the president's handling of the economy and promoting of economic growth. The fact that the widely used index registering economic growth, the Gross National Product, does not accurately factor in the environmental costs of such growth influences presidential initiatives and the administrative presidency in environmental policy.

In the face of a nagging recession, relatively high unemployment, and an impending election, the Bush Administration increasingly shifted its emphasis toward the development of natural resources, altering environmental laws, easing up on pollution control regulations, and limiting citizens' appeals to prevent private enterprise activities in public lands. The White House concerns about the possible loss of traditional Republican support in Rocky Mountain states and its desire to regain the Pacific Northwest states of Oregon and Washington led to a proposal to amend the Endangered Species Act. In addition, the Departments of the Interior and Agriculture adopted rules to limit citizen and environmental groups in appealing and preventing mining and oil drilling and sales of timber on public lands. The Administration's plan to narrow the definition of the nation's wetlands, its steps to allow firms to increase toxic air pollution above levels allowed by their permits without informing the public, and Bush's executive order extending the four-month moratorium on new regulations and review of existing environmental regulations were to boost the economy and enhance the president's chances for reelection.[44]

The Bush administrative presidency has reflected the president's pragmatic and reactive decision-making style and priorities. It has maintained and extended the system of centralized review of regulatory policy built up over three previous administrations. In order to ensure Bush's reelection, the tools of the administrative presidency have also been selectively used to "balance" environmental policy with competing economic objectives to the detriment of the environment on some key problems.

NOTES

1. James A. Strock, "The Congress and the President: From Confrontation to Creative Tension," *Environmental Law Reporter* 17 (1987): 10006–9.

2. 463 U.S. 29, 1983.

3. 452 U.S. 490, 1981.

4. *Public Citizen Health Research Group* v. *Rowland*, 796 F.2d 1479, D.C. Cir. 1986.

5. *Environmental Defense Fund* v. *Thomas*, 627 F. Supp. 566 D, D.C., 1986.

6. 467 U.S. 857, 1984.

7. *Heckler* v. *Chaney* (105 S. Ct.) 649 (1985).

8. *Presidential Management of Rulemaking in Regulatory Agencies*, Report (Washington, D.C.: National Academy of Public Administration, 1987), 19.

9. Joel D. Aberbach, "The President and the Executive Branch," in *The Bush Presidency: First Appraisals*, ed. Colin Campbell, S.J., and Bert A. Rockman (Chatham, N.J.: Chatham House Publishers, 1991): 352.

10. David Hoffman, "Bush Calls Civil Servants Unsung Heroes," *The Washington Post*, 27 January 1989, A7.

11. James P. Pfiffner, "Establishing the Bush Presidency," *Public Administration Review* 50 (January/February 1990): 71.

12. Philip Shabecoff, "In Thicket of Environmental Policy, Bush Uses Balance as His Compass," *New York Times*, 1 July 1990, 20.

13. Interviews of Conservation Organization officials, 4 March 1991.

14. Special Report, President Bush's FY 1990 Budget Amendments, Environmental and Energy Study Institute, Washington, D.C., 1990: 1.

15. *President Bush's Midterm Report on the Environment*, League of Conservation Voters, March 1991, 1.

16. *Congressional Quarterly Weekly Report* 48 (3 February 1990): 313; and *Congressional Quarterly Weekly Report* 48 (9 February 1991): 348.

17. *President Bush's Midterm Report*, 9.

18. Ibid.

19. Margaret E. Kriz, "Boosting Nuclear," *National Journal* 23 (23 February 1991): 440.

20. OMB, *Regulatory Program of the United States Government 1991*, 1990: 646.

21. Ibid., 636.

22. Elizabeth Dole, Secretary of Labor et al., *Petitioners* v. *United Steel Workers of America et al.*, U.S. 110 S. Ct. 929 (1990), 937.

23. Ibid., 936.

24. Linda Greenhouse, "High Court Holds OMB Overstepped Authority," *New York Times*, 22 February 1990, B8; Ruth Marcus, "Court Curbs OMB's Ability to Block Disclosure Rules," *The Washington Post*, 22 February 1990, A2, A6.

25. S. Jay Plager, OIRA Administrator, in *Reauthorization of the Paperwork Reduction Act*, Senate Hearing 101–106, Senate Committee on Governmental Affairs, 101st Cong., 1st sess., 266.

26. Testimony, Sherry Ittelson, Public Citizens Congress Watch, in *Reauthorization of OMB's Office of Information and Regulatory Affairs*, Senate Hearing 101–588, Senate Committee on Governmental Affairs, 101st Cong., 2d sess., 46, 415.

27. Letter of Bruce C. Navarro, acting assistant attorney general, Office of Legislative Affairs, U.S. Department of Justice, to Senator John Glenn, chairman, Senate Committee on Governmental Affairs, 20 February 1990, *Reauthorization of the Paperwork Reduction Act*, Senate Hearing 101–166, Senate Committee on Governmental Affairs: 880–88.

28. Kirk Victor," Quayle's Quiet Coup," *National Journal* 23 (7 July 1991): 1676, 1680.

29. George Hager, "Republicans Cry Foul as House Changes Rules for 'Scoring,' " *Congressional Quarterly Weekly Report* 49 (5 January 1991): 45.

30. Margaret E. Kriz, "Owls 1, Timber 0," *National Journal* 23 (4 May 1991): 1056, 1059.

31. Editorial, *New York Times*, "The Swamp President," 14 August 1991, A18.

32. Dr. Joseph S. Larson, Environmental Institute, University of Massachusetts/Amherst, *New York Times*, 15 October 1991, C4.

33. *New York Times*, 3 August 1991, 35.

34. Margaret E. Kriz, "Swamp Fighting," *National Journal* 23 (3 August 1991): 1921.

35. *New York Times*, 15 October 1991: C4.

36. Robert W. Crandell and John D. Graham, "New Fuel Economy Standards?" *The American Enterprise* 1 (March/April 1991): 69.

37. Department of Energy, *National Energy Strategy: Powerful Ideas for America*, 1st ed., Washington, D.C.: (1991/1992), 79–80.

38. Ibid., 172, 181, 183–4.

39. "Policy Implications of Global Warming, National Academy of Sciences," *New York Times*, 11 April 1991, B12.

40. Critical Mass Energy Project, Public Citizen, "Sustainable Energy: Future Principles and Goals for a National Energy Strategy," Washington, D.C., 31 January 1991, 2.

41. The Wilderness Society, "George Bush at Two Years, Not 'the Environmental President': An Assessment by the Wilderness Society," Washington, D.C., 23 January 1991, 1.

42. *President Bush's Midterm Report*, 1.

43. Philip Shabecoff, "In Thicket of Environmental Policy," 20.

44. Keith Schneider, "Environmental Laws are Eased by Bush as Election Nears," *New York Times*, 20 May, 1992, A1, 18.

7

Conclusion

Advocates of a strong presidency maintain that the president as the only nationally elected leader and as chief executive with broad power derived from the Constitution is justified in directing the execution of the laws and supervising and coordinating the activities of the federal bureaucracy. These advocates perceive the buildup of the institutional presidency and deployment of a vigorous administrative presidency strategy as vehicles to harness the bureaucracy toward realizing objectives articulated in the presidential election.

However, difficulties can occur when presidents and their lieutenants act on the claim that they received a popular mandate to translate some of their specific proposals and their broader goals into government policy. The claim of a policy mandate rests on the presumption that national policy issues have been clearly debated by candidates and presented to the voters. However, even if issues are addressed, other factors such as candidates' previous records, their rhetoric and personalities, and the voters' party affiliations and socioeconomic backgrounds may play a significant role in the final electoral outcome. Moreover, the claim of a presidential mandate may not be confirmed by survey voting research and public opinion polls. For example, there was no evidence indicating a significant popular shift to the political right in the 1980 presidential election. President Reagan did not obtain a clear popular mandate for his conservative objectives; rather, there was an overwhelming rejection of President Carter given his inability to deal with economic and some foreign policy problems.[1] Public opinion polls indicated that Reagan could not claim a specific mandate for his New Federalism policy and for drastic reduction of funding and enforcement of environmental and health and safety regulations.[2] Survey research of voters' preferences in 1980 indicated that a plurality favored greater expenditures in environmental protection rather than less expenditures, which was Reagan's priority. Reagan's formidable reelection victory in 1984 was interpreted as a popular mandate of approval of his economic and foreign policies, but once again his approach did not square with the public's views concerning environmental protection.[3]

An aggressive administrative presidency strategy exemplified by the Reagan Administration can increase the tensions, distrust, and political gridlock between the presidency and Congress. Such a strategy faces the danger of the politicization of advisory and regulatory agencies to the extent that technical rationality, organizational memory, and the legitimacy of agency operations may be undermined. In bypassing the expertise of career officials in policy formation and implementation planning, the president's appointed agency heads may be implementing political priorities of a president and his chief lieutenants based on their simplistic values and misinformation—with potentially serious policy consequences. Moreover, substantive policy may be achieved through administrative means that are less open to public discussion, debate, and correction, thereby increasing public mistrust.

Politicization and centralization of the institutional presidency are viewed as appropriate means of providing greater coordination and control of the executive branch. They are perceived as realistic ineludible approaches in coping with the incongruence between the demands, incentives, and resources of the presidency in the American political system. Moe contends that "in the real world they [presidents] embrace politicization and centralization because they have no attractive alternative. The causes are systemic—they are rooted in the way the larger institutional system is put together."[4] The appropriate degree of politicization and centralization is difficult to determine without undermining the contributions of the career bureaucracy. At the same time, however, the causes of congressional counterreaction to these trends are also systemic, bolstered by the structure and incentives of Congress, particularly under divided party control of Congress and the presidency.

Nathan maintains that politicization of the bureaucracy is justifiable, not only because of the requisites of presidential leadership but also because it advances popular control of the administrative state. However, Aberbach and Rockman note that

> politicization of the federal bureaucracy is justified thereby as being either in the broader public interest or at least in the president's own interest. We argue that neither is likely to be the case and that such efforts invite retaliation on the part of Congress.[5]

The short-term and long-term political costs and benefits of administrative presidency strategies were analyzed in case studies dealing with Nixon and the Department of Housing and Urban Development, Carter and the Interstate Commerce Commission, and Reagan and the Environmental Protection Agency and the Nuclear Regulatory Commission. After examining the use of presidential administrative tools of appointment, removal, budget powers, reorganization, and delegation of program authority to the states in these case studies, Waterman concluded that a more cooperative, rather than a confrontational, administrative presidency strategy was clearly preferable, given the constraints of the American political system and the higher long-term political costs associated with an aggressive administrative strategy.[6] He considered Nathan's vigorous administrative presidency strategy as counterproductive in long-term influence over the federal bureaucracy. Rather, he maintained that, following Neustadt's model, presidential power and influence over the administrative state rest fundamentally on the politics of persuasion. The logic of Neustadt's model of presidential influence over the career bureaucracy is that the politics of bargaining and persuasion are inescapable since political control of the career service is legally and politically jointly shared by the president and Congress, and that the bureaucracy, too, has its vantage points and allies in its interaction with the presidency.

Aberbach and Rockman also seem to support a less confrontational administrative presidency strategy. They note that effective administrative leadership rather than the antibureaucratic rhetoric of recent presidents can encourage bureaucratic compliance with presidential requests.

> Although a good many claims have been made about the recalcitrance of career civil servants to follow the policy and program course that a presidential administration is embarking on, little evidence supports these assertions when effective administrative leadership is brought to bear. . . . No evidence shows that good management is incompatible with effective politics unless the imposition of stringent command procedures is regarded as an integral part of a presidential administration's political style.[7]

On balance, Reagan's administrative presidency strategy had a blighting impact on environmental and natural resources policies. However, several other presidents used their administrative presidency resources to advance conservation and environmental policy objectives. The president's appointment power, for example, was a major instrument, reflecting presidential influence and concern in these policy areas. Theodore

Roosevelt appointed Gifford Pinchot as head of the Forest Service and relied heavily on him and Secretary of the Interior James Garfield to implement his stewardship approach in conservation policy. Franklin Roosevelt appointed a number of conservationists, including Secretary of the Interior Harold Ickes and Secretary of Agriculture Henry Wallace, to promote conservation policy, including it in the New Deal agenda. Lyndon Johnson retained Stewart Udall as secretary of the interior, endorsing much of Udall's preservationist goals in the Administration's new conservation policy. President Carter relied on Interior Secretary Cecil Andrus to advance the Alaska Lands bill and appointed a number of environmentalists and consumer protection and safety activists to subcabinet posts, including Douglas Costle as EPA administrator, Eula Bingham as OSHA director, and Gus Speth as Council on Environmental Quality (CEQ) chairman.

The president's budget power served as another key administrative tool affecting environmentally related programs and reflected an administration's priorities and fiscal commitment for agency operating expenditures, research and development funding, and enforcement operations. F.D.R.'s public works budget requests included funds for conservation and water pollution control activity in the New Deal. Presidents Nixon and Ford submitted substantial budget requests in EPA's initial years; Carter expanded research and development requests for energy conservation and solar energy options; and President Bush increased budget requests for EPA and natural resources agencies after their budgetary blight in the Reagan presidency. However, environmental critics noted that, even before the Reagan presidency, presidential budget requests for EPA fell short of meeting the increased responsibilities and deadlines piled on the agency by new and revised environmental statutes.

Presidents had mixed results in promoting administrative reorganization of natural resources and environmental agencies. Presidents Nixon and Carter were forced to abandon their plans for a cabinet-rank Department of Natural Resources, which included environmental and natural resources agencies. The Nixon Administration succeeded in negotiating the establishment of EPA by presidential executive order. President Bush supported the elevation of EPA to cabinet status and adopted environmental organizations' recommendations for a revived and reorganized CEQ.

Presidential proclamations and presidential executive orders also advanced conservation and environmental objectives. Theodore Roosevelt issued a number of presidential proclamations under a broad interpretation of the Antiquities Act of 1906 creating eighteen national monuments, including the Grand Canyon and several other areas later incorporated by

Congress as national parks. He also used presidential withdrawal powers to create additional national forest reserves and withdrew water power sites, preventing their development by public utility firms. Lyndon Johnson considered Secretary of the Interior Udall's recommendations designating millions of additional acres as national monuments, but eventually decided to preserve national monuments in 300,000 acres. Jimmy Carter also designated fifty-six million acres as national monuments under the Antiquities Act as a factor in forestalling commercial development until the boundaries of the Alaska Lands Act could be settled by Congress. President Nixon's executive orders promoted enforcement of air and water pollution control and strengthened CEQ's authority to implement the National Environmental Policy Act (NEPA). Carter's executive orders included the protection of flood plains and wetlands and the requirement that American vendors notify importing nations of the risks of hazardous imported products. Another Carter executive order empowered CEQ to issue regulations dealing with federal agency implementation of the procedural requirements by NEPA. President Reagan later revoked those executive orders that did not square with his views on the role of the federal government, federal regulation, and the federal system. While some gains were realized in conservation and environmental policy through presidential administrative powers, there is always the danger that they may be temporary, as in the case of executive orders, or subject to congressional rejection or retaliation.

The more immediate challenge for the environmental community and its allies in the 1990s is to withstand pressures to curb environmental regulations and to neglect the implementation of key environmental laws as a means of alleviating the nation's troubled economy. President Bush, for example, alarmed the environmental community by issuing a presidential order requiring a ninety-day moratorium on any new federal regulations, unless they promoted economic growth or were deemed emergencies by the White House, or were required by court order or statutory deadlines. This directive placed more than forty proposed regulations dealing with consumer, environmental, health, and safety matters in regulatory limbo during the ninety-day period. Authority to monitor and approve regulations under the moratorium rested with the President's Council on Competitiveness, chaired by Vice President Quayle.[8] Additional challenges for the environmental forces in 1992 and tests of presidential support and congressional commitment lie in the reauthorizations of the Endangered Species Act and the Clean Water Act and in implementing the Clean Air Act of 1990. Another gauntlet for environmental supporters in the 1990s and a test of presidential and congressional commitment to environmental programs exists in the growing property rights backlash to environmental regulations and statutes.

Assuming there is a modest economic revival in the near future, the resources of the administrative presidency can be selectively employed in some relatively low cost but important ways to promote environmental objectives in the remaining years of this century. Presidents can appoint competent, resourceful, and experienced officials to the EPA and other regulatory agencies who can revaluate existing regulatory programs and consider a new mix of regulatory strategies. These might include market-type incentives, monitored to ensure that they are benefiting environmental goals more than business and industry interests. A president's budgetary commitment is also essential to ensure that EPA has an expanded data base and adequate scientific work force to study complex environmental problems, to provide environmental forecasting, and to substantiate risk assessments and costly environmental regulations. Sustained presidential political and budgetary support is also necessary for U.S. participation in international agency programs examining global environmental problems. In an era of tight budgets and enormous deficits, it makes economic and environmental sense to spend less or defer spending on massive projects, such as the projected $8 billion supercollider project, and provide an increased research and development commitment to less expensive alternative energy options, such as the development of solar technology to obtain hydrogen as a fuel source.

A president can also advance environmental goals by promoting Department of Education grants and technical assistance to state and local governments to advance environmental education in primary and secondary levels in both science and social science curricula. Although many state governments were committed to environmental education in 1991, the federal government's Department of Education had no full-time personnel involved in promoting environmental education in the nation's classrooms. In 1990 an Office of Environmental Education was established in EPA with responsibilities to provide environmental education grants and to establish federal internship positions and awards for environmental achievement. However, the agency had only $12 million in 1992 to allocate for a large number of requests for environmental education grants.[9]

The resources of the presidency, including budget and reorganization powers, executive orders and directives, and the president's role as the nation's chief diplomat, can be used to harness the bureaucracy to broaden the concept of national security to address issues of international and global environmental security and safety. Some significant steps have been taken to protect the stratospheric ozone layer by hastening the phase-out of CFCs and Halons. However, the Bush Administration has been criticized for its reluctance to pledge specific commitments to reduce CO_2 emissions, for its failure to become a signatory to the Law of the Sea, and for its last-minute reservations before approving a treaty banning mineral exploration in Antarctica.

There are opportunities, but there are also significant problems, in providing leadership in environmental policy through a president's administrative powers and his role as legislative leader. The bulk of a president's time, effort, and agenda is primarily concerned with economic problems, foreign policy, and national security matters. Environmental policy advocates compete with other domestic policy constituencies for limited access to the Oval Office. Environmental and natural resources issues may not reach the president's short priority agenda unless crises or scandals occur or there is an impending reauthorization of a major environmental law. Presidents since the Nixon Administration have increasingly used administrative means in attempting to contain the costs of social and environmental regulations. They have played a significant role in approving or bargaining over proposed environmental legislation, but the initiative and germination of most environmental legislation has emerged from Congress.

It is difficult to determine how influential a candidate's previous environmental record or his campaign pledges have been in the final outcome of a presidential election. Candidate Carter emphasized his commitment to environmental goals in 1976, citing his record as governor of Georgia, and there were clearcut differences between the positions of Ford and Carter on environmental and energy reserves. However, it is not evident how much voters' environmental concerns tipped the election in favor of Carter. Instead, President Ford's ineffective stewardship of the economy was considered a major factor, along with other circumstances, in his defeat. In the 1988 presidential campaign, the condition of the economy was more of an asset than a liability for the Republicans, but George Bush's chief pollster and close advisers thought that quality-of-life issues might be critical electoral factors in some swing states. This led to candidate Bush's strategic pledge to be an environmentalist president in the tradition of Theodore Roosevelt and to deal with some specific environmental problems. It is not clear how significant Bush's environmental commitments were in winning some of those critical swing states, but from an environmental perspective both candidates eventually produced specific proposals to deal with the nation's environmental and energy problems.[10]

When it comes to a president's reelection bid, however, his success usually depends heavily on the public's perception of his handling of the nation's economic problems and his effectiveness in promoting economic

growth. There is less public concern about a president's record and
attention to more consensual environmental protection matters.[11]

> Both political parties are committed to economic progress, and for
> both that means an increased GNP (Gross National Product). When
> alarm is expressed about stimulating adequate growth today, this
> means that the policies adopted have not adequately increased the
> GNP. The general public also accepts this and is more likely to keep
> a party in power when it believes the economy—and that means
> chiefly the GNP—is growing.[12]

According to the GNP index, the most widely used measure estimating
economic growth, the two-billion-dollar expenditures for labor and equipment
for the Valdez oil spill cleanup in Alaska in 1990 raised the nation's GNP, but
there was no accounting for the considerable amount of environmental
destruction caused by the accident. The GNP index is also value-neutral
concerning expenditures undertaken to prevent or mitigate pollution in the
production process, compared to expenditures for pollution cleanup operations. Under the current national accounts system, the measurement of net
national product accounts for depreciation of factories, buildings, and other
equipment but does not include estimates for the depreciation or deterioration
of natural resources of forests, soil, and air and water quality. The government
undertakes estimates of projected costs of environmental regulations, but still
does not fully account for the deterioration of biological capital upon which a
sustainable economy must depend. Thus, continued reliance on the GNP index
and the present national accounts system sends misleading signals to the public
and to policy makers, including the president and Congress, concerning the
nature and consequences of economic growth.[13]

The United States is planning to develop an alternative index that takes
environmental factors into account, but it will not be uniformly available
until the mid-1990s. The GNP index will not be replaced, but at least a
more realistic index will be available to the public and to those policy
makers concerned about the capacity of the biosphere to sustain present
patterns of economic growth.

While there are opportunities for presidential leadership in environmental
policy through the resources of the administrative presidency, the record of
presidential leadership as well as congressional commitment since Earth Day
in 1970 has been uneven, overshadowed by economic and national security
concerns, and undercut by energy policy initiatives. Presidential leadership
has been reactive, often to crises, and shaped by a political economy whose
leading measurements of economic growth do not fully account for environ-

mental and natural resources losses. The major challenges of the 1990s and the next century require major reconsideration by Congress and the presidency of the institutional capability and reform of the regulatory system to cope with interrelated national and global environmental problems.

Unfortunately, limits on political incentives of the president as administrative and legislative leader in environmental policy render such leadership problematic and uncertain for the major challenges the nation faces in the foreseeable future.

NOTES

1. Gerald M. Pomper, "The Presidential Election," in *The Election of 1980: Reports and Interpretations*, ed. Gerald M. Pomper with colleagues (Chatham, N.J.: Chatham House Publishers, 1981), 86–87. See also Michael E. Kraft, "A New Environmental Policy Agenda: The 1980 Presidential Campaign and Its Aftermath," in *Environmental Policy in the 1980s: Reagan's New Agenda*, ed. Norman J. Vig and Michael E. Kraft (Washington, D.C.: CQ Press, 1984), 43–44.

2. Michael D. Reagan, "The Reagan 'Mandate,' Public Law and the Politics of Change," *Congress and the Presidency* 12 (Autumn 1985): 187.

3. Riley E. Dunlap, "Public Opinion and Environmental Protection," in *Environmental Politics and Policy*, ed. James P. Lester (Durham, N.C.: Duke University, 1989), 114–16.

4. Terry M. Moe, "The Politicized Presidency," in *New Directions in American Politics*, ed. John E. Chubb and Paul E. Petersen (Washington, D.C.: Brookings Institution, 1985), 246.

5. Joel Aberbach and Bert Rockman, "Mandates or Mandarins? Control and Discretion in the Modern Administrative State," *Public Administration Review* 48 (March/April 1988): 608.

6. Richard W. Waterman, *Presidential Influence and the Administrative State* (Knoxville: University of Tennessee Press, 1990): 13, 192.

7. Aberbach and Rockman, "Mandates or Mandarins," 609.

8. Michael Waldron, "Deep Freeze the Regulatory Freeze," *The New York Times*, 2 February 1992, F, 13.

9. Holly Brough, "Nature's Classroom," *World Watch* 4 (May/June 1991): 8.

10. Norman J. Vig, "Presidential Leadership from the Reagan to the Bush Administration," in *Environmental Policy in the 1990s: Toward a New Agenda*, ed. Norman J. Vig and Michael E. Kraft (Washington, D.C.: CQ Press, 1991): 45–47.

11. Riley E. Dunlop, "Public Opinion and Environmental Policies," in *Environmental Politics,* 133–34.

12. Herman E. Daly and John Cobb, Jr., *For the Common Good: Redirecting the Economy toward Community, the Environment and a Sustainable Future* (Boston: Beacon Press, 1989), 62.

13. Sandra Postal, "Toward a New 'Eco-nomics,' " *World Watch* 3 (September/October 1990): 25; Robert Repetto and William B. Magrath, *Wasting Assets: Natural Resources in the National Income Accounts* (Washington, D.C.: World Resources Institute, 1989), 1–2.

Selected Bibliography

BOOKS, ARTICLES, PAPERS, AND REPORTS

Aberbach, Joel D. "The President and the Executive Branch." In *The Bush Presidency: First Appraisals*, ed. Colin Campbell, S.J., and Bert A. Rockman. Chatham, N.J.: Chatham House Publishers, 1991.

Aberbach, Joel D., and Bert A. Rockman. "Mandates or Mandarins? Control and Discretion in the Modern Administrative State." *Public Administration Review* 48 (March/April 1988): 606–12.

Andrews, Richard N. L. "Risk Assessment: Regulation and Beyond." In *Environmental Policy in the 1990s*, edited by Norman J. Vig and Michael E. Kraft. Washington, D.C.: CQ Press, 1990.

Ball, Howard. *Controlling Regulatory Sprawl: Presidential Strategies from Nixon to Reagan*. Westport, Conn.: Greenwood Press, 1984.

Bardach, Eugene, and Robert A. Kagan. *Going by the Book: The Problems of Regulatory Reasonableness*. Philadelphia, Penn.: Temple University Press, 1982.

Carter, Jimmy. *Keeping Faith: Memoirs of a President*. New York: Bantam Books, 1982.

Cartwright, Paul Russell. *Theodore Roosevelt: The Making of a Conservationist*. Urbana: University of Illinois Press, 1985.

Cash, Robert B. "The President: Use and Enforcement of Executive Orders." *Notre Dame Lawyer* 39 (December 1963): 44–55.

Caulfield, Henry P. "The Conservation and Environmental Movements." In *Environmental Politics and Policy*, ed. James P. Lester. Durham, N.C.: Duke University Press, 1989.

Chamberlain, Lawrence H. *The President, Congress and Legislation*. New York: Columbia University Press, 1946.

Chambers, Raymond. "The Executive Power: A Preliminary Study of the Concept and Efficacy of Presidential Directives." *Presidential Studies Quarterly* 7 (Winter 1977): 21–37.

Chubb, John E. *Interest Groups and the Bureaucracy: The Politics of Energy*. Stanford, Calif.: Stanford University Press, 1983.

Chubb, John E., and Paul E. Peterson. "American Institutions and the Problem of Governance." In *Can the Government Govern?* ed. John E. Chubb and Paul E. Peterson, 1–43. Washington, D.C.: Brookings Institution, 1988.

Cooper, Joseph, and William F. West. "Presidential Power and Republican Government: The Theory and Practice of OMB Review of Agency Rules." *Journal of Politics* 50 (November 1988): 864–92.

Cooper, Philip J. "By Order of the President, Administration by Executive Order and Proclamation." *Administration and Society* 18 (August 1986): 233–62.

Crandall, Robert W., and John D. Graham. "New Fuel Economy Standards." *The American Enterprise* 2 (March/April 1991): 68–69.

Cross, Frank B. "Executive Orders 12291 and 12498: A Test Case in Presidential Control of Executive Agencies." *Journal of Law and Politics* 4 (Spring 1988): 483–541.

Daly, Herman E., and John B. Cobb, Jr. *For the Common Good: Redirecting the Economy toward Community, the Environment, and a Sustainable Future.* Boston: Beacon Press, 1989.

Dunlop, Riley E. "Public Opinion and Environmental Protection." In *Environmental Politics and Policy*, ed. James P. Lester. Durham, N.C.: Duke University Press, 1989.

Eads, George C., and Michael Fix. *Relief or Reform: Reagan's Regulatory Dilemma.* Washington, D.C.: Urban Institute Press, 1984.

Fuchs, Edward Paul. *Presidents, Management and Regulation.* Englewood Cliffs, N.J.: Prentice-Hall, 1988.

Gaines, Sanford. "Environmental Effects Abroad of Major Federal Actions: An Executive Order Ordains a National Policy." *Harvard Environment Law Review* 3 (Spring 1979): 136–59.

Goodman, Marshall R., and Margaret T. Wrightson. *Managing Regulatory Reform: The Reagan Strategy and Its Impact.* New York: Praeger, 1987.

Hadden, Susan G. "Risk Policy in American Institutions." In *Risk Analysis, Institutions and Public Policy*, ed. Susan G. Hadden. Port Washington, N.Y.: Associated Faculty Press, 1984.

Hargrove, Erwin C. *Jimmy Carter as President: Leadership and Politics of the Public Good.* Baton Rouge: Louisiana State University Press, 1988.

Harris, Richard A. *Coal Firms, under the New Social Regulation.* Durham, N.C.: Duke University Press, 1985.

Harris, Richard A., and Sidney M. Milkus. *The Politics of Regulatory Change: A Tale of Two Agencies.* New York: Oxford University Press, 1989.

Hays, Samuel P. *Beauty, Health and Permanence: Environmental Politics in the United States.* Cambridge: Cambridge University Press, 1987.

Heclo, Hugh. "The Emerging Regime." In *Remaking American Politics*, ed. Richard A. Harris and Sidney M. Milkus. Boulder, Colo.: Westview Press, 1987.

Ingraham, Patricia W. "Political Direction and Policy Change in Three Federal Agencies." In *The Managerial Presidency*, ed. James F. Pfiffner. Pacific Grove, Calif.: Brooks Cole, 1991, 180–93.

Jackson, Jerry, and Lyle D. Albaugh. "A Critique of the Takings Executive Order in the Context of Environmental Regulation." *Environmental Law Reporter* 18 (November 1988): 10463–73.

Jasonoff, Sheila. *Risk and Political Culture.* New York: Russell Sage Foundation, 1986.

Jones, Charles O. *The Trusteeship Presidency: Jimmy Carter and the United States Congress.* Baton Rouge: Louisiana State University Press, 1988.

Kirshstein, Richard. "Can Government Place a Value on Saving a Human Life?" *National Journal* 11 (7 February 1979): 252–55.

Kraft, Michael E., and Norman J. Vig. "Environmental Policy in the Reagan Presidency." *Political Science Quarterly* 99, no. 3 (1984): 413–39.

Kriz, Margaret E. "Swamp Fighting." *National Journal* 23 (3 August 1991): 1919–23.

Landy, Marc, Marc J. Roberts, and Stephen R. Thomas. *The Environmental Protection Agency: Asking the Wrong Questions. New York: Oxford University Press, 1990.*

Lave, Lester. *Quantitative Risk Assessment in Regulation.* Washington, D.C.: Brookings Institution, 1982.

League of Conservation Voters. *President Bush's Midterm Report on the Environment* (March 1991): 1–11.

Lester, James P. "New Federalism and Environmental Policy." *Publius* 16 (Winter 1986): 149–65.

McElfish, James M., Jr. "The Takings Order: Constitutional Jurisprudence or Political Philosophy?" *Environmental Law Reporter* 18 (November 1988): 10474–81.

McGarity, Thomas O. "Regulatory Reform and the Positive State." *Administrative Law Review* 38, no. 4 (1986): 399–425.

Marcus, Alfred A. "Risk, Uncertainty and Scientific Judgment." *Minerva* 26 (1988): 138–52.

Melnick, R. Shep. *Regulation and the Courts: The Case of the Clean Air Act.* Washington, D.C.: Brookings Institution, 1983.

Melosi, Martin V. "Lyndon Johnson and Environmental Policy." In *The Johnson Years*, vol. 2, *Vietnam, the Environment and Science*, ed. Robert A. Divine. Lawrence: University of Kansas Press, 1987.

Milkus, Sidney M. "The Presidency, Policy Reform, and the Rise of Administrative Politics." In *Remaking American Politics*, ed. Richard A. Harris and Sidney M. Milkus. Boulder, Colo.: Westview Press, 1989.

Moe, Terry M. "The Politicized Presidency." In *New Directions in American Politics*, ed. John E. Chubb and Paul E. Peterson, 235–71. Washington, D.C.: Brookings Institution, 1985.

Morgan, Ruth P. *The President and Civil Rights: Policy Making by Executive Orders.* New York: Oxford University Press, 1970.

Nathan, Richard P. *The Administrative Presidency.* New York: John Wiley and Sons, 1983.

———. "Institutional Change under Reagan." In *Perspectives on the Reagan Years*, ed. John L. Palmer. Washington, D.C.: Urban Institute Press, 1986, 121–45.

———. "The Presidency after Reagan: Don't Change It—Make It Work." In *Looking Back on the Reagan Presidency*, ed. Larry Berman. Baltimore, Md.: Johns Hopkins University Press, 1990.

National Academy of Public Administration. *Presidential Management of Rulemaking in Regulatory Agencies.* Washington, D.C., 1987.

Neustadt, Richard E. *Presidential Power and the Modern Presidents: The Politics of Leadership from Roosevelt to Reagan.* New York: The Free Press, 1990.

Olson, Erik. "The Quiet Shift of Power: Office of Management and Budget Supervision of Environmental Protection Agency Rulemaking under Executive Order 12291." *Virginia Journal of Natural Resources Law* 4, no.1 (Fall 1984): 1–80.

"OMB Control of Government Information," *OMB Watch*, 27 January 1986.

Pfiffner, James P. "Establishing the Bush Presidency." *Public Administration Review* 50 (January/February 1990): 64–73.

Pomper, Gerald M. "The Presidential Election." In *The Election of 1980: Reports and Interpretations*, ed. Gerald M. Pomper with colleagues. Chatham, N.J.: Chatham House Publishers, 1981.

Reiss, Albert, Jr. "Selecting Strategies of Social Control over Organizational Life." In *Enforcing Regulation*, ed. Keith Hawkins and John M. Thomas. Boston, Mass.: Kluver Nijhoff, 1983.

Rockman, Bert A. "The Modern Presidency and Theories of Accountability: Old Wine and Old Bottles." *Congress and the Presidency* 3 (Autumn 1986): 135–55.

Rosenbaum, Walter A. *Environmental Politics and Policy*, 2d ed. Washington, D.C.: CQ Press, 1990.

———. "The Bureaucracy and Environmental Policy." In *Environmental Politics and Policy Theories and Evidence*, ed. James P. Lester. Durham, N.C.: Duke University Press, 1989.

Rosenberg, Morton. "Presidential Control of Agency Rulemaking: An Analysis of Constitutional Issues Raised by Executive Order 12291." *Arizona Law Review* 23 (Summer 1981): 1199–1234.

Rosenfield, Ann. "Note: Presidential Policy Management of Agency Rules under Reagan Order 12498." *Administrative Law Review* 38 (1986): 63–101.

Rourke, Francis. "Presidentializing the Bureaucracy: From Kennedy to Reagan." In *The Managerial Presidency*, ed. James P. Pfiffner. Pacific Grove, Calif.: Brooks Cole, 1991, 123–34.

Rushefsky, Mark. "The Misuse of Science in Governmental Decision-making." *Science, Technology and Human Values* 9 (Summer 1984): 47–59.

———. *Making Cancer Policy*. Albany: State University of New York, 1988.

Salamon, Lester, and Alan J. Abramson. "Governance: The Politics of Retrenchment." In *The Reagan Record: An Assessment of America's Changing Priorities*, ed. John L. Palmer and Isabel V. Sawhill. Lexington, Mass.: Ballinger Books, 1984.

Schramm, Sarah Slavin. *The Politics of Executive Orders*. Ph.D. diss., American University, 1981.

Shabecoff, Philip. "In Thicket of Environmental Policy, Bush Uses Balance as His Compass." *New York Times*, 1 July 1990: 20.

Shanley, Robert A. "Presidential Executive Orders and Environmental Policy." *Presidential Studies Quarterly* 13 (Summer 1983): 405–16.

———. "Franklin D. Roosevelt and Water Pollution Control Policy." *Presidential Studies Quarterly* 18, no. 2 (Spring 1988): 319–30.

Sheridan, Sue D. "The Extraterritorial Application of NEPA under Executive Order 12114." *Vanderbilt Journal of Transnational Law* 13 (Winter 1980): 173–218.

Shick, Allen. *The Capacity to Budget*. Washington, D.C.: Urban Institute Press, 1990.

Strauss, Peter L. "The Place of Agencies in Government: Separation of Powers and the Fourth Branch of Government." *Columbia Law Review* 84 (Spring 1984): 573–669.

Skowronek, Stephen. *Building a New American State: The Expansion of National Administrative Capacities, 1879–1920*. New York: Cambridge University Press, 1982.

Tulis, Jeffrey. *The Rhetorical Presidency.* Princeton, N.J.: Princeton University Press, 1987.

Vietor, Richard H. K. *Energy Policy in America since 1945: A Study of Business–Government Relations.* Cambridge, Mass.: Cambridge University Press, 1984.

Vig, Norman J. "The President and the Environment: Revolution or Retreat?" In *Environmental Policy in the 1980s,* ed. Norman J. Vig and Michael E. Kraft. Washington, D.C.: CQ Press, 1984.

―――. "The Courts: Judicial Review and Risk Assessment." In *Risk Analysis, Institutions and Public Policy,* ed. Susan G. Hadden. Port Washington, N.Y.: Associated Faculty Press, 1984.

―――. "Presidential Leadership: From the Reagan to the Bush Administrations." In *Environmental Policy in the 1990s: Toward a New Agenda,* ed. Norman J. Vig and Michael E. Kraft. Washington, D.C.: CQ Press, 1991.

Waterman, Richard W. *Presidential Influence and the Administrative State.* Knoxville: University of Tennessee Press, 1989.

Wilderness Society. *George Bush at Two Years Not 'the Environmental President': An Assessment by the Wilderness Society.* 31 January 1991: 1–11.

Wood, B. Dan. "Principals, Bureaucrats and Responsiveness in Clean Air Enforcements." *American Political Science Review* 82 (March 1988): 213–34.

PUBLIC DOCUMENTS

Bonnen, James T. "Federal Statistical Coordination Today: A Disaster or a Disgrace?" In *Federal Government Statistics and Statistical Policy.* Hearings before the House Subcommittee on Legislation and National Security. House Committee on Government Operations, 97th Cong., 2d sess.

Griffith, Jeanne E. "Oversight of Statistical Policy." In *Office of Management and Budget: Evolving Roles and Future Issues.* Congressional Research Service, 99th Cong., 2d sess., Committee Print 97–131.

Rosenberg, Morton. "Regulatory Management at OMB." In *Office of Management and Budget: Evolving Roles and Future Issues.* U.S. Congress, Congressional Research Service, 99th Cong., 2d sess., Committee Print 97–131.

U.S. Congress. House Committee on Energy and Commerce. *EPA's Asbestos Regulations: A Report on a Case Study on OMB Interference in Agency Rulemaking.* Hearings before the Subcommittee on Oversight and Investigation, 99th Cong., 1st sess., Committee Print 99–U.

―――. *OMB Review of EPA Regulations.* Hearings before Subcommittee on Oversight and Investigation, 99th Cong., 2d sess.

U.S. Congress. House Committee on Government Operations. *Office of Surface Mining: Beyond Reclamation.* 99th Cong., 1st sess., H. Rept. 99–206.

―――. *Surface Mining Law: A Promise Yet to Be Fulfilled.* 100th Cong., 1st sess., H. Rept. 100–183.

―――. *The Paperwork Reduction Act of 1980.* Hearings on H.R. 6410 before the Subcommittee on Legislation and National Security, 96th Cong., 2d sess.

―――. *Implementation of the Paperwork Reduction Act of 1980.* Hearings before the Subcommittee on Legislation and National Security, 97th Cong., 1st sess.

―――. *The Federal Statistical System, 1980 to 1985.* Study prepared by Baseline Data Corporation, 98th Cong., 2d sess.

————. *The Paperwork Reduction Act of 1980.* 96th Cong., 2d sess., H. Rept. 96–835.

U.S. Congress. House Committee on Interior and Insular Affairs. *Oversight and Reorganization of the Office of Surface Mining.* Hearings before Subcommittee on Energy and Environment, 97th Cong., 1st sess.

U.S. Congress. House Committee on Science and Technology. *The Risk Analysis Research and Demonstration Act of 1982.* 90th Cong., 1st sess., H. Rept. 97–625.

————. *The Risk Assessment Research and Demonstration Act of 1983.* Hearings on H.R. 4192 before House Subcommittee on Natural Resources, Agriculture Research and Environment, 98th Cong., 2d sess., H. Rept. 97–625.

————. *EPA's Office of Research and Development and Related Issues.* Hearings, 98th Cong., 2d sess.

U.S. Congress. Congressional Budget Office. *The Environmental Protection Agency: Overview of the Proposed 1984 Budget.* Washington, D.C.: GPO, 1984.

U.S. Congress. Environmental and Energy Study Conference. *Special Report, President Bush's Fiscal 1992 Budget Proposal.* Washington, D.C.: GPO, February 1991.

U.S. Congress. General Accounting Office. *Program to Follow Up Federal Paperwork Commission Recommendations Is in Trouble.* GGD 80–36. Washington, D.C.: GPO, March 1980.

————. *Paperwork Reduction, Mixed Effects on Agency Decision Processes and Data Availability.* Washington, D.C.: GPO, September 1989.

U.S. Congress. Office of Technology Assessment. *Identifying and Regulating Carcinogens.* Washington, D.C.: GPO, November 1987.

U.S. Congress. Senate. *Office of Management and Budget Influence on Agency Regulations.* Senate Committee on Environment and Public Works, 99th Cong., 2d sess., Committee Print 99–156.

————. *Paperwork Reduction Act Amendments of 1984.* Senate Committee on Governmental Affairs, Subcommittee on Information Management and Regulatory Affairs, 98th Cong., 2d sess., Senate Hearing 90–888.

————. *Reauthorization of the Paperwork Reduction Act.* Senate Committee on Governmental Affairs, 101st Cong., 1st sess., Senate Hearing 101–166.

————. *Reauthorization of OMB's Office of Information and Regulatory Affairs.* Hearings on S. 1742 before Senate Committee on Governmental Affairs, 101st Cong., 1st sess.

U.S. Commission on Federal Paperwork. *Information Resources Management: A Report of the Commission on Federal Paperwork.* Washington, D.C.: GPO, 1977.

U.S. Council on Environmental Quality. *Eleventh Annual Report.* Washington, D.C.: GPO, 1980.

————. *Fifteenth Annual Report.* Washington, D.C.: GPO, 1984.

U.S. Department of Energy. *National Energy Strategy: Powerful Ideas for America.* 1st ed., 1991/1992. Washington, D.C.: GPO, 1991.

U.S. Environmental Protection Agency. *Summary of Enforcement Accomplishments, Fiscal Years 1985–86.* EOA Office of Enforcement and Compliance Monitoring. Washington, D.C.: GPO, 1987.

U.S. Office of Management and Budget, Executive Office of the President. *Federal Statistics: A Special Report on the Statistical Programs and Activities of the U.S. Government, Fiscal Year 1986.* Office of Information and Regulatory Affairs. Washington, D.C.: GPO, 1985.

————. *Information Collection Budget of the U.S. Government, Fiscal Year 1986.* Washington, D.C.: GPO, 1986.

————. *Management of Federal Information Resources, OMB Circular No. A–130.* Federal Register 55, No. 247, 24 December 1985. Washington, D.C.: GPO, 1986.

————. *Regulatory Program of the United States Government.* 1 April 1985–31 March 1986. Washington, D.C.: GPO, 1986.

————. *Regulatory Program of the United States Government.* 1 April 1986–31 March 1987. Washington, D.C.: GPO, 1987.

————. *Regulatory Program of the United States Government.* 1 April 1987–31 March 1988. Washington, D.C.: GPO, 1988.

————. *Regulatory Program of the United States Government.* 1 April 1988–31 March 1989. Washington, D.C.: GPO, 1989.

————. *Regulatory Program of the United States Government.* 1 April 1989–31 March 1990. Washington, D.C.: GPO, 1990.

————. *Regulatory Program of the United States Government.* 1 April 1990–31 March 1991. Washington, D.C.: GPO, 1991.

U.S. President. *Public Papers of the Presidents of the United States: Jimmy Carter.* Vol. 2, 1979. Washington, D.C.: GPO, 1980.

————. President's Task Force on Regulatory Relief. *Regulatory Policy Guidelines: Reagan Administration's Regulatory Achievement.* Washington, D.C.: GPO, 13 August 1983.

Index

IRLG. *See* Interagency Regulatory
  Liaison Group

Jackson, Henry, 51
Johnson, Lyndon B., 11, 17, 158, 159

Kagan, R. A., 110
Kalur v. *Resor*, 53
Kennedy, Edward, 31

Larson, Joseph S., 147
Lave, Lester, 64, 97, 103
League of Conservation Voters, 138,
  139, 140, 150
Legislation: Bush and, 137, 144–45;
  presidential role in, 15, 161; Reagan
  and, 23; reauthorization of environmental laws and, 132, 142;
  regulatory management system and,
  78; risk assessment and, 105–6;
  Theodore Roosevelt and, 14, 15; vs.
  executive orders, and president's
  goals, 50–51. *See also specific laws*
Levins, Carl, 77
Litigation, and enforcement, 112, 124–27
Local governments, 113
Lujan, Manual, 137–38, 146

Metzenbaum, Howard, 120
Miller, James, 34, 63
Moe, Terry M., 156
Morgan, R. P., 50
Mount Sinai School of Medicine, 2, 35,
  38
Muskie, Edmund, 51, 56
Myers v. *United States*, 64

NAPA survey. *See* National Academy
  of Public Administration
NAS. *See* National Academy of Sciences
Nathan, Richard P., 10–11, 156, 157
National Academy of Public Ad-
  ministration (NAPA), 98
National Academy of Sciences (NAS),
  46, 93, 149
National Energy Strategy (NES), 147–
  50

National Environmental Policy Act
  (NEPA), 21, 51, 53–57, 159
National Industrial Control Council, 52
National Industrial Recovery Act, 15
National monuments, 14
National Oceanic and Atmospheric Ad-
  ministration, 52
National Resources Planning Board,
  16–17
Natural resources policy, in Bush Ad-
  ministration, 139–40, 145–46
NEPA. *See* National Environmental
  Policy Act
NES. *See* National Energy Strategy
Neustadt, Richard E., 157
New Deal, 158
New Federalism, 5, 82–83, 112–14,
  123, 155–56
Nixon, Richard M.: environmental
  policy and, 51–53; executive orders
  of, 51–53, 58, 137; use of administra-
  tive resources by, 10, 51–53, 58,
  137, 158, 159
Nollan v. *California Coastal Commis-
  sion*, 80
Northern spotted owl, 146, 150
NRC. *See* Nuclear Regulatory Commis-
  sion
Nuclear power, 20, 59, 141
Nuclear Regulatory Commission
  (NRC), 20, 59

Occupational Safety and Health Administration (OSHA), 21, 45–46, 92,
  103
Office of Information and Regulatory
  Affairs (OIRA), 22; Bush Administration and, 143; cancer risk
  guidelines and, 100–102; Congress
  and, 101, 102, 143; disposition of
  agency information requests and, 34–
  37; documentation and, 66–67;
  GAO study of agency information requests and, 38–40; limitations of, 2,
  4, 35–38, 103; reauthorization of,
  67, 102, 135; regulatory review and,
  43, 62–72; responsibilities of, 31;

About the Author

ROBERT A. SHANLEY is Associate Professor of Political Science at the University of Massachusetts, Amherst. He is the co-author of *Busing in the Political and Judicial Process* (Praeger, 1974) and has published journal articles on the presidency, public administration, community leader attitudes, and citizen participation in environmental policy making.